LEARNING SOFT MANAGEMENT SKILL

JOHN LOK

Copyright © John Lok
All Rights Reserved.

ISBN 979-888606008-9

This book has been published with all efforts taken to make the material error-free after the consent of the author. However, the author and the publisher do not assume and hereby disclaim any liability to any party for any loss, damage, or disruption caused by errors or omissions, whether such errors or omissions result from negligence, accident, or any other cause.

While every effort has been made to avoid any mistake or omission, this publication is being sold on the condition and understanding that neither the author nor the publishers or printers would be liable in any manner to any person by reason of any mistake or omission in this publication or for any action taken or omitted to be taken or advice rendered or accepted on the basis of this work. For any defect in printing or binding the publishers will be liable only to replace the defective copy by another copy of this work then available.

Contents

Preface

Introduction

Management science is a popular business, economic and psychological method to be applied to help any business organizations, societies to solve problems. Whether what are the real functions or advantages that management science methods or strategies can help our societies or organizations to solve any problems ?

In my this book first part, I shall attempt to indicate some real social or organizational problems how and why managers can attempt to apply management science methods or strategies to help their organizations or our societies to solve any kinds of common or complex problems. Readers can learn some real management science knowledges to attempt and judge whether some social or organizational problems can be solved by management science knowledge easily.

This book second part brings readers feel you are organizational outsourcing strategic professionals. You need to help your organizational different departments to implement outsource strategy or insource strategy or help government to inplement any human resource , economic development strategies. Although, nowadays, outsourcing is popular strategy to any global organizations. But they neglect outsourcing strategy has also disadvantages to some organizational departments. This book concerns to explain why outsourcing strategy can bring benefits to some organizational departments, but it can also bring disadvantages to some organizational departments. Also, I shall indicate how to implement management strategies to solve social problems.

This book third part concerns how to apply how facility management methods to attempt to explain whether your organization can be influenced to raise your employee individual productive efficiency as well as improve service performance to achieve to let your clients feel more satisfaction by effective human resource training or/and facility management methods. My research question includes:

(1)Can effective human resource training or/and facility management influences your organization's employee individual productive efficiency raising and/or service performance improving?

(2)How and why does organization's facility management in-house department or outsourced department can assist employees to improve its office or warehouse working environment to be more comfortable to let employees to feel in order to influence their productive efficiencies to be raised or improving their service performance to bring customers' more satisfactory feeling?

This part aims to let any organization leaders can attempt to apply psychological methods to predict whether their in-house facility management service is enough or/and human resource management strategy and training course program strategies which both have relationship to influence their employees' productive efficiency and service performance in order to achieve aim to raise more satisfactory feeling to their customers. I believe that effective facility management can improve better workplace environment to influence employee individual productive efficiency raising as well as effective human resource training course program can improve employee individual service performance in order to achieve customers to feel more satisfactory service performance in consequence for the organization's service.

Whether do any organizations need facility management department? What function of benefits will bring when the organization sets up one facility management department? If the organization lacked one facility management department, what the disadvantage it will bring to influence the organization's operation? Does it has relationship between raising efficiency or improving performance and facility management department? I shall indicate some evidences and causations to explain what will be occurred when the organization owns one facility management department or it lacks one facility management department in its organization. Any readers can make judgement whether in what situations , the organization needs to set up one facility management department in order to bring advantages or waste essential human resource or raise service cost from the facility management department.

In fourth part, I shall explain why organizations need to concern how economic influence to them to meet sociology in strategic management, to bring why organizations need one efficient strategic plan reasons. After, I shall explain why public institutions need to apply strategic management concept to manage organizations as well as indicate what disadvantages and advantages are influenced to business successful factors. I shall indicate school organizations example, to explain the reasons why which do not prepare any strategy plans will have any weakness or disadvantages to influence any short term or long term educational plans to achieve aim or mission more successfully. Then, I shall explain the reasons how to apply strategic management concept to any service business more efficient and effective as well as to indicate why service attitude and service performance which will influenced to fall down service quality if any service organizations lack strategic management concept to be applied. Next, I shall indicate why hospital organizations (electronic record system) is needed one effective and efficient strategy management plan to achieve if which expect administration can work more efficient and effective daily. Finally, I shall indicate why benefits of rationalization can be achieved to reduce costs and improving service for strategic plan in some business organizations.I shall compare what the differences are between product and corporate brand strategy as well as explain why it will bring benefits to some organizations if which had effective and efficient product and/ or brand strategy. Then, I shall explain how European space exploration can implement effective and efficient strategic human resource plan to achieve space exploration mission more successful. I shall explain why some organizations need one efficient strategic communication plan to achieve which objectives or goals more successful. Then, I shall explain what "Strategic Management Theory" means, what its benefits are to influence organizational operation and indicate why organization needs to revisit to compare non-strategic plan and strategy plan of this two stages to evaluate what their differences are. Thus , to identify the reasons why organizations need strategic plan.

In fifth part,I shall discuss whether future soft or hard skills which is more important to raise organizational competitive effort.. Any employers will expert their employees own different skills to know how to do their jobs efficiently and effectively and easily. So, future any organization employees ought considere how to learn different kinds of skills or knowledges in order to prepare to satisfy their future employers' different new tasks needs. However, if future any new skillful needs or demands will be raised to future employers' demands. It brings these questions: what skills do global any organization employees need own in general? How to improve or raise employees themselves skills more easily and efficiently? What will happen if future employees do not learn new knowledge to improve or raise themselves skills? Why is learning any new skillful knowledge important ? What will be the possible negative and /or positive consequence if future the organizations do not need their employees to learn any new kinds of skillful knowledge? I shall indicate some actual technological skills or soft skills to explain why the organizational employees need to spend time and nervous to learn the kind of new skillful knowledge. I shall also explain the influential consequences are for the organization, if the organization does not need employees to learn any kinds of technological skillful knowledge or soft knowledge. However, I believe explain why any organizational technological innovations and employees' technical learning knowledge, these both factors , which will raise any organizational productivities and efficiencies more easily.

This book is suitable to any students who expect to learn why strategic plan organizations still fail or strategic direction professionals who expect to prepare efficient and effective strategic plans to achieve their organizational mission successfully. I will explain how any why effective facility management can influence department communication, excellent technological input, effective human resource developement training, good employee motivation strategy and effective performance measurement strategy can influence any organization's overall performance to be more effective

Prologue

- Facility management influences
consumer satisfactory service
feeling
- Facility management how influences
employee Psychology to raise
productive efficiency

- How to impact of workplace
management on well-being and
productivity
- Facility management technological
factor how influences workers
performance in construction industry
- How organizational facility environment
factor influences new and old employees
long term performance
Chapter SIX
Psychosocial and medical interventions
for mental and physical health facility
management strategy

- What is the new model of healthcare facility
management p.121-140
- What is the tradition facilities management
model to hospitals
- Approach to reducing costs
- The path to a solution
Reference
Chapter SEVEN
Strategy plan implement
- Economic factors influence
to meet strategic management?

Management factors influence organizational strategic plans

- Organization strategic plan challenges p.141-160
School strategic plan challenges
Service organizationsveffectiveness

and efficiency challenges
Electronic health record system
to health care organization challanges
● Benefits of rationalization from
strategic plans
Reducing costs and improving
service for strategic plan
to service organizations
Brand strategy
Human resource plans to space
exploration organization
The direction between business
and tactic models and tactics
Strategic communication
plan
● Reasons need strategic plan

Why organizations need strategic plan
What is strategic management?
Why needs strategic versus
non-strategic cooperation
Strategic plan tangible and
intangible benefits

● Reference

Chapter EIGHT
Soft or hard skill need to organization
● Skills shortages on developing
country market p.161-178

● Future global skillful labor
soft knowledge skill need
2.1 Why do future labours need to
learn worldwide readiness skills
2.2 Why these occupations need
readiness skills
2.3 Data -analysis skill needs

2.4 What are regional dynamic skills
of global labour market demand
● Future organizational skillful needs
how to influence workforce
change to what kinds of employees
Reference

CHAPTER ONE

Management science problems solution cases

Case 1

How reduces transport cost of shipping or road transportation to the most minimum level in warehouse, factory locations

linear programming management science solution method :

Researching the main shipping or /and road transport problem to bring cost rising to between either warehouse or/and factory or both and the goods transfer transport destinations.

Inventory Models management science method helps warehouse, factory locations to reduce road or shipping transporation cost between goods transfer locations. For certain types of inventory control problems, certain models that attempt to minimize the cost associated with ordering and carrying inventories have been developed.

Transportation problem is a particular class of linear programming, which is associated with day-to-day activities in our real life and mainly deals with logistics. It helps in solving problems on distribution and transportation of resources from one place to another. The goods are transported from a set of sources (e.g., factory) to a set of destinations (e.g., warehouse) to meet the specific requirements. In other words, transportation problems deal with the transportation of a single product manufactured at different plants (supply origins) to a number of different warehouses (demand destinations). The objective is to satisfy the demand at destinations from the supply constraints at the minimum transportation cost possible. To achieve this objective, we must know the quantity of available supplies and the quantities demanded. In addition, we must also know the location, to find the cost of transporting one unit of commodity from the place of origin to the destination. The model is useful for making strategic decisions involved in selecting optimum transportation routes so as to allocate the production of various plants to several warehouses or distribution centers. Suppose there are more than one centers, called 'origins' , from where the goods need to be transported to more than one places called 'destinations' and the costs of transporting or shipping from each of the origin to each of the destination being different and known. The problem is to transport the goods from various origins to different destinations in such a manner that the cost of shipping or transportation is minimum. Thus, the transportation problem is to transport various amounts of a single homogenous commodity, which are initially stored at various origins, to different destinations in such a way that the transportation cost is minimum.

Inventory Models Management Science Solution Method
A tyre manufacturing concern has many factories located in many different cities transport cost case

For certain types of inventory control problems, certain models that attempt to minimize the cost associated with ordering and carrying inventories have been developed. The objective of the transportation model is to determine the amount to be shipped from each source to each destination so as to maintain the supply and demand requirements at the lowest transportation cost.

For example: A tyre manufacturing concern has many factories located in many different cities. The total supply potential of manufactured product is absorbed by retail dealers in different cities of a country. Then, transportation problem is to determine the transportation schedule that minimizes the total cost of transporting tyres from various factory locations to various retail dealers.

The transportation model can also be used in making location decisions. The model helps in locating a new facility, a manufacturing plant or an office when two or more number of locations is under consideration. The total transportation cost, distribution cost or shipping cost and production costs are to be minimized by applying the model. How do you calculate the cheapest way to ship goods between several warehouses and stores? In this lesson, you will explore the transportation problem and its solutions.

Searching What Is The Transportation Problem to cholocate retail stores case

Mathematical Programming Management Science Solution Method:
It attempts to maximize the attainment level of one goal subject to a set of requirements and limitations. It has extensive use in business, economics, engineering, the military and public service, mainly as an aid to the solution of allocation problems.

Imagine yourself owning a small network of chocolate retail stores. To run a successful business, you will also have to own or rent a warehouse where you will store the goods ready to be delivered whenever the stores need them. If you have only one warehouse, it will be supplying all your stores. However, as soon as you expand and open a second warehouse, you will have to make an important decision: which warehouse will deliver which goods to each of your stores? Depending on the choice you make, you might save or spend a significant amount of money.

The transportation problem is a distribution-type problem, the main goal of which is to decide how to transfer goods from various sending locations (also known as origins) to various receiving locations (also known as destinations) with minimal costs or maximum profit. As long as the number of origins and destinations is low, this is a relatively easy decision. But as the numbers grow, this becomes a complicated linear programming problem. Think about Walmart. In 2016, it had 5,229 stores and 166 distribution centers in the US! It would be impossible to calculate the optimal shipping routes without a computer algorithm.

General transportion problem types
Transportation problems can be classified into different groups based on their main objective and origin supply versus destination demand. Transportation problems whose main objective is to minimize the cost of shipping goods are called minimizing. An alternative objective is to maximize the profit of shipping goods, in which case the problems are called maximizing.

In a case where the supply of goods available for shipping at the origins is equal to the demand for goods at the destinations, the transportation problem is called balanced. In a case where the quantities are different, the problem is unbalanced.

When a transportation problem is unbalanced, a dummy variable is used to even out demand and supply. A dummy variable is simply a fictional warehouse or store. For example, if total supply at all warehouses is 50 units, but total demand at all stores is only 40 units, we create a fictional store with an additional demand of 10 units. The cost of shipping to the fictional store is usually zero. Now, the transportation problem becomes balanced. It is worth noting that sometimes problems that are solved using the transportation method have nothing to do with an actual movement of goods. What is crucial for applying the method is to recognize the network of connected elements.

Case 2

Management science solves public transport passenger queue problem Waiting Line (Queuing) Models: solution imbalanced taxi and passenger queue in urban public transportation service case

The Four Problems Of Urban Transportation (And The Four Solutions)

The fixed-route bus and the bicycle solve at least one urban problem better than new technologies urban transportation problem case. There are four main problems in urban transportation that require four separate solutions. Some urban transportation design recommendion argued that technology can solve some problems, but not the same problem that public transit solves."The city has four separate problems of urban transportation which have four separate kinds of solutions, and it is very important to not mistake the solution for one problem for the solution for a different problem."

The first solution :

Bus stop time real -time information technology and apps solution method Friction arises between a transit system and its users when the users don't have the information they need when they need it. That problem has been largely solved, Walker said, by information technology and apps. "That has been a fantastic transformation. Some of you may not be old enough to remember what life was like without real-time information, when you just went right out into the snow and wondered when the bus was coming."

The second solution:

Innovation method

The innovation method solves the city has four separate problems of urban transportation may include: Emissions and Energy Efficiency: "for which we're currently working on electric vehicles, and that's fantastic." Labor and Safety: The cost of labor is the primary driver of operation costs for passenger transport, Walker said. "It is why your bus doesn't come more often, and it is also why Uber can't make money." Autonomous vehicles will address that and the accident rate. "There is a problem with the efficient use of labor, and also a colossal problem of safety for which we are talking about autonomous vehicles, and that's fantastic." Space: "And there is a fourth problem which is the efficient use of space, for which the solution is on the one hand, cycling and walking, and on the other, public transit provided by big vehicles."

The third soution:

The fixed-route bus or train solutione method is the best solution reason

The fixed-route bus or train is the vehicle of the future, because it remains the most efficient way to move large numbers of people through the congested space of a city. In his critique of public transit, Musk pointed out that people prefer "individualized transport, that goes where you want, when you want," like the Tesla Model S. But Walker contends individualized transport that goes where you want when you want can't move people through a congested city as efficiently as a fixed-route bus.

"We are always going to need vehicles sized to the appropriate capacity requirement, which means big buses in big cities," he said. "Our friends in the tech industry, including many of you here, and I love what you're doing, are always trying to sell us stories about how everything will fit together into a magnificent fusion. They want us to mix it up, to think about how it combines. And I'm always saying, but wait a minute, if you're going to be a smart customer you have to think about how they work separately as well."

Instead of above technological methods to solve public transport problem. The queue control management method will be one good solution How do I conduct queue management of passengers in waiting taxi or bus area for Public transportation Vehicles?

Are there existing design projects and studies that a public transportation vehicle (Taxi or Bus) would know the number of passenger in waiting area/ shed through long range network? I am conducting a design project for buses in my country that would know the number of passenger in waiting area and this information will be sent to the terminal or bus which will they used to pick up these passengers. Thus, congestion of buses and passenger can be lessen

I think that there are 2 technical issues: a) how to collect and transmit information, b) how to manage public transportation to minimize queue. About the 1st question you probably need either to do it manually (operator sitting at every station and making phone calls like "please send one more bus urgently, we have 100 of people waiting here", but this may be too expensive, at least for city buses) or to do it automatically (video camera, some image recognizing software that calculates people and then sends a message to the center) in this city has four separate problems of urban transportation concerns taxi and bus queue case.

Conclusion of the best solution method

As I know, there is not such a system design yet. but you may devise one by using the queue theory and optimizing the performance of the system by the following pattern:

- defining a objective function corresponding to the total passengers awaiting time.

- optimizing the objective function by finding the best set of assigning the available buses to the stations (considering the routes)

Case 3

Waiting Line (Queuing) Models: solution imbalanced taxi and passenger queue in airport case

Predicting Imbalanced Taxi and Passenger Queue Contexts in Airport management problem

For certain types of problems involving queues, special descriptive models have been developed to predict the performance of service systems such as car garages – cars standing in queue for servicing.

The taxi and passenger queue contexts indicate the various states of queues related to taxis and passengers (i.e. taxis are waiting for passengers, passengers are waiting for taxis, both are waiting for each other, none is waiting). Predicting these queue contexts in a future time is very important for better airport ground transport operations. However, queue context prediction at the airport is a challenging problem due to the presence of different contextual factors i.e., time, weather, taxi trips, flight arrivals and many more. Also these taxi and passenger queue contexts at the airport are imbalanced since some of the contexts are very infrequently occurring compared to others. In this paper, we address the problem of predicting imbalanced taxi and passenger queue contexts at the airport. First, we investigate different contextual factors, including time, taxi trips, passengers and weather for queue context prediction. Then we propose a detailed step by step solution to address this problem. To support the effectiveness of our detailed approach, we generate a queue context dataset by fusing three real world datasets including taxi trip, passenger wait time and weather condition that represent the taxi and passenger queue contexts at any major international airport in any country City. The experimental results demonstrate that our developed queue context prediction framework provides detailed solutions to deliver higher accuracy in queue context prediction.

Therefore, context-aware mobility analytics enables the provision of intelligent analysis on mobility contexts considering different user perspectives. The success of many applications such as transport management and location recom- mendation requires the discovery of valuable knowledge through extensive analysis of related factors . For example, an airport can be regarded as the first and last impression of a city. Since a longer passenger wait time for a taxi ride can diminish the satisfaction rating of an airport , the authorities try hard to maintain a higher customer satisfaction rating by providing various mobility services such as easy and comfortable airport transfer to the city using taxicabs. However, the demand-supply equilibrium of taxis is highly dependent on the taxi drivers' decisions to make airport trips. The ubiquitous data can help with managing the mobility of airport users by detecting different mobility contexts (i.e. situa- tions of the concurrent queues related to passengers and taxis) . The intelligent analysis and prediction of different mobility contexts can help with making mobility decisions for airport passengers and taxis at different times of the day.

We argue that by incorporating the temporal deviation of taxi drivers' moves as the feature importance score can identify good quality neighborhoods and thus significantly boost the taxi-passenger queue context prediction accuracy. We utilize a real world queue context data set that includes information from taxi trip logs, airport passenger arrivals and weather conditions which are relevant to the different queue contexts. Then we propose a temporal driver-knowledge deviation based feature importance scheme to select a quality neighborhood for predicting taxi and passenger queue contexts.

As we extract more features by computing the deviations of all feature values from its hourly mean along with the current features of the queue context dataset , it is necessary to check the relevancy of all features. The reason is that the use of all these features may degrade the prediction performance significantly due to the inclusion of some irrelevant and redundant features. Also, for different stations, the configurations such as lane numbers, and maximum queue length of taxis and passengers can affect the solution of the passenger-taxi queue problem.

The proliferation of pervasive devices in smart cities has enabled the development of many smart mobility applications . Smart parking is one of the innovations that provides easy to use parking services to the urban commuters by leveraging pervasive sensors and flexible payment systems.

Inferring a situational awareness map using clustering methods has become a popular research topic in recent years. GPS trajectory has been utilised in smart mobility applications. In this section, we briefly review the related work which can be separated into two categories: points clustering and trajectory clustering. For example, intelligent reminders of user activities and notifications for major transporta- tion delays due to the current situation of the users. This outcome can also be leveraged for the applications of discovering user rou- tines based on personal contexts of mobile users. In an intelligent healthcare scenario, a robust and simultaneous recogni- tion of multiple user contexts would be important to be considered for elderly and disabled people, while travelling through various accessible paths .

Case 4

Management games model solves salespeople emotion problem in store environment

Any organizations can let salespeople feel happy to sell their products. Then their sale performance will also raise. The question concerns that how to make them to feel happy to help the organization to sell their products? I shall explain how to apply managment games or management psychological methods to solve this organizational problem as below:

How to manage sales for predictable revenue?

In order to hold salespeople sale psychology whether they feel happy or unhappy, executives need to understand the essential activities, sales managers must focus on to be analysts for change, foster continuous improvement and create a sales culture that drives results. Sale executives need to know how to achieve top objectives of sales management is to drive sales, capture new revenue and exceed monthly sales and margin objectives, e.g. performing sale straregy development with each salesperson on Monday morning at a minimum, and in a formal one-on-one meeting during the week;using strategy tools and questioning techniques to ensure the prospects are qualified and the strategy is valid; knowing the ratio between future values and future monthly quotos to raise sale opportunities; six month on-going sale plan aims to make sure there are coordinated to achieve sale to various market segments; developing on ongoing series of networking events to build market awareness in order to ensure all salespeople attend specific events involved in networking by salespeople to, understanding the market how to influence salespeople sale method to sale number, understanding trends and seeking some channels to raise additional sales opportunities; how to create trained or warm sale environment to let sales teams feel happy to sell.

How to design and utilize efficient control sale procedures?

The sale cycle procedure may include these market activities, such as advertising, sales promotion, market research, physical distribution, pricing , sale place, sale staffs seeking. SO, any organizations need have good sale planning, direction and control of the personnel, selling activities of a business with including recruiting, selecting, training, rating, supervising, paying or reward system, motivating strategy , as all these tasks apply to the personnel sales-force.

The factors may influence salespeople psychology, they may include fair income reward system, or appreciation methods and sale career development plan to every salesperson. It aims to encourage them to achieve the highest sale effort. Anymore, methods to train sale managers have the right direction to guide, lead and motivate their salespeople, e.g. knowledge of salespeople psychology needs how to satisfy them, understanding why they choose to do or act themselves sale behaviors in order to improve their weakness to motivate salespeople to achieve company's sale target goal every month easily, e.g. raising profitability, sales volume, market share, growth and corporate image building raise clients' confidence to choose to buy this company's any products more easily.

The sales organization is required for the following purposes, they may include: enabling top-management, to devote to more time in policy making for the growth and expansion of business to divide and fix authority among the subordinates , so that they may shirk work, to avoid repetition of duties and functions, so that there may not be any confusion among them to locate responsibility of each and every employee , so that they can complete the whole work in stipulated time, if not then the particular person must be responsible, to establish the sales effort to enforce proper supervision of sales force.

What does the concept of salespeople replacement value mean?

What is a sales force turnover management tool?

Sales force turnover is defined as the rate at which salespeople leave an organizations, resignations, retirements or dismissals. So, if the organization can raise the sales force turnover ratio, because many salespeople can be promoted or the retirement, or the sales force turnover ratio raising reasons as well as they are not resignation or dismissal reasons. I believe that the organization ought have good sale environment and reasonable reward and welfare strategy to let its salespeople feel happy to help this company to sell its products every day.

However, sales management's actions have direct or indirect effects to impact on turnover. Direct effects may include the firm's firing or dismiss policy. The indirect effects on sale turnover may include new salesperon recruiting and selecting policies affect the quality and performance of the sale force as well as the speed at which salespeople are replaced. The same policies have an impact on the sales force turnover rate through the characteristics of the newly recurited salespersons and the promotion , training, retraining policies, support, supervision, compensation. ALl of those factors have an impact on salesperson's personal satisfaction or dissatisfaction absolutely. So, any sale organizations need to concern how and why whether any one of above these factors may influence their salespeople how to perform or act sale behaviors in order to excite their sale number more effective in long term.

How to achieve sale force management effectively?

Sale management is one strategy to many organizations, because organizations expect their salespeople can only raise product sale number. So , they will consider whetther how to implement the sale management strategy to be the most suitable to themselves sale organizations in order to excite their sale teams to sell their products to achieve sale growth aim effectively. So for organization's long term sale growth development, it seems that one excellent sale management strategy can help the organization has stable sale number growth in long term possible.

However, the term " selling" includes a variety of sales situations and activities. For example, those sales positions where the sales representative is required primarily to deliver the product to the customer on a regular or periodic basis. The emphasis is this type of sales activity is very different to the sales position where the sales representative is dealing with sales of capital equipment to industrial purchasers. IN additions some sales representatives deal only in export markets whereas others sell direct to customers in their homes. So, sale organizations need to sell to local or overseas market as well as its target customer is businessmen or individual consumer or both in order to implement to choose their most suitable sale management strategy to train their salespeople more effective or achieving sale growth objective only. Because these its sale major target and where sale market place both factors will influence how it ought train its salespeople, so any organization's training method ought be influenced to change by whom is its major sale target and where is its major sale market location factors.

How to know the psychology of salesmanship?

When the organization can predict or find reasons to explain why its salespeople feel unhappy to help
this organization to sell its products. Then, it can attempt to improve its weaknesses in order to let its salespeople to feel more sale service satisfactory feeling to continue to help this organization to sell its products. Then, it won't need not often to train or recruit new salespeople to replace its old salespeople in consequence.

How to know what its salespeoples' real need in order to raise their sale service satisfactory feeling ?

Psychology means that " science of the mind" and psychology plays to important part in business and it is quite worth to bring to influence any organization salespeoples' posivitive or negative sale emotion in their every sale process between themselves and their every client in personal. For example, if the salesperson often have negative emotion or he feels unhappy in every sale process, then he will encounter or increase many times of sale failure possibilities. He will feel that he is one poor verbal advertiser or seller or promotor to help his organization to promote its products to sell again as well as he will lose confidence to sell any products next sale chance, because his failure sale experiences are accumulated to influence his sale emotion to be poor or difficult sale.

Hence, the poor performance salesperson needs have more successful sale experiences to compensate his / her prior many sale failure times feeling, if the organization hopes this poor performance salesperson can raise sale number easily. Overall, any organizations need to concern how to improve or raise the more failure times of sale experience salespeoples' sale techniques or methods or attitudes more than choose to fire or dismiss them as well as finding another new salesperson to replace him/her. Because it is possible that the salesperson 's poor sale performance that is not due to himself/herself poor sale effort and sale knowledge or lacking sale experience to the product, it may be due to the poor sale team cooperation relationship , feeling poor or not comfortable sale physcial shop environment, poor sale manager and other salespeople working relationship, the sale manager lacks leadership effort, poor family relationship etc. external factors more than himself/herself personal poor or negative emotion or poor health etc. personal factors. Hence, the organization ought enquire him/her why he/she feels unhappy to sell its products and it needs to attempt to find methods to solve his/her challenges immediately. If his/her challenges can be solved. It is possible that his/her sale efforts can be also raised for. So, if the organization can know how to utilize positive sale emotion psychological methods to predict or know why and how every salesperson perform his/her sale behavior in whose daily sale tasks, then it can concentrate on implementing effective and the most suitable sale training to raise their sale abilities more easily.

However, the sale training may include: How to build or improve long term good salesperson and his/her customer sale service relationship between every salesperson and every client in every buying and selling cycle process, how to using right communicating styleds for better understanding every client's real needs, powers and negotiating, e.g. every salesperson needs to review why there are many clients do not choose to buy any products from his sale presentation or promotion, finding every time sale failure reasons can let the salesperson makes himself/herself sale failure reasons evaluation or judgement in order to find what is the major reason influences his/her sale failure, e.g. lacking product knowledge, he/she often let many clients to feel that he lacks patience to listen the client's enquiry or feedback, his sale presentation is not attractive to let many clients like to stay longer time to listen his sale presentation in whole sale process, the salesperson himself/herself emotion is negative and he /she can let many clients feel he / she is not happy or does not enjoy to sell this product from himself/herself face impression or sale behavior impression easily, lacking enough sale techniques to persuade his/her clients why he/she ought choose to buy this product in whole sale process etc. these factors may influence the salesperson's sale failure chance to be raised. Hence sales manager ought need to spend long time to meet the poor sale performance salesperson to discuess what his/her sale challenges are the most major to influence his/her every sale successful chance in order to improve his/ her sale performance more successfully.

In conclusion, the reasons why salespeople often encounter sale failure possibilities. The factors may include these aspects, such as they lask the desire to help customers to make satisfactory purchase decisons, they only concern how to achieve sale final objective or aim only, it will cause clients feel they do not real concern their real needs. They only concern to sell the product in success. They do not know how to describe the product whether what characteristics or features it owns accurately in order to increase sale chance to persudade them to make final decision to by the product, they do not attempt to participate the whole sale process to help them to choose the most right product in order to satisfy their any purcahse needs, they ought avoid deceptive or manipulative influence tactics, avoid the use of high pressure sales techniques etc. Thus, if any organizations can spend time to investigate what factors cause why any one of salespeople choose perform his/her sale behavior often in order to know or understand their salespeople' sale psychology absolutely. Then, I believe that their sale number will only grown more easily.

Case 6

Management science classical theory solves internet invention to raise smart phone sale number increases

Why does internet can influence smart mobile phone consumers' purchase desire? Has internet have direct relationship to influence smart mobile phone buyers' purchase desires ? Can the smart mobile phone talking product still attract phone buyers' preference choice, if it lacks internet function? Can internet raise smart phone sale number and create many mobile phone inventors and manufacturer occupations to raise GDP real GDP when smart phone buyers number and smart phone related occupation needs increase. I shall apply behavioral economic theory to attempt to explain the reasons how and why internet has direct relationship to influence smart mobile buyers' preference talking product choice in this traditional home telephone talking product market as below:

Is the internet putting up a barrier between people, even in bed? Does internet influence mobile phone consumers have not choose to buy because they are influenced to use mobiles when they use mobile to link internet to see any movies, or phones or news and influence their sleeping time in habit and they won't have nervous to work or learn on day time. We compulsively carry our smartphones with us wherever we go. The classroom, the bathroom, the bedroom, the outdoors — our phone is always in hand as if it were some magic self-defense tool capable of protecting us from all that is evil in the world. It all happened so fast. We didn't have the time to set any boundaries for smartphone usage, and now we find ourselves unable to save our relationships and form meaningful interactions with those dear to us.Smartphones are very useful in many circumstances. However, although not ruining your relationships per se, they can harm it in devious ways.

A smartphone is a modern day distraction that is so common, it's hardly noticed any more. It accompanies us wherever we go, demanding our attention multiple times a day. A phone call, a Facebook notification. We become irrevocably immersed in our digital lives, prioritizing the virtual world over anything else. Is it really that important to Instagram your dinner, rather than actually savoring it and sharing your impressions – or maybe a forkful of the dish – with the person next to you?Smartphones get in the way of our relationships, making it impossible for us to wholeheartedly devote our attention to the present moment. As a result, we lose many moments of wonder that are unique and never to be lived again.

Addiction to smartphone usage is a common problem among adults worldwide. It manifests itself in the excessive usage of their phones, while engaged in other activities such as studying, driving, social gatherings and even sleeping. However, many people fail to realize that addiction to smartphone usage is a serious issue that can have a negative effect on the person's thoughts, behavior, tendencies, feelings, and sense of well-being. In particular, it can be a risk factor for depression, loneliness, anxiety and sleep disturbances. As per the Mental Health Foundation in the United Kingdom, people with depression experience an unhappy mood, loss of interest or pleasure, feelings of guilt or low self-worth, disturbed sleep or appetite, low energy, and poor concentration. Depressive and anxiety disorders are two main common disorders that are highly prevalent globally, as over 300 million people are estimated to suffer from depression, which is equivalent to 4.4% of the world's population. It is speculated that not only addiction to smartphone usage can affect one's mental and behavioral status, but also that those with mood disorders are more likely to become addicted to using their smartphones .

Numerous tools have been utilized in literature to assess the same phenomenon, but with different terms such as excessive smart phone usage, smartphone addiction, dependency on smart phones, internet addiction, problematic mobile phone usage, and so on. Remarkably, there was a tendency to use a non-pathological terminology, such as "Problematic Smartphone Use," rather than the term smartphone addiction. Addiction manifests itself in various forms such as preoccupation, tolerance, lack of control, withdrawal, mood modification, conflict, lies, excessive use and loss of interest. Several studies have found that women are more likely to develop an addiction to smartphone usage than men. This was viewed as a positive way for people to stay connected in social relationships. One study clarified that women like to show affection to their families using their smartphones while men use phones for efficiency and practicality . Though there are several studies on this topic, no study has proven this connection so far. Smartphone addiction has been found to be correlated with various physical and psychological issues, as indicated in a number of studies that tested this relationship among various age groups. For example, one study found that people with depression, social anxiety and loneliness had different uses for their smartphones compared to others. People with social anxiety made fewer outgoing calls, as well as, fewer text messages than those without social anxiety. It was reported that high levels of smartphone addiction were correlated with low self-esteem, loneliness, depression and shyness.

Although, internet can bring smart mobile phone users to spend sleeping time to use this kind of mobile product to watch movies, watch TV, listen music, social media communication, searching etc. non-talking communication behaviors. It seems that internet may influence smart phone users to change their phone purchase choice to buy the kind common mobile product more. But, in behavioral economic view, internet can bring smart mobile phone product has more attractive strengths to influence common mobile phone kind product users to chooce to use smart mobile phone products in preference. Internet can also bring these positive emotion to persuade the common mobile users to choose to use them.

Convenient applying: Any smart phone users can apply smart phone to link to internet to replace home computers to link to internet to watch movies, watch TV, listen music, social media communication, searching etc. non-talking communication behaviors in anywhere and any time conveniently. It is one kind of small size and light talking communication tool, but it can also help any mobile users to apply smart phone product to apply internet to do the same computer tasks in any time and any places. Hence, smart mobile can bring many computer users to feel that they can apply computer to do similar internet search behaviors at home. Convenient internet search function is one attract function to influence traditional computer users to choose to apply smart phone tools to replace computers tools to apply internet to search information, news, watch TV, movie, lisen music etc. social media communication behaviors at homes. When they bring smart phone to any where, then they can apply this tool to click to internet to do the same computer and internet link tasks in order to enjoy their entertainment needs. So, they do not need to apply computer tool to link to internet to enjoy their visal entertainment at homes. They can bring smart phone to go to anywhere to link to internet to enjoy their visal entertainment in any time conveniently. So, smart phone can be replaced to home computer tool to solve any visal entertainment enjoyers' needs.

● Internet brings smart phone users to feel more visal entertainment enjoyment

The Internet has revolutionized direct communication, lead to the digitization of books and film, as well as made convenience even more important. Companies have developed strategies that capitalize on the growing desire for easily accessible goods and services in only a few mouse clicks. As technology grows increasingly local and more connected to all aspects of the customer purchasing process, small business owners need to be more efficient in how they target their markets. Understanding why convenience plays such a large role in the purchasing process is vital in growing a successful business. Here are five trends that have popped up in recent years as businesses looked for ways to help their customers take advantage of well-timed opportunities. Internet can bring more attract to smart phone users, instead of visal enjoyment needs, the reasons may include as below:

1. Prior Consumer Knowledge

In today's digital world, consumers are looking for retail solutions which allow them to maximize their free-time and to stretch their disposable income. Due to this economic climate, small businesses which are able to provide their customer with a more convenient experience than a large retailer, are cashing in. H.M Cole, a custom clothier, offers its customers an entire planned wardrobe for the upcoming year after an hour's consultation. Other convenience services such as Trunk Club and Stitch Fix, personalized styling sites for men and women respectively, take that one step further in creating a complete look. These levels of convenience take a simple fitting and turn it into a way for consumers to spend less time deciding outfits, and more time doing other things they value.

2. Direct-to Store Delivery

Due to the "larger-than-life" nature of big box stores, they have begun to develop strategies which combat the convenience of a smaller retailer.

The newest trend among these chains is to offer direct-to store delivery. Shoppers are able to find what they are looking for online, and purchase directly on the site. Rather than having to wait the 3-5 days for delivery, chains are making their purchases available (sometimes at discounted rates) for pick up at their local store. Essentially, customers are taking part in shopping services where the store physically groups together the inventory, saving the individual time in their purchases.

3. Personalized Billing, Shipping Info

Customer profiles across frequently visited webpages allow for consumers to not only keep their billing information in one place, but also have access to similar products or content. Businesses are able to not only track purchases, but to specifically target an individual with the information provided for convenience sake. A user does not usually choose to re-enter billing or shipping information on a site they frequent, and so by saving this information, a company is removing an obstacle that might otherwise influence the purchase.

4. Time is Money

Fast food and drive-thru options have changed the world's nutritional demands, creating a society of cheap convenience foods. Although the nutritional value of these highly-processed foods is lacking, the demand for them has been on the rise across the globe. While these types of businesses are growing at a record rate, the pressure to remain affordable and convenient has driven them online.

Some innovative restaurant chains have transitioned to online ordering which provide an easy, personalized interface for their customers to select and buy all from the website portal. A restaurant receives the order digitally, packages the food, and then sends it out to delivery, often for an additional fee. Both Google and Amazon , as well as many startups, have launched services that deliver meals and groceries to your home. Time has shown that customers are willing to spend a little more for the convenience of having food arrive at their doorstep.

5. Subscription Services

Another recent convenience service trend is through subscription services.

This can include streaming goods such as TV shows, movies, audio books, or music tracks. Companies charge their customers a fee to have access to a database of content whenever, wherever they want. Some providers have included commercials as a means to generate more income. Other subscription services include coffee of the month clubs, or deliver gift boxes. These companies charge a monthly (or yearly) subscription fee and compile a box of themed goodies for their customers.While some very big companies have struggled to make convenience a larger part of their customers' experiences, many small businesses that offer niche products and services have an advantage in this area. The Internet is helping them to level the playing field in a way. It provides a platform for small businesses to capitalize on the demand for goods by using convenience to win fans and new customers.

On conclusion, internet can bring smart phone users to do any activities when they need to apply computer tools at home in any time and anywhere. So, internet has direct relationship to persuade mobile phone or computer users to choose to buy mobiles for communication uses or internet uses in preference nowadays as well as internet can bring the different kinds of new or unique mobile phones design needs increase to achieve the creating mobile phone inventors and mobile phone manufacturers occupations need. So, it seems that internet can influence mobile phone product's occupations needs and mobile phone consumers number increase to raise real GDP growth to the smart phone maufacturing and sale country really.

Reference

Bigne, Enrique (2005). The impact of internet user shopping patterns and demographics on consumer mobile buying.

Falk, Louis, K. et. al (2005) " E-commerce and consumer's expectations: What makes a website work". Journal of website promotion, 1(1), 65-75.

Parasuraman, A., Zeithaml, V.A. and Berry L.L. (1988) SERVQUAL: A multiple-item scale for measuring consumer perceptions of
service quality. Journal of retailing, 64, 12-40.

Case 7

GAME THOERY SOLUTION IBM AND MICROSOFT COMPUTER LARGE COMPANIES COOPERATION MANAGEMENT PROBLEM CASE

Economics is just as much about consumer and producer behavior as it is about finance or the allocation of resources. With that in mind, game theory will explain one of the most fundamental tools economists use to frame competitive decision making. It provides a systematic approach to decision-making in competitive environments and a framework for the study of conflict.

Game theory solves the Prisoner's social criminal behaviors

Two small-time criminals are out breaking into cars, stealing what they can. They are working together in the same area of town. Fortunately, they get caught and booked down at the station. The detective goes in to question them separately and offers them both the same deal: they can either confess or stay silent. Their punishment will be determined by what action they take and what action the other perp takes. Here's what could happen:

a) If both perps confess, they each get 3 years.

b) If both perps stay silent, they each get 1 year.

c) If perp #1 stays silent and perp #2 confesses, perp #2 serves NO time and perp #1 serves 10 years.

d) If perp #2 stays silent and perp #1 confesses, perp #1 serves NO time and perp #2 serves 10 years.

So, if you were perp #1, what would you do? You could stay quiet and count on only getting one year, hoping that your friend stays quiet as well, and you'll both only serve 1 year. But, what if you admit to being involved and they admit being involved as well, then you'll both get 3 years. Or, what if you stay silent but your friend admits? Then you'll get 10 years; that wouldn't be good! Well, it is if your friend stays quiet.

The lesson to be learned from the prisoner's dilemma described above is how difficult it is to make an optimal decision when two competitors - and that's what these two perps are right now - can't collaborate. Typically, the economic man (or woman) is someone who makes decisions based on their own self-interest and chooses that which maximizes their own benefits. The entire idea behind game theory is that the result of your decision isn't known to you until you find out what your friend (or competitor) is going to do, so you have to make the best decision you can based on the information you have.

Game Theory in Real Life

We know how game theory works in a fictional situation that would never really happen, but what about how game theory applies to real life? Well, we can talk about that, too. Think about any strategic decision a business might make. The success or failure of that decision may very well depend on how the competition reacts. Perhaps a fast food restaurant wants to build a new location on the corner of a popular intersection. They complete their analysis of traffic flow, demand, other options in the area, etc., and ultimately decide it's a good idea. Then, once construction begins, another restaurant opens up a new location across the street, with a new building plan that includes drive-through ordering. What does our first restaurant do now?

Technology marketing cooperative strategy

Future when the thinking capabilities of computers approach our own is quickly coming into view. Raid process in coming decades will bring about machines with human –level intelligence capable of speech and reasoning, with a myriad of contributions to economics, politics and warcraft. The birth of true artificial intelligence will profoundly affect humankind's future. In our future technological development market, what it will bring much influences to economy. I shall indicate these several aspects, they may include as below:

On artificial intelligent invention brings high unemployment to low skill employees aspect, from the time the last artificial intelligence break through was reached in the last 1940s, scientists around the world have looked for ways of this " artificial intelligence" to improve technology, raising efficiency and productivity beyond what even the most sophisticated of today's artificial intelligence programs can achieve. Even now, research is ongoing to better understand what the new AI programs will be able to do, when remaining within the intelligence such as human brain. Most AI programs currently programmed have been limited primarily to making simple decisions or performing simple operations on relatively small amounts of data.

AI technological invention will bring much contribution to influence our future economic development. It had unique characteristics to compare common machines and it can help many industries to raise efficiency, productivity and improve performance as well as consumer individual self use. Such as the network is not taught to understand prose in any human sense. Instead, during its training phase, it adjusts the internal connections in its simulated neural networks to best anticipate the next word. It can be applied to read any article and understand any meaning to write any article as same to authors' mind and writing ability. For example, in the future, any one entered the first few sentences of any article, you are reading, the algorithm spewed out two paragraphs that sounded liked a freshman's effort to recall the gist of an introductory lecture on machine learning during which she was daydreaming. The output contains all the right words and phrases , not bad. So, (AI) technology can be applied to become just one more example of programs that do things thought to be uniquely human playing the real-time strategy game, translating text, making personal recommendations for books and movies, recognizing people in images and videos. But with the invention, of deep neural networks and the massive computational of the tech industry, computers improved until their outputs to longer appeared . In the future, algorithms can best humans, (AI) can help human to do any things in possible. Then, our society will encounter one automobile machine working environment. Does (AI) innovation will low skill employees lose their jobs because robotic can replace to any human to do simple jobs in any industries.

Whether machines can become sentient matters for ethical reasons. If computers experience life through their own senses, they cease to be purely a means to an end determined by their usefulness to us humans. Then our society will have many jobs which are needed to be worked by human, due to (AI) or robotic invention, it can replace human to do many simple jobs, e.g. factory manufacturing jobs, warehouse deliver jobs, public transportation , e.g. tram, train, ferry, underground train, bus etc. driving tasks, they are replaced by robotic auto driving, even pilot flying job will be also replaced to drive air planes by (AI) driving on sky impossible. Although, (AI) can help businesses to raise efficiency, increase productivity and improve performance, but it also bring these jobs to be replaced by (AI) and it will cause many people lose jobs when (AI) is invented to be applied in popular in our future societies. On business benefits aspect, (AI) can bring working efficiency and productivity improvement, but it can also bring unemployment ratio raises as the same time when employers accept to apply (AI) to replace human to any simple or difficult tasks.

So, we need to limit or prohibit (AI) invention to exceed human's extent in possible. I mean that we do not need to limit to invent any (AI) skill, but we need to concern human need to work in the same time. If (AI) was real replaced to do any simple jobs in any industries, then there are many low skill workers , such as factory workers, clean workers, drivers ,even high skill workers, such as lawyer, teacher, pilot. They will lose their jobs in possible. So, how to invent (AI) technology will influence our future global employment chance to provide us to continue to work in any organizations. So, (AI) will may bring high unemployment ratio, if it is applied to any low skill , even high skill jobs aspects to different industries in global.

On conclusion , in economist view, technology market development must need, such as (AI) invention because it can help any industries to raise efficiency, productivity and improve performance, but we need to know how it can be applied to avoid human to lose jobs, due to (AI) is replaced to do their tasks for any industries in possible. Whether (AI) invention can create jobs or bring job lose? (AI) scientists must need to consider how to invent their skill to be applied to which tasks aspect if they hope human won't lose many jobs to do in future one day.

● How to apply robotic to raise efficiency and productivity and improving performance for manufacture as well as bringing long term productive economic benefit to manufacturers?

It is one good question. Can scientists only concentrate on researching artificial intelligent for raising productivity, efficiency and improving performance to businesses aspect, so neglecting on research other scientific researching aspects? Technological marketing economy is as a play between independent individual subjects. However, it has also become clear that the notion of play has to be interpreted within a different framework than that of classical functionalism. In mainstream classical economics, interaction or exchange is understood as the effect of the ends-means rationally of individuals. Smith's sympathy –based view of man and society avoids this functionalistic reduction of interaction and exchange. For example, the utilitarian or functional aspect of , the social process of producing and distributing wealth through free exchange, is in Smith's view on part of the value and belief system which people in ordered and prosperous societies employ to give sense and meaning to their experiences.

Hence, in our business society, technology can bring marketing economic change to be better. One free technology marketing economic society must have these advantages to bring to influence our living, such as below:

It interprets and explains improving social processes of producing and distributing to business, such as (AI) skill invention , it can help businesses to improve performance and efficiency and productivities for their manufacturing aim only, but (AI) ought not be applied to replace to do all low skill workers' jobs in any positions in any factories or warehouses. So, any employers ought not dismiss all workers and they are replaced by all robotics. They will need to consider overall economic benefit. I mean that avoiding low skill workers unemployment ratio raises. For example, one factory can still keep 50% workers and 50% robotics to cooperate to work together. Because some human workers can be such as assistants to do any simple tasks in factory every teams. Human workers can discover any errors to let manager to know in order to improve in their cooperation process with robotics. So, human workers and robotics cooperation , it is more efficient manufacturing method to compare any manufacturing process is needed to finish from robotics only in any future factory or warehouse working environment. So, robotics and human workers cooperation can bring the most efficient production and distribution benefits to future manufacturers in any factories or warehouses because human can help robotics to find any error in order to improve. Otherwise, if the factory or warehouse has only all robotics to work. Although, they may bring raising productivities or improving performance and efficiencies. But they can not know whether how to improve their errors or revises their every time productive performance to be better every day. SO, the most efficient manufacturing method is that human workers and robotics cooperate to work together in any factories or warehouses.

On innovation and information economic influence aspect, one of the most important topics in economics is the economics of information. Information includes things as varied as e-mail, and even the text book you are reading. Information is a very different kind of commodity from things like pizza and shoes because information is expensive to produce , but cheap to reproduce. Because of the unusual nature of information, it is subject to market failure, so we need to develop different kinds of public politics to regulate it, the law of " intellectual property".

We are encountering the essence of economic development is innovation and that monopolists are in fact of innovation in a capitalist economy. What does the economics of information mean ? Who do we need to develop information economy? Modern economics emphasizes the special problems involved in the economics of information. Information is a fundamentally different commodity from normal goods. Because information is costly to produce , but cheap to reproduce, markets in information are subject to serve market failures.

For the production of software program industry example, the windows software, developing this program took several years and cost Microsoft many money of dollars. You can purchase a legal copy for $5. The same phenomenon is at work in pharmaceutical, entertainment and other areas where much of the value of a good comes from the information it contains. In each of these areas, the research and development to software on the product may be an expensive process that takes years. But once, the information is recorded on paper, in a computer or on a compact disc, it can be reproduced and used by a second person essentially for free.

The inability of firms to capture the full monetary value of their invention is called inappropriability. Inventions are not fully appropriable because other firms may imitate an invention, in which case the other firms may derive some of the benefits of the inventive investments. Sometimes, imitators may drive down the price of the new product, in which case consumers would get some of the rewards. Information consumers can earn these benefits when the value of an invention to all consumers and producers is many times the appropriable private return to the inventor (the monetary value of the invention to the inventor).

However, information is expensive to produce but cheap to reproduce. To the extent the rewards to invention are inappropriable, we would expect private research and development to be underfunded, with the most significant underinvestment in basic research because that is the least appropriable kind of information. The inappropriability and high social return on research can lead most governments to subsidize basic research in the fields of health and science and to provide special incentives for other creative activities. Thus, special laws governing patents, copyrights, business and trade secrets and electronic media create intellectual property rights. The purpose is to give the owner special protection against the material's being copied and used by others without compensation to the owner or original creator.

On the Internet information economic market influence hand, inventions that improve communications are hardly limited to the modern age. But the rapid growth of electronic storage, access and transmission of information highlights of providing incentives for creating new information. Many new information technologies have large sunk costs but virtually zero marginal costs. With the low cost of electronic information systems like the internet, it is technologically possible to make the large amounts of information available to everyone, everywhere, at close to zero marginal cost. Perfect competition is nowadays different e-commerce internet information business competitive feature, and any e-commerce merchants can not survive here because a price equal to a zero marginal cost will yield zero revenues and therefore no viable firms.

Hence, the economics of the information economy highlights the conflict between efficiency and incentives. On the one hand, all information ,might be provided free of charge, e.g. free e-book download, e-song download e-movie download from internet. Free provisions of information looks economically efficient because the price would thereby be equal to the marginal cost, which is zero. But a zero price on intellectual property would destroy the profits and therefore reduce the incentives to produce new books from authors, movies and songs from creators would earn little rewards from their creative activity. But with the costs reproduction and transmission so much lower for electronic information than for traditional information, so the future any electronic publishing industry 's products, e.g. e-books, e-songs , e-music, e-movies prices will be lower than traditional paper books, pack of songs and movies price, either consumers go to shops to buy them or consumers pay visa card to enter websites to buy any e-books , songs, e-music , e-movies from internet channel. Then, it will cause these traditional publishing and entertainment industries' competition to be raised because these e-publishers or e-entertainment can reduce their price to sell from their websites when their costs are nearly to zero. Hence, information technology can raise competition to the traditional publishing and entertainment industries. The traditional paper book, music, movie business merchants need to any authors or creators to help them to create any unique movies, songs, paper books to sell from their shops and they need to ensure their authors or music , movie creators won't give these creative book, song, movie products to any e-music, e-publisher, e-movie merchants to sell from their websites absolutely.

On conclusion, information technology influence any music, publish, movie creative product competitive raising to the traditional paper book publishers, music or movie publishers when many book publishers or music or movie creators choose e-commerce to replace traditional shop visiting sale method. So , it is possible to influence overall publishing and music and movie creative industries will change to e-commence consumption model. Then the traditional book and music and movie visiting stores will disappear and the online websites to these merchants will increase and their price also will reduce in global e-publishing and e-creative product consumption environment. So, information technology will bring some traditional store visiting number decreases and online merchant e-store number increases and consumers can pay less price to buy these creative products from internet.

New trade game theory explains IBM and Micro software both compaines cooperative advantages

New trade theory (NTT) suggests that a critical factor in determining international patterns of trade are the very substantial economies of scale and network effects that can occur in key industries.

These economies of scale and network effects can be so significant that they outweigh the more traditional theory of comparative advantage. In some industries, two countries may have no discernible differences in opportunity cost at a particular point in time. But, if one country specialises in a particular industry then it may gain economies of scale and other network benefits from its specialisation.

Another element of new trade theory is that firms who have the advantage of being an early entrant can become a dominant firm in the market. This is because the first firms gain substantial economies of scale meaning that new firms can't compete against the incumbent firms. This means that in these global industries with very large economies of scale, there is likely to be limited competition, with the market dominated by early firms who entered, leading to a form of monopolistic competition.

Monopolistic competition is an important element of New Trade Theory, it suggests that firms are often competing on branding, quality and not just simple price. It explains why countries can both export and import designer clothes. This means that the most lucrative industries are often dominated in capital-intensive countries, who were the first to develop these industries. Therefore, being the first firm to reach industrial maturity gives a very strong competitive advantage. (some may say unfair advantage) New trade theory also becomes a factor in explaining the growth of globalisation. It means that poorer, developing economies may struggle to ever develop certain industries because they lag too far behind the economies of scale enjoyed in the developed world. This is not due to any intrinsic comparative advantage, but more the economies of scale the developed firms already have.

Examples of New Trade Theory

•Specialisation of IT in Silicon Valley – the US. Hewlett and Packard started their computer business. Success attracted more IT firms to that area. Not because of any particular intrinsic benefit but new firms start to get the network benefits of being around other IT setups.'

•Globalisation has led to increased variety for consumers. The proliferation of brand clothing labels. Firms competing in the model of monopolistic competition and heavy branding. Neither UK or Italy has a particular comparative advantage in producing clothes, but consumers are attracted to brand image of Italian and British fashion labels.

Moral hazard influences to Macrosoft or Microcorp and IBM software cooperational success problem

Moral hazard is when one party can take risks knowing the other party will bear the consequences. It describes the risk present when two parties don't have the same information about actions that take place after an agreement is in place. The situation creates a temptation to ignore the moral implications of a decision: doing what benefits you most instead of doing what is right.

Example of Moral Hazard in Insurance

Moral hazard is a term that originated in the insurance industry and spread to the financial sphere. To illustrate the concept, imagine you rent a car and opt for the maximum insurance coverage possible. Damaging the vehicle does not have significant negative consequences for you, because the insurance company pays for repairs—or a replacement car—if something happens.

The insurance company uses statistics to estimate how likely the vehicle is to suffer damage, and they price their services accordingly. You pay much less for insurance than it would cost to repair a car because, in most cases, the insurance company won't have to pay for any repairs. But there are times when you might have an unfair information advantage over your insurance company. That's where moral hazard comes in.

You plan to drive into the mountains on rough, narrow roads. So, you get the most generous insurance coverage possible, and you don't worry about bouncing over rocks or scratching the paint in thick brush along the side of the road. You might even have a perfectly good car available at home, but there's no way you're going to drive your vehicle up that road—so you rent a car and buy insurance. The low cost of insurance means you have no incentive to protect the car you rented, but the insurance company doesn't know you're driving it under such conditions.

Moral hazard happens when you have an incentive to take risks that somebody else will pay for. You get to do whatever brings you the greatest potential benefit, and you don't suffer the consequences. In this example, the insurance company bears the risk: the cost of repairing or even replacing the car. The more insulated you are from risk, the more temptation you face.

Examples of Moral Hazard in Lending

Moral hazard became a significant factor during (and after) the financial crisis that began in 2007. The concept can apply to both lenders and borrowers.

Lenders were eager to approve loans before the mortgage crisis. Some mortgage brokers encouraged "subprime" borrowers to lie on loan applications, or they altered documents to make it appear that borrowers were able to afford loans that they really couldn't afford. For example, sometimes they reported inaccurate income numbers or the brokers did not require documentation that would demonstrate a borrower's ability to repay the loan.

Why would lenders hand out money when they don't know if the borrower can afford the payments—especially if they have to commit fraud to get the loans approved? In many cases, the lenders were only originating, or selling, the loans. After approving and funding loans, lenders would sell the loans to investors, who eventually suffered the losses. In other words, the lender took little or no risk. But lenders had an incentive to keep making new loans because that's how originators generate revenue.

When things turned sour, lawmakers and the public got scared. They worried that if major banks collapsed (some of them were loan originators, while others held risky investments), they would bring down the U.S. economy—not to mention the global economy. Because these banks were considered "too big to fail," the U.S. government provided funding to help some of them to weather the economic storm. If those banks suffered significant losses, the government promised to protect deposits (in some cases through the FDIC). Of course, taxpayers fund the U.S. government, so the taxpayers were ultimately bailing out the banks. The moral hazard was the lenders and investment banks taking risks that had consequences not for themselves, but for taxpayers and others.

Borrowers

Moral hazard can occur in almost any agreement, whether it's an informal understanding or a formal contract. If one party has the opportunity to benefit from taking "risks"—while risking almost nothing—moral hazard is at play.

During the financial crisis, as millions of homeowners struggled to pay their mortgages and loan defaults skyrocketed, government programs offered relief. People could avoid foreclosure thanks to money and guarantees from the U.S. government.

The moral hazard in these cases was that borrowers, increasingly underwater on their home loans, would be tempted to walk away from their mortgage rather than repay it. Such an action would put risk back onto the lender. The hazard is that the borrower no longer had an incentive to do the right thing—to pay back the mortgage as agreed.

Hence, such as moral hazard applies to Macrosoft or Microcorp and IBM software cooperational case . If Macrosoft and Microsorp and IBM do not decide to co-operate to help themselves to expand their software strengths to achieve the aim to improve their software quality and feature and function, then they can not bring any software innovation to let future software users to raise any new softwares invention or improvement useful benefits. Then, global software market can not be improved to let any software users to raise high techological software products choices number. Because they are competitors, they won't hope themselves softwares' quality, feature and function and improvement are worse to compare other softwares companies among them. So, global software users will have moral hazard to enjoy any kinds of new softwares products invention in short time. But, if they can cooperate to buy and sell themselves both shares, then they both will be another softwares owners, they won't hope the another software company loses many software customers because itself new software inventions to attack the another software company. They must hope themselves any new software invention products , they can still attract many new software products customers together. Then, global software users won't have moral hazard to enjoy any new software invention products in short time, because they must cooperate to help themselve to improve their any new softwares ' qualities , features and functions in order to they can have many software customers share in these software market when they are global large software firms.

What are Principal-Agent Problems to Microsoft and IBM both large computer companies cooperation?

For example, a company's stock investors, as part-owners, are principals who rely on the company's chief executive officer (CEO), as their agent, to carry out a strategy in their best interests. That is, they want the stock to increase in price or pay a dividend, or both. If the CEO opts instead to plow all the profits into expansion or pay big bonuses to managers, the principals may feel they have been let down by their agent. There are a number of remedies for the principal-agent problem, and many of them involve clarifying expectations and monitoring results. The principal is generally the only party who can or will correct the problem.

Understanding the Principal-Agent Problem

The principal-agent problem has become a standard factor in political science and economics. The theory was developed in the 1970s by Michael

Jensen of Harvard Business School and William Meckling of the University of Rochester. In a paper published in 1976, they outlined a theory of an ownership structure designed to avoid what they defined as agency cost and its cause, which they identified as the separation of ownership and control.The trend has been towards contracts with the agent that link compensation directly to performance measurements set by the principal.

This separation of control occurs when a principal hires an agent, The principal delegates a degree of control and the right to make decisions to the agent. But the principal retains ownership of the assets and the liability for any losses.

Factoring in Agency Costs

Logically, the principal cannot constantly monitor the agent's actions. The risk that the agent will shirk a responsibility, make a poor decision, or otherwise act in a way that is contrary to the principal's best interest, can be defined as agency costs. Additional agency costs can be incurred while dealing with problems that arise from an agent's actions. Agency costs are viewed as a part of transaction costs.

Agency costs may also include the expenses of setting up financial or other incentives to encourage the agent to act in a particular way. Principals are willing to bear these additional costs as long as the expected increase in the return on the investment from hiring the agent is greater than the cost of hiring the agent, including the agency costs.

Examples of the Principal-Agent Problem

The principal-agent problem can crop up in many day-to-day situations beyond the financial world. A client who hires a lawyer may worry that the lawyer will wrack up more billable hours than are necessary. A homeowner may disapprove of the City Council's use of taxpayer funds. A home buyer may suspect that a realtor is more interested in a commission than in the buyer's concerns. In all of these cases, the principal has little choice in the matter. An agent is necessary to get the job done.However, there are ways to resolve the principal-agent problem.

Solutions to the Principal-Agent Problem

The onus is on the principal to create incentives for the agent to act as the principal wants. Consider the first example, the relationship between shareholders and a CEO. The shareholders can take action before and after hiring a manager to overcome some risk. First, they can write the manager's contract in a way that aligns the incentives of the manager with the incentives of the shareholders. The principals can require the agent to regularly report results to them. They can hire outside monitors or auditors to track information. In the worst case, they can replace the manager.

Contract Clauses

In recent years, the trend has been towards employment contracts that connect compensation as closely as possible with performance measurements. For managers of businesses, incentives include performance-based awards of stock or stock options, profit-sharing plans, or directly linking management pay to stock price. At its root, it's the same principle as tipping for good service. Theoretically, tipping aligns the interests of the customer, or the principal, and the agent, or the waiter. Their priorities are now aligned and are focused on good service.

Hence, such as this IBM and microsoft large both companies, if they hope to cooperate , they need to solve which company can have more management authority and which company can have more share owming or investing authory. If IBM can have more management authority to control their both companies, but IBM has less shares number to Microsoft, e.g. IBM has 30 % shares to Microsoft, whether IBM ought earn more profit or less profit to 30% profits from Microsoft, if IBM have more management authory, but IBM can not cooperate to Microsoft to assist it to raise more computer buyers number. So, agent problem will cause IBM and Microsoft cooperation more easily together in nowadays computer market. But, if IBM can help Microsoft to increase computer buyers number after IBM participates to manage Microsoft's internal organizational management , then IBM can increase Microsoft computer buyers number in long time. Then, their cooperation can be more success, it means that their principle and agent problem will solve between them.

Management Science Dependency Theory Solves Macrosoft and IBM software cooperational success method

● Macrosoft or Microcorp and IBM software cooperational strategy

What is information technologic game strategy? How and why information technological game strategy can influence economic growth? I shall explain as below:

Nowadays, Macrosoft and Microcorp are the global information technological big companies. They own much market share in global information technological industry. Whether what factors influence they can still be global information technological products leaders. Why does computer software consumers still choose their products to compare other software products in preference? I suppose that Macrosoft and Microcorp, their hypothetical any software games have developed a clever new computer game that is certain to be very popular. Although Microcorp have the unique competitive advantage with its own software game engineers and compete against Macrosoft, but it can so it cheaper and better if it can hire any Macrosoft's software game engineers. So, in economic view, it needs to pay high salary (higher cost) to hire Macrosoft's engineers (labor), but Macrosoft's engineers can help Microcorp to invent any new kinds of software games to compete Macrosoft. Although, Microsorp needs to pay higher labor cost, but when it can raise its any software games' design and game playing methods to attract any game players. Then, these new and exciting software games can help it can bring many game entertainment players and then it can sell cheaper price to raise more attractive effort to win its competitor (Macrosoft). So, higher software game designing engineers (skill labor), their game designing effort will be the major factor to influence any one information technological companies in success. If one software designing company can employ one high software game designing effort profession to help it to design any kinds of attractive software games. Although, it may pay high salary (labor cost), but it have much chance to attract many software game buyers to compare that if it pays less salary to employ one poor game software designing profession. Because the poor software game designing profession may need to spend long time to research how to design any kinds of attractive game software to excite game players' playing desires in this playing software game industry market. Long time research to the poor software game designer may be one none any reward to compensate to the software game designing firm when it needs to pay long time salary to employ him. Otherwise, if the software game designing firm can accept to pay higher salary to the higher software game designer, he will have higher chance to help it to design any more attractive software games to influence game players' playing game entertainment desires. So, any software game designing companies their game designers (labor) must be the major factor to influence their business succeeds or fails in this software game entertainment market.

On the employing method hand, Microcorp can choose to include in its contracts with its software engineers that from working for another Macrosoft software company for a certain period of time if they resign from Macrosoft. A move such as this is sometimes called a preeptive move. Its propose is to alter its rivals' payoffs in order to alter their employing strategies. Preemptive moves are usually costly (high slaary), and this one is no exception. In its employment contracts makes Macrosoft a less attractive to let its old game software engineers want to leave their current employer, such as Macrosoft. As a result, Macrosoft must pay its software game designing engineers above the going market salary if it hopes their employment contracts can be continue between Macrosoft and its software game engineers.

Should Macrosoft must need to decide how to react. It can choose to fight Microcorp by aggressively advertising its game, which is costly high, but gives it a larger market share in the game player entertainment market, when Macrosoft had any one profession game software engineer(s) leave(s) his company and he/they change(s) to the another Microcorp software game designing company to work, or it can forego the expense of an advertisement campaign and simply share the market 50/50 with its major competitor, Microcorp to be partners.

Their competition has close relationship to influence economic growth because it will have many game players number to be increase if they can cooperate to be partners in success when they can design any new kinds of software game products to satisfy software game players' entertainment feeling. Otherwise, if they can not be one good partners and they only consider their every business benefits and neglect themselves business benefits. Then, their software playing games sale price can either to be reduced in order to attract any software game players when their software games can not be designed to have much new playing methods to attract many game players. Consequently, the GDP income to this software game entertainment market must reduce because any kinds of entertainment software games prices are reduced as well as the game players number is also decreasing. Due to they are the major software entertainment game suppliers in global. Any game players will only choose either Microcorp or Macrosoft to buy their any kinds of entertainment software game products to play majorly. So, their software game manufacturing and sale number must influence global GDP income increases or decreases in macro economy view. It implies that any countries technological software game industry's GDP income will depend on these both Microcorp and Macrosoft software game's cooperation relationship whether they have good or bad cooperation relationship. If their cooperation relationship is good, then they can manufacture high quality and attractive entertainment software games as well as raising sale price and exciting many game players' entertainment desires to achieve the increase to game players number aim more easily.

How to achieve their cooperation relationship more easier. I suppose that, in the software game entertainment industry, over its lifetime, the computer game will generate $500,000 in new income (income minus production cost) for all the firms producing it or its clones. Macrosoft must pay its software engineers an additional $100,000 to get them to agree to accept a contract containing an anticompetition clause. It costs Microcorp $100,000 to develop the software if it can hire Macrosoft's engineers and $200,000 otherwise. Aggressive advertising costs Macrosoft $70,000 and has the effect of giving it a 80% market share if it restricts its engineers' employment and a 72% market share if it does not. So, the fall in total market share is caused by the fact that without some of Macrosoft's advertisements. If however, Macrosoft passively acquiesces to Microcorp's entry and shares the market, then both firms can still achieve a 50% market share fairly. Hence, they must need to achieve 50/50 market share if they hope to achieve the cooperation relationship in success. Otherwise, they will not achieve cooperation relationship in success.

However, the spending advertisement factor will also their cooperation chance in success. For example, it would be more realistic to recast the Software Game as one in which Macrosoft chooses how much to spend on advertising with sales depending continuously on the amount spent. Other examples of continuous cooperation choices may include: the productive capacity of an electrical power plant; the salary to offer a prospective employee; or the insurance premium to charge a prospective policyholder. So, the amount to any of these expenditure factor will influence whether they will decide to cooperate to sell their software games products in global game entertainment market.

How and why Macrosoft and Microcorp's cooperation can influence global economic growth? It is significant that Macrosoft and Microcorp both technological software game designing companies are global the largest firms, they are doing international software game trade business to many countries and they have large market share in the software entertainment game sale market. Aside from trade based on technological gaps and software game product cycles, software game entertainment industry is dynamic in nature or game players' entertainment taste will change any time in completely static in nature. That is, given the nation's game players' playing taste and game entertainment factor, such as game playing designing technological method and game player individual playing game taste both.

We proceeded to determine the nation's comparative advantage and the gains from the different kinds of entertainment software game designing supply factor and the game player individual game taste changing factor. So, any nation's software game players number will depend on these both factors to influence whether their number will either increase or decrease in the year in this global software game entertainment market. However, these factors can be changed by time, technology usually can improve any software game playing methods and game player individual playing taste will also change any time. As a result, the nation's comparative advantage also changes over time, such as when the nation has many game players lose their interest to buy any software games to play, then the nation ought not only consider how to develop its software entertainment game in the technological industry, it is right time to research any other new technological industries to develop if it still hopes its GDP income can rise in the technological industry overall aspect. Such as dynamic trade theory is still in its infancy. However, our comparative statics analysis can carry us a long way in analyzing the effect on international trade resulting from changes in factor technology, and tastes over time, such as entertainment software game case.

The growth of factors of production will also influence the software game entertainment industry development, through time, a nation's population usually grows and with its size of its labor force , such as China and India. Similarly, by utilizing part of its resources to produce capital equipment, e.g. India needs to utilize its technological resources, technological engineers and technological material can need to be used to manufacture either new software game products or computers. But, its technological resources will be shortage (both labor and technological material). So, many technological companies choose to apply more technological material and technological engineers to use much time and money to manufacture any new software game products. Then, these labor and material resources will be reduced to be spent time and material to manufacture any new computer products in the year. In this technological industry case, capital refers to all the man-made means of production, such as machinery, factories, communication and education and training of labor force, all of which greatly enhance the nation's ability to produce either computer products or software game products. So, the national will also continue to assume that it can experiencing economic growth is producing two commodities, such as software game and computer both kinds of technological products under the constant returns to scale. So, if India can not raise the rapid technical process to skill labor and supply technological material supplying number to satisfy to manufacture the enough software game and computer products to supply them to sell to any countries' playing game players and computer users every month. Then, its technological industry will lose many clients, due to it can not supply enough software games and computers number to sell to any countries.

Several empirical studies have indicated that most the increase in real per capita income in technological industrial nations is due to technical progress and much less to capital accumulation. However, the analysis of technical progress is much more complex than the analysis of factor growth because there are several definitions and types of technical progress, and they can take place at different rates in the production of either or both commodities, such as software game and computer.

Technical progress is usually classified into neutral, labor saving , or capital saving. All technical progress , regardless of its types reduces the amount of both labor and capital required to produce any given level of output. So, if India could have good technical progress to raise its technological labor skill and reducing the technological material to be used to manufacture the software games and computers. Then, it will have chance to keep the maximum manufacturing level number to software game and computer products as the same time.

CHAPTER TWO

Wrong management science methods bring what advantages and disadvantages to societies and organizations

In management science view, any organizations or societies need to know why our organizations or societies need to apply any kinds of management science method to help our organizations or societies to solve some problems, even all problems when our organizations or societies are encountering any kinds of problems. I shall explain what management science means and how and why one effective management organization or management society will let its citizen or its staffs to bring more welfares or benefits in its organization or society.

One effective or efficient or successful organization or society , it has these characteristics in its organization or its society.

1.It helps in Achieving Group Goals - It arranges the factors of production, assembles and organizes the resources, integrates the resources in effective manner to achieve goals. It directs group efforts towards achievement of pre-determined goals. By defining objective of organization clearly there would be no wastage of time, money and effort. Management converts disorganized resources of men, machines, money etc. into useful enterprise. These resources are coordinated, directed and controlled in such a manner that enterprise work towards attainment of goals.

2.Optimum Utilization of Resources - Management utilizes all the physical & human resources productively. This leads to efficacy in management. Management provides maximum utilization of scarce resources by selecting its best possible alternate use in industry from out of various uses. It makes use of experts, professional and these services leads to use of their skills, knowledge, and proper utilization and avoids wastage. If employees and machines are producing its maximum there is no under employment of any resources.

3.Reduces Costs - It gets maximum results through minimum input by proper planning and by using minimum input & getting maximum output. Management uses physical, human and financial resources in such a manner which results in best combination. This helps in cost reduction.

4.Establishes Sound Organization - No overlapping of efforts (smooth and coordinated functions). To establish sound organizational structure is one of the objective of management which is in tune with objective of organization and for fulfillment of this, it establishes effective authority & responsibility relationship i.e. who is accountable to whom, who can give instructions to whom, who are superiors & who are subordinates. Management fills up various positions with right persons, having right skills, training and qualification. All jobs should be cleared to everyone.

5.Establishes Equilibrium - It enables the organization to survive in changing environment. It keeps in touch with the changing environment. With the change is external environment, the initial co-ordination of organization must be changed. So it adapts organization to changing demand of market / changing needs of societies. It is responsible for growth and survival of organization.

6.Essentials for Prosperity of Society - Efficient management leads to better economical production which helps in turn to increase the welfare of people. Good management makes a difficult task easier by avoiding wastage of scarce resource. It improves standard of living. It increases the profit which is beneficial to business and society will get maximum output at minimum cost by creating employment opportunities which generate income in hands. Organization comes with new products and researches beneficial for society.

Any organizations or our societies can attempt to apply any kinds of management science knowledge to solve our organizational or social problems, but if our organizations or societies apply the wrong management science method to attempt to help our societies or organizations to solve our any problems. Then, the kind of wrong management science method will not bring advantages to our organizations or societies , even it can bring extra disadvantages to our organizations or societies. So, how to choose the most suitable management science method to solve our organizational or social problem, it is very important consideration to ourselves, when we feel that we have need to find the most suitable management science method to solve the kind of social or organizational problem.

Management science solves organizational problems

One successful or efficient or effective organization or society ought have good knowledge management strategy

I shall explain what is knowledge management and knowledge management will bring what advantages or disadvantages to our organizations or societies. Management science is one kind of knowledge management, it can help any organizations or societies to solve any simple or complex problems. Knowledge management is a systematic approach to capturing and making use of a business' collective expertise to create value. The potential advantages of effective knowledge management are significant but, as with most processes, there are certain challenges to consider.However, althouh, Knowledge management ought help business growth, but it also bring disadvantage when our societies or organizations apply this knowledge management method to attempt to solve their problems, they may include:

● Advantages and disadvantages of knowledge management
Advantages of knowledge management. Some of the common benefits of knowledge management include:

I. improved organisational agility

II. better and faster decision making

III. quicker problem-solving

IV. increased rate of innovation

V. supported employee growth and development

VI. sharing of specialist expertise

VII. better communication

VIII. improved business processes

A good knowledge management system will make it easy to find and reuse relevant information and resources across your business.

I. create better products and services

II. develop better strategies

III. improve profitability

IV. reuse existing skills and expertise

V. increase operational efficiency and staff productivity

VI. recognise market trends early and gain an advantage over your rivals

VII. benchmark against your competitors

VIII. make the most of your collective intellectual capital

Resourceful collaboration will bring more views, diverse opinions and varied experiences to the process of decision-making, helping your business to make decisions based on collective knowledge and expertise.

● Disadvantages of knowledge management

The key to any successful knowledge management system is knowing its limitations. Some of the common challenges include:

I. finding ways to efficiently capture and record business knowledge

II. making information and resources easier to find

III. motivating people to share, reuse and apply knowledge consistently

IV. aligning knowledge management with the overall goals and business strategy

V. choosing and implementing knowledge management technology

VI. integrating knowledge management into existing processes and information systems

To overcome these challenges, before any organizations or our societies decide to apply knowledge management to solve our problems, we ought need to consider these issues.

I. develop clear processes to capture, record and share business knowledge

II. define the scope and objectives of any knowledge management initiatives

III. create a corporate culture of knowledge sharing between employees and management

IV. set clear goals and strategies to help you utilise the collective knowledge (otherwise, it will be of no use to your business)

V. consider budget, strategy and training needs for any new knowledge management system

VI. consider change management strategies for introducing new knowledge management practices

Strategic management in management science view

Instead of knowledge management, we also need to know how we choose the most suitable strategic management method in order to help our societies or our organizations to solve any social or organizational problems in success.

Strategic Management is all about identification and description of the strategies that managers can carry so as to achieve better performance and a competitive advantage for their organization. An organization is said to have competitive advantage if its profitability is higher than the average profitability for all companies in its industry. Strategic management can also be defined as a bundle of decisions and acts which a manager undertakes and which decides the result of the firm's performance. The manager must have a thorough knowledge and analysis of the general and competitive organizational environment so as to take right decisions. They should conduct a SWOT Analysis (Strengths, Weaknesses, Opportunities, and Threats), i.e., they should make best possible utilization of strengths, minimize the organizational weaknesses, make use of arising opportunities from the business environment and shouldn't ignore the threats.

Strategic management is nothing but planning for both predictable as well as unfeasible contingencies. It is applicable to both small as well as large organizations as even the smallest organization face competition and, by formulating and implementing appropriate strategies, they can attain sustainable competitive advantage. It is a way in which strategists set the objectives and proceed about attaining them. It deals with making and implementing decisions about future direction of an organization. It helps us to identify the direction in which an organization is moving.

Strategic management is a continuous process that evaluates and controls the business and the industries in which an organization is involved; evaluates its competitors and sets goals and strategies to meet all existing and potential competitors; and then reevaluates strategies on a regular basis to determine how it has been implemented and whether it was successful or does it needs replacement.

Strategic Management gives a broader perspective to the employees of an organization and they can better understand how their job fits into the entire organizational plan and how it is co-related to other organizational members. It is nothing but the art of managing employees in a manner which maximizes the ability of achieving business objectives. The employees become more trustworthy, more committed and more satisfied as they can co-relate themselves very well with each organizational task. They can understand the reaction of environmental changes on the organization and the probable response of the organization with the help of strategic management. Thus the employees can judge the impact of such changes on their own job and can effectively face the changes. The managers and employees must do appropriate things in appropriate manner.

They need to be both effective as well as efficient.

One of the major role of strategic management is to incorporate various functional areas of the organization completely, as well as, to ensure these functional areas harmonize and get together well. Another role of strategic management is to keep a continuous eye on the goals and objectives of the organization.

Following are the important concepts of Strategic Management, when you are your country's social leader or you are your organization's business leader, you need to consider these steps in your strategic management arrangement, such as below:

Strategy - Definition and Features
Components of a Strategy Statement
Strategic Management Process
Environmental Scanning
Strategy Formulation
Strategy Implementation
Strategy Formulation vs Implementation
Strategy Evaluation
Strategic Decisions
Business Policy
BCG Matrix
SWOT Analysis
Competitor Analysis
Porter's Five Forces Model
Strategic Leadership
Corporate Governance
Business Ethics
Core Competencies
Advantages and Disadvantages of Cooperative Society

In micro view, organizational management science aspect, one successful cooperative social organization can create innovation advantages to any organizations, such as when one organization can apply management science to let it become one successful cooperative social organization. Although, it seems that one cooperative society is one sucessful management organization, but it also has disadvantages when the organization becomes one successful cooperative social organization.

An cooperative social management organization's

Advantages:

1. Easy Formation:

Compared to the formation of a company, formation of a cooperative society is easy. Any ten adult persons can voluntarily form themselves into an association and get it registered with the Registrar of Co-operatives. Formation of a cooperative society also does not involve long and complicated legal formalities.

2. Limited Liability:

Like company form of ownership, the liability of members is limited to the extent of their capital in the cooperative societies.

3. Perpetual Existence:

A cooperative society has a separate legal entity. Hence, the death, insolvency, retirement, lunacy, etc., of the members do not affect the perpetual existence of a cooperative society.

4. Social Service:

The basic philosophy of cooperatives is self-help and mutual help. Thus, cooperatives foster fellow feeling among their members and inculcate moral values in them for a better living.

5. Open Membership:

The membership of cooperative societies is open to all irrespective of caste, colour, creed and economic status. There is no limit on maximum members.

6. Tax Advantage:

Unlike other three forms of business ownership, a cooperative society is exempted from income-tax and surcharge on its earnings up to a certain limit. Besides, it is also exempted from stamp duty and registration fee.

7. State Assistance:

Government has adopted cooperatives as an effective instrument of socio-economic change. Hence, the Government offers a number of grants, loans and financial assistance to the cooperative societies – to make their working more effective.

8. Democratic Management:

The management of cooperative society is entrusted to the managing committee duly elected by the members on the basis of 'one-member one -vote' irrespective of the number of shares held by them. The proxy is not allowed in cooperative societies. Thus, the management in cooperatives is democratic.

Disadvantages:

In spite of its numerous advantages, the cooperative also has some disadvantages which must be seriously considered before opting for this form of business ownership.

The important among the disadvantages are:

1. Lack of Secrecy:

A cooperative society has to submit its annual reports and accounts with the Registrar of Cooperative Societies. Hence, it becomes quite difficult for it to maintain secrecy of its business affairs.

2. Lack of Business Acumen:

The member of cooperative societies generally lack business acumen. When such members become the members of the Board of Directors, the affairs of the society are expectedly not conducted efficiently. These also cannot employ the professional managers because it is neither compatible with their avowed ends nor the limited resources allow for the same.

3. Lack of Interest:

The paid office-bearers of cooperative societies do not take interest in the functioning of societies due to the absence of profit motive. Business success requires sustained efforts over a period of time which, however, does not exist in many cooperatives. As a result, the cooperatives become inactive and come to a grinding halt.

4. Corruption:

In a way, lack of profit motive breeds fraud and corruption in management. This is reflected in misappropriations of funds by the officials for their personal gains.

5. Lack of Mutual Interest:

The success of a cooperative society depends upon its members' utmost trust to each other. However, all members are not found imbued with a spirit of co-operation. Absence of such spirit breeds mutual rivalries among the members. Influential members tend to dominate in the society's affairs.

Advantages and Disadvantages of Diversity in the Workplace

In micro organization view, management science can bring advantages of diversity in the workplace to the organization, but it also being disadvantages to the organization. They may include as below:

People like to stay in their comfort zones. That is why routines develop over time. When we feel safe, then the idea is that we can be more creative in every element of our life. This process envelopes our personal and professional lives. There are ways that we try to become comfortable at work on our own, like bringing a potted plant to the office or taping a favorite comic strip to the computer. About 2 out of every 5 employees also say that they love their job because of the presence of their co-workers. When there is a supportive team and supervisor in place, it is easier to pursue what we are passionate about as a career.

The issue with diversity is that it takes some people out of their comfort zone. Some professionals define the composition of the perfect team as people who come from the same culture, ethnicity, educational experience, or social status. If someone on the team has a different set of life experiences, then the unknowns that come about because of it can feel scary. When people are afraid, then their focus is on survival instead of productivity. Even though the pros and cons of diversity in the workplace show that teams can by over 30% more productive when they focus on uniqueness, some people are not ready to step outside of their comfort zone. They would rather trade short-term comfort for long-term profit losses.

How do you feel about having diverse teams present in the modern workplace?

Advantages of Diversity in the Workplace

I. This design allows each team member to focus on their strengths.

If an employer can create diversity in the workplace, then each worker will have their strengths complement those of everyone else on the team. That means assignments can be handed out with greater specificity so that the quality of the work improves. Supervisors aren't forced to guess at who might be the best option for an assignment because each person has a unique skill that they bring to the table. Diversity in the workplace allows for strengths and weaknesses to be spread out so that their effects are maximized and minimized respectively. No matter what the requirements of a project might be, there is someone who can step up to lead the team toward a successful result.

II. It increases the number of job opportunities for minority workers.

Diversity in the workplace looks at all population demographics when hiring for an open position. That means employers have an opportunity to find the best possible person for a job because they are not limited to a specific group of individuals. This advantage makes it possible to have more women working in society and promotes the hiring of minority groups. It applies at all levels of employment, from the local small business to multinational firms. When everyone has a chance to work if that's what they want to do, then a secondary benefit of this advantage is that it diversifies the wages and productivity of the economy. This process reduces the amount of risk communities face if an unexpected recession were to occur.

III. Employers have more chances to cross-train workers and teams.

Diversity in the workplace creates teams where each person brings a unique strength to work every day. Individuals can specialize in their career, which means their skills and wisdom can be passed along to other team members. Everyone gets to learn and grow each day because there are higher levels of information exposure thanks to the varying backgrounds and educational opportunities each person accomplished. This advantage also has a secondary benefit that involves cultural awareness. When we can understand the complexities of other ethnicities and perspectives, then it becomes easier to find common ground. This process eventually leads to a higher level of innovation and fewer silos and echo chambers.

IV. Companies have access to more talent.

When diversity in the workplace is a top priority for an organization, then supervisors and hiring managers can expand their applicant screening processes to include more people. There are fewer restrictions on geographic location, educational accomplishments, or previous work histories. The top priority in the hiring process focuses on the talent and skills of the individual, and then how that person could fit into the team. Instead of trying to hire the best possible candidate from a group of applicants, diversity in the workplace encourages managers to find the best person for the job.

V. This perspective can help companies to start growing bigger and faster.

Almost 70% of hiring managers in the United States say that the implementation of a diversity initiative was a contributing factor to the growth of their organization. This advantage helps the organization to create new opportunities for existing team members, install new positions, and raise wages as productivity and creativity levels rise to encourage a stronger sales atmosphere. Hiring managers need the tools that can help them to find the best candidates for each person to take advantage of this opportunity. About 90% of supervisors think that the use of cross-border communication allows their company to grow bigger and faster. Nearly half focus on recruiting as a way to improve diversity.

VI. Diversity in the workplace creates more revenue-earning opportunities.

The companies which focus on diversification are the businesses which tend to see more sales and revenues because of their efforts. Emphasizing multiple language fluency for a team can boost their profits by 10% for every fluent language that is spoken. Gender diversity can help revenues grow by 40% in the first year of this effort. This advantage can open new markets for the organization that can help profits to start climbing as well without a significant increase in the work of the team. Diversity in the workplace goes beyond skin color or gender. These benefits occur when lifestyle differences, spiritual perspectives, and other unique life factors are taken into account during the hiring process. You cannot exclude employees from a job because of their differences, but you can look for people who can fit into a specific role for you.

VII. It is a way to increase the creativity of an entire team.

Almost 80% of employees working in the United States say that they are not using their creativity to its full potential. Diversity is one of the best environments to encourage this approach to a career because it offers numerous perspectives that can enhance the brainstorming sessions. The biggest complainers about a lack of creative energy in the modern workplace are those who limit the diversity of their teams. Having different perspectives can create conflict at times, but the unique interpretation of life that each person brings is invaluable to the employer and their team. The need to create change or embrace differences is what leads to an environment that encourages innovation.

VIII. Diversity in the workplace exposes societal bias.

Bias is what destroys diversity in the workplace before it can establish itself. Hiring managers tend to bring men on more than women, even if the qualifications of each candidate are equal. During a study funded by Harvard and Princeton, managers were given a set of applications and qualifications, but they did not reveal the gender of each identity. During this blind process, women were preferred over their male counterparts when gender was not part of the hiring process. Because of this issue, women could be under-represented in the labor force by over 50%. People with an alternative gender identity (outside of male or female) can see even more struggles in this area. It is a problem for racial minorities around the world as well.

IX. Customers are attracted to diversity in the workplace.

Over 40% of employees say that their company has the right amount of diversity or that their teams should try to become more unique. Although it can be challenging to share a workplace environment with someone who is uniquely different, the advantages typically outweigh the problems which can develop over time. When everyone comes from the same perspective, then the daily routine becomes dull. Going to work becomes a boring experience. People can even lose their passion for what they do because there is a lack of diversity present on their team. There are immediate benefits to consider when hiring managers make diversity a top priority. It can lower the levels of burnout which are present in the workplace, improve the quality of each project, and boost the levels of community exposure that are present.

X. Productivity levels improve because of diversity in the workplace. Even when a team doesn't like the idea of being diverse, their productivity levels can rise by more than 30%. When people have co-workers who are different from them, then there is an increase in the sensitivity levels that are present in the workplace. People start to look for ways to find common ground. There is more time given to each team member to share ideas, and a higher emphasis on hiring women occurs. The fastest way for an employer to encourage a higher level of productivity is to add diversity throughout their organization. Even when there are moments where the work levels decline, the overall benefit never disappears.

List of the Disadvantages of Diversity in the Workplace

I. Hiring managers focus on leadership qualities too often. Diversity in the workplace seeks out experts who excel in their chosen career, job function, and team environment. The goal is to create a series of strengths that allows everyone to grow over time. These are all advantages, but it can become a problem if hiring managers are bringing in people who all want to be in charge. Competition can be healthy, but it can also be dangerous when it spirals out of control. When the goal is to promote the individual instead of the team, then a diversity initiative fails. You must go beyond what you see to create a team that complements one another. That means there must be leaders, people who are content with their current position, and individuals who come to work because of their passion. There must be emotional diversity too.

II. Diversity can create workers who are over-qualified for some jobs. Communities grow and decline naturally as the economy settles into a comfortable pattern. Diversity in the workplace can create stable circumstances and more job security, but it can also create a series of problems where workers become over-qualified for what they are doing. If that individual were to lose their job for some reason, then it could become a struggle for them to find new employment elsewhere. We saw this problem throughout the United States during the Great Recession years.

Employers were hiring people who were willing to work for almost any wage. You had people who had earned a Ph.D. trying to fill cashier positions at fast-food establishments because there were no job opportunities in their area.

III. Diversity in the workplace can create too many opinions.
When hiring managers focus on diversity, then they are creating a series of differing opinions that can make it easier to find the right journey to take for forward progress. There are also times when the sheer number of available opinions can create a problem for the organization. When everyone gets a chance to be heard, then the speed of a project can slow down just as quickly as it can increase.

IV. Offshoring can become a point of emphasis with diversity in the workplace.
Domestic diversity can become an expensive proposition. It costs a lot, between salary and benefits, to hire the best people for your open positions. Because of this issue, it is not unusual for companies to look for offshoring opportunities that can help them to add unique perspectives to their corporate identity without a significant labor expense. This issue can create a lack of job security for existing workers, which can limit their focus and productivity. Platforms like Upwork and Fiverr bring freelancers into this mix as well. If a company can hire independent contractors at a lower rate to receive equal or superior work, then they will do so. The reason why the middle class is growing around the world is because of diversity initiatives, which means fewer local jobs might be available.

V. Diversity in the workplace can lessen the amount of trust that exists.
When an organization decides to make a diversity initiative a top priority, then there is an immediate decrease in the amount of trust that is present in the workplace. This disadvantage impacts every population demographic – including people who come from the same culture, educational background, and career experience. Although this disadvantage doesn't create silos or team isolation, it can create roadblocks to collaboration. Some people will interact less often with others, experience fear if they are forced to do so, and this issue eventually can limit productivity.
Different perspectives create unique opinions and approaches to life that can create severe disagreements in the workplace. It is not unusual for every person to believe that their individual perspectives are the correct one, so they will share that information with others. If someone should happen to disagree, then some people will take that as a personal attack against their

character more easily.

VI. Diversity in the workplace can create communication problems.
People from different cultures may not speak the same language as their primary communication option. Hiring people from different areas can provide unique perspectives, but it can also cause issues with how co-workers speak with one another. Even when the same language is spoken, there can be differences in the meaning of certain words or jargon understanding problems that can create confusion in the workplace.

VIII. Diversity initiatives are usually left to a single person to implement. About 2 out of every 5 companies leave their diversity initiatives in the hands of a single individual or sponsor. That person is usually the Chief Executive Officer or another member of the leadership team. This assignment is fine if the CEO or another member of the C-suite doesn't have a lot on their plate, but this process is usually put on the back burner of priorities. It is easier to talk about making this issue a priority than to create new policies and procedures that can make it a reality. For the remaining companies that use multiple people to create diversity in the workplace, there can be silos created that individualize this process so that a similar result occurs. There must be complete leadership buy-in for this process to be effective.

IX. Complaint levels often rise with a diversity initiative.
There tends to be more conflict between individual team members in a diverse environment when compared to one where most people come from the same perspective. Different habits and working styles can create bothersome results. Imagine sitting next to a co-worker who needs to click a pen constantly to think, and that's how some people see this process. Without proactive management, an increase in complaints and grievances typically occurs, which means there is more time and money spent on investigations. This disadvantage can become so severe that some companies will see a surge in resignations because they don't like being placed into an "uncomfortable" situation. That means an organization must cope with the necessary costs to replace the lost workers, so it may take months (or years) to recoup the investments made.

On conclusion, diversity in the workplace requires a commitment from every level of the chain of command for it to be a successful experience. If the CEO doesn't buy into the process, then neither will the entry-level worker. Then there must be a monetary commitment given to the process to ensure its successful completion. We live in a society that expects instant results. Diversity can provide unique perspectives, but it may take time for revenue and productivity increases to arrive. Many initiatives stop before they can be successful because there is a lack of patience with this process. The advantages and disadvantages of diversity in the workplace must be carefully managed for the results to be successful.

Management science solves social problems

What is our social problem?
Updated with recent issues such as the national debate on health care reform, this Second Edition of How Can We Solve Our Social Problems? Social problems, also called social issues, affect every society, great and small. Even in relatively isolated, sparsely populated areas, a group will encounter social problems. Part of this is due to the fact that any members of a society living close enough together will have conflicts. It's virtually impossible to avoid them, and even people who live together in the same house don't always get along seamlessly. On the whole though, when social problems are mentioned they tend to refer to the problems that affect people living together in a society.

The list of social problems is huge and not identical from area to area. In the US, some predominant social issues include the growing divide between rich and poor, domestic violence, unemployment, pollution, urban decay, racism and sexism, and many others. Sometimes social issues arise when people hold very different opinions about how to handle certain situations like unplanned pregnancy. While some people might view abortion as the solution to this problem, other members of the society remain strongly opposed to its use. In itself, strong disagreements on how to solve problems create divides in social groups.

Other issues that may be considered social problems aren't that common in the US and other industrialized countries, but they are huge problems in developing ones. The issues of massive poverty, food shortages, lack of basic hygiene, spread of incurable diseases, ethnic cleansing, and lack of education inhibits the development of society. Moreover, these problems are related to each other and it can seem hard to address one without addressing all of them.

It would be easy to assume that a social problem only affects the people whom it directly touches, but this is not the case. Easy spread of disease for instance may tamper with the society at large, and it's easy to see how this has operated in certain areas of Africa. The spread of AIDs for instance has created more social problems because it is costly, it is a danger to all members of society, and it leaves many children without parents. HIV/AIDs isn't a single problem but a complex cause of numerous ones. Similarly, unemployment in America doesn't just affect those unemployed but affects the whole economy.

It's also important to understand that social problems within a society affect its interaction with other societies, which may lead to global problems or issues. How another nation deals with the problems of a developing nation may affect its relationship with that nation and the rest of the world for years to come. Though the United States was a strong supporter of the need to develop a Jewish State in Israel, its support has come at a cost of its relationship with many Arabic nations.

Additionally, countries that allow multiple political parties and free expression of speech have yet another issue when it comes to tackling some of the problems that plague its society. This is diversity of solutions, which may mean that the country cannot commit to a single way to solve an issue, because there are too many ideas operating on how to solve it. Any proposed solution to something that affects society is likely to make some people unhappy, and this discontent can promote discord. On the other hand, in countries where the government operates independently of the people and where free speech or exchange of ideas is discouraged, there may not be enough ideas to solve issues, and governments may persist in trying to solve them in wrongheaded or ineffective ways. The very nature of social problems suggests that society itself is a problem. No country has perfected a society where all are happy and where no problems exist. Perhaps the individual nature of humans prevents this, and as many people state, perfection many not be an achievable goal.

On conclusion, social problem-solving might also be called 'problem-solving in real life'. In other words, it is a rather academic way of describing the systems and processes that we use to solve the problems that we encounter in our everyday lives. The word 'social' does not mean that it only applies to problems that we solve with other people, or, indeed, those that we feel are caused by others. The word is simply used to indicate the 'real life' nature of the problems, and the way that we approach them.

A Model of Social Problem-Solving

One of the main models used in academic studies of social problem-solving was put forward by a group led by Thomas D'Zurilla.

This model includes three basic concepts or elements:

•Problem-solving

This is defined as the process used by an individual, pair or group to find an effective solution for a particular problem. It is a self-directed process, meaning simply that the individual or group does not have anyone telling them what to do. Parts of this process include generating lots of possible solutions and selecting the best from among them.

•Problem

A problem is defined as any situation or task that needs some kind of a response if it is to be managed effectively, but to which no obvious response is available. The demands may be external, from the environment, or internal.

•Solution

A solution is a response or coping mechanism which is specific to the problem or situation. It is the outcome of the problem-solving process.

Once a solution has been identified, it must then be implemented. D'Zurilla's model distinguishes between problem-solving (the process that identifies a solution) and solution implementation (the process of putting that solution into practice), and notes that the skills required for the two are not necessarily the same. It also distinguishes between two parts of the problem-solving process: problem orientation and actual problem-solving.

Problem Orientation

Problem orientation is the way that people approach problems, and how they set them into the context of their existing knowledge and ways of looking at the world. Each of us will see problems in a different way, depending on our experience and skills, and this orientation is key to working out which skills we will need to use to solve the problem.

An Example of Orientation

Most people, on seeing a spout of water coming from a loose joint between a tap and a pipe, will probably reach first for a cloth to put round the joint to catch the water, and then a phone, employing their research skills to find a plumber. A plumber, however, or someone with some experience of plumbing, is more likely to reach for tools to mend the joint and fix the leak. It's all a question of orientation.

Problem-solving includes four key skills:

1.Defining the problem,

2.Coming up with alternative solutions,

3.Making a decision about which solution to use, and

4.Implementing that solution.

Based on this split between orientation and problem-solving, D'Zurilla and colleagues defined two scales to measure both abilities.

They defined two orientation dimensions, positive and negative, and three problem-solving styles, rational, impulsive/careless and avoidance.

They noted that people who were good at orientation were not necessarily good at problem-solving and vice versa, although the two might also go together.

It will probably be obvious from these descriptions that the researchers viewed positive orientation and rational problem-solving as functional behaviours, and defined all the others as dysfunctional, leading to psychological distress.

The skills required for positive problem orientation are:

Being able to see problems as 'challenges', or opportunities to gain something, rather than insurmountable difficulties at which it is only possible to fail. Believing that problems are solvable. While this, too, may be considered an aspect of mindset, it is also important to use techniques of Positive Thinking; Believing that you personally are able to solve problems successfully, which is at least in part an aspect of self-confidence. Understanding that solving problems successfully will take time and effort, which may require a certain amount of resilience; and motivating yourself to solve problems immediately, rather than putting them off.

Those who find it harder to develop positive problem orientation tend to view problems as insurmountable obstacles, or a threat to their well-being, doubt their own abilities to solve problems, and become frustrated or upset when they encounter problems.

The skills required for rational problem-solving include:

a. The ability to gather information and facts, through research. There is more about this on our page on defining and identifying problems;

b. The ability to set suitable problem-solving goals. You may find our page on personal goal-setting helpful;

c. The application of rational thinking to generate possible solutions. You may find some of the ideas on our Creative Thinking page helpful, as well as those on investigating ideas and solutions;

d. Good decision-making skills to decide which solution is best. See our page on Decision-Making for more; and

e. Implementation skills, which include the ability to plan, organise and do. You may find our pages on Action Planning, Project Management and

Solution Implementation helpful.

Potential Difficulties

Those who struggle to manage rational problem-solving tend to either:

a. Rush things without thinking them through properly (the impulsive/careless approach), or

b. Avoid them through procrastination, ignoring the problem, or trying to persuade someone else to solve the problem (the avoidance mode).

c. This 'avoidance' is not the same as actively and appropriately delegating to someone with the necessary skills (see our page on Delegation Skills for more). Instead, it is simple 'buck-passing', usually characterised by a lack of selection of anyone with the appropriate skills, and/or an attempt to avoid responsibility for the problem.

An Academic Term for a Human Process?

You may be thinking that social problem-solving, and the model described here, sounds like an academic attempt to define very normal human processes. This is probably not an unreasonable summary. However, breaking a complex process down in this way not only helps academics to study it, but also helps us to develop our skills in a more targeted way. By considering each element of the process separately, we can focus on those that we find most difficult: maximum 'bang for your buck', as it were.

How Technology Can Help Solve Societal Problems

What Are Science and Technology?

Science and technology have completely changed the world over the last 200 years. Human life expectancy has doubled. We've learned how to communicate and travel rapidly across the entire globe. We're surrounded by televisions, computers, electric lights, cars, cell phones, and all kinds of things that would have been unimaginable even a century ago. And none of it would be possible without science and technology.

Science is the systematic study of the natural world, through observation and experiment. Technology is the use of scientific knowledge for practical purposes, to complete tasks that wouldn't be possible without it. Technology can be super simple, like the wheel, or super complicated, like the personal computer. Either way, we are surrounded by it in our modern lives.

Can applying management technoloigcal science method to solve Society's Problems, artificial intelligence, computer, mobile, big data digial internet etc. high technological methods?

Sometimes it might seem like technology only causes problems or complicates things. People yearn for a simpler life, without cell phones beeping, traffic jams, and dangerous weapons. But the truth is, science and technology have solved a lot of society's problems and will continue to do so in the future.

However, nowadays, human is encountering " The Network Revolution" stage. And so is it today. The Fourth Industrial Revolution — what Klaus Schwab (founder of the World Economic Forum) defines as the fusion of technologies blurring the lines among the physical, digital and biological spheres — is upon us. Meanwhile, nationalism is colliding with globalism, machine learning and artificial intelligence advancing geometrically, and global warming is on a direct path to changing the very nature of our planet. Despite these many challenges, this revolution, like the many that have preceded it, also comes with a great promise of opportunity.

To be sure, there are reasons for great optimism. In just the past 30 years, the global poverty rate halved with many of the poorest people in the world becoming significantly less poor. These gains mirror dramatic improvements in health and education including advances in life expectancy, child mortality, health care provision, among other important areas. Moreover, most of these gains predate the effective integration of digital technologies into the cause. In short, it is reasonable to argue that the potential for social 'changemakers' armed with today's digital platforms in partnership with large and growing virtual networks can dramatically improve the human condition.

Some management scientists beleive that "The potential for social 'changemakers' armed with today's digital platforms in partnership with large and growing virtual networks can dramatically improve the human condition."

I shall indicate how " Self-organization Powered by Technology" technological management scinece method , it can be applied to help any organizations, even our societies to solve many organizational or social problems nowadays.

What is our nowadays Civil society ? What are the differences or changes between our traditional civil society and nowadays civil society? How and why does technological innovation influence our civil social change, e.g. internet, ecommerce, smart phone ?— the network of institutions that define us as actors in the civil sphere independent of governments — is supposed to serve as the leader in promoting pluralism and social benefit.

As Klaus Schwab notes that "a renewed focus on the essential contribution of civil society to a resilient global system alongside government and business has emerged." Unfortunately, nonprofit groups, academic institutions and philanthropic organizations engaged in social change are struggling to adapt to the new global, technological and virtual landscape.

This new direction starts with social organizations fundamentally rethinking the core assumptions driving their attitudes, behaviors and beliefs about creating long-term sustainable value for their constituencies in an exponentially networked world. Rather than using an organization-centric model, the nonprofit sector and related organizations need to adopt a mental model based on scaling relationships in a whole new way using today's technologies model.

Embracing social change as a platform is more than a theory of change, it is a theory of being — one that places a virtual network or individuals seeking social change at the center of everything and leverages today's digital platforms (such as social media, mobile, big data and machine learning) to facilitate stakeholders (contributors and consumers) to connect, collaborate, and interact with each other to exchange value among each other to effectuate exponential social change and impact.

Civil society is grounded in exploiting new digital technologies, but extends well beyond them to focus on how organizations think about advancing their core mission — do they go at it alone or do they collaborate as part of a network? Nowadays, many business organizations or public organizations require thinking and operating, in all things, as a network. It requires updating the core DNA that runs through social change organizations to put relationships in service of a cause at the center, not the institution. When implemented correctly, SCaaP will impact everything — from the way an organization allocates resources to how value is captured and measured to helping individuals achieve their full potential.

Digital Platforms Empower Social Change at Scale

To be sure, early adopters are already using technology to effectuate change at a pace and scale not previously available in the physical and digitally disconnected world. The marginal cost of delivery remains too high. But with today's technologies, with support from the board and management to make it happen, social change at scale is possible. Just as Apple chose a platform approach when launching their App Store, these organizations are enabling their partners and contributors to share and co-create in the value chain they co-inhabit. Each has moved beyond allowing supporters to donate and promote, toward sharing real value through stakeholders' talents and assets.

The future of social change as a platform is a world of connected platforms working to solve society's most pressing challenges more effectively as fast as possible. These platforms will supersede and encompass existing social change organizations. Those organizations that embrace social change as a platform will lead the way in helping to usher in this new era of connected social change platforms.

The core assets needed today to advance social change — ideas, individuals and institutions — continue to be the primary ingredients. What is changing and will continue to change, however, is the way these assets are assembled to deliver maximum social impact. Organizations can achieve SCAAP to the extent that those with a shared cause can gradually maximize shared capability (platforms) and minimize organization products. This represents a radical shift in approach.

Every organization relies on its information, capabilities and assets to be effective, but their networks are largely untapped or underutilized. Creating more value and scaling social impact requires the organizations' leaders to leverage their networks, tapping into new sources of value, both tangible and intangible. Value in the social impact supply chain will continue to come from new sources, for those who allow that to happen. Existing stakeholders in social change organizations will add value in new ways and new stakeholders will interact in new ways with the community's resources and assets via the platform. SCaaP will increasingly bring all those actors and sectors together.

Some management scienists indicated that "The future of social change as a platform is a world of connected platforms working to solve society's most pressing challenges more effectively as fast as possible."

How technological innovation impacts our social change?

Our future social change will be impacted to these several aspects:

Social change organizations that leverage their stakeholder's networks as well as their tangible (programs and services) and intangible (expertise and relationships) assets will gain these and other advantages from embracing the SCaaP business model.

•Decreases costs: Stakeholders willing to share their opinions, skills, relationships and even real assets for shared value to the cause, at a very low or near-zero cost, stretch an organization's very scarce resources. Moreover, reinventing the wheel each time social change products and services are created lead to duplication and waste.

•Deepens community engagement: Enabling meaningful ways for stakeholders to add value increases engagement and deepens understanding and strengthens these relationships. SCaaP enables anyone with a good idea to build innovative services that connect citizens to the cause of their choice, allowing citizens to more directly participate.

•Increases organizational flexibility and decreases risk: Operating as a network increases an organization's adaptability and speed. Work is more distributed and lends itself to self-organizing, which makes it highly responsive to changing needs. Allowing common functions to be implemented as shared utilities across social change organizations instead of replicating them in each silo also reduces risk.

•Enhances transparency and accountability: SCaaP fundamentally shifts the power dynamic within the social change community. Grant makers work with community stakeholders as peers, helping them achieve full potential as individuals and their organizations.

•Expands impact: Ultimately, scaling relationships lets an organization secure more value, which helps maximize social impact. As co-creating partners who have a vested interest in advancing a cause, stakeholders' incentive to add value is clear. The platform's success is their success.

How technological management science method of internet platform ,which can impact our social change as well as it can be the best technological management method to help our societies to solve many social problems

Social change as a platform is first and foremost a business strategy, a theory of change that needs to be integrated into every organization's five-year strategic plan. That effort begins by identifying how and where an organization can accelerate the transition to a network-model across the entire organization. Specifically, organizations must assess their business model and inventory network assets, and start to reallocate resources and capital to networks as well as develop network key performance indicators (KPIs).

•Choose the right platform. Platforms that embrace intelligence, speed, productivity, mobility, and connectivity empower social change organizations to take advantage of the most significant transformations taking place in enterprise software.

•Select the relationships to scale. Identify all the key stakeholders for advancing your mission and indicate which relationships are the most important to scale. Be sure to include existing and potential relationships, including other partners and organizations that can add value.

•Connect programs and services. Plot the organization's various offerings — programs and services offers to various stakeholders — and map how each contributes value to advance the relationships with different stakeholders.

•Convert the data into intelligence. A unified view of relationships and programs creates troves of data. Convert the data into useful, real-time intelligence integrated into the organization's processes in real-time.

•Drive one-to-one engagement. Real-time intelligence lets organizations engage more effectively with all.

•Track what matters. It's not just financial performance that matters, but also engagement, sentiment and co-creation. Create KPI's for each of these items and add them to daily performance reviews.

•Keep platforms, networks and intelligence at the center. Products and services are helpful, but in the final reckoning, it is the breadth and depth of the network that will create the scale of social change desired.

On conclusion, I believe that internet platform is the best technological management method to help our, the nonprofit world will have the potential to enact social change on a scale previously unimagined. It is time to take up the mantle because doing so can unlock the future potential of every human being because human can gather any useful data to attempt to compare which is the best in order to solve any social problems in the short time as well as internet platform, e.g. big data gathering method will still be the most accurate and the most rapid speed to help any management scientists to learn how to analyze and conclude the problem solution in the most useful way more than other high technological methods nowadays.

CHAPTER THREE

Information Technology Outsourcing

Information technology outsourcing advantages

In any organization information technology department, information system operations remain the predominant function outsourced, other functions are also being performed by external service providers and the relationship is between outsourcing and certain demographics: size, industry is formation intensity. The results suggest that system operations remain being performed by external service providers. Further, industry and information intensity has some influence on the extent of outsourcing of certain functions.

Information technology department outsoucring benefits may include as below:

The first reason is cost reduction, trying to remain competitive and up-to-date is becoming a financial burden to many organizations. This is true particularly in fields, such as banking and financial services, health care and manufacturing. Hiring outsiders to handle part or even all of its information system often helps an organization to provide better services and maintain a competitive advantage. The information technology industry choice of outsourcing factor is related to size, industry type and information technology.

The second reason is technological and/or human resources in the management of the information technology infrastructure skill improvement. The information technology department outsourcing service to external service provider, includes the degree of internalization of technological resources and the degree of internalization of human resources. Some economists defined internalization of outsourcing service is as ownership is by the focal organization which takes on full control with profit and loss responsibility. Also who define outsourcing is as involving a significant use of resources, either technological and/or human resources, external to the organizational hierarchy in the management of the information technology infrastructure.

So the information technology external service providers includes: applications development and maintenance, systems operations, networks/telecommunications management and user computing support, system planning and management purchase of application software, but excludes business consulting services, after-sale vendor services and the lease of telephone lines etc. outsourcing services.

The third reason is economics of scale in areas of hardware, software. This pressure is seen as the most significant factor driving today's corporate interest. An outsourcing service provision might be in a position to exploit economics of scale in areas of hardware, software and staff since it pools different kind of technological projects from many service receivers. Outsourcing information technological service can reduce the corporate's cost with the high level of IT investment, there are increasing pressures to move away from fixed expenditure, corporate overhead towards a more direct variable cost approach to control the IT operations.

The IT costs can become predictable for overruns is often placed on the service provider. Outsourcing service can allow the service to gain immediate access to competitiveness in delivering products or services as well as to avoid of obsolescence risk, due to the changes in the nature of the IT infrastructure, the risk of obsolescence is high. Outsourcing can allow the service provider has the ability to diversify these risks across a broad range of service receivers. However, long term contracts might in spread the risk, the weakness is back to the receiver.

It seems outsourcing IT service has also these disadvantages: such as, loss of flexibility or managerial control. Outsourcing reduces real or perceived control over both quality real or perceived control over both the quality of software and the timetable of project since the work is now being carried out by people not under direct supervision.

It also threats to long term career prospects to information system professionals because many of them do not find suitable. Is jobs or promising career paths in both areas of the corporation. Outsourcing also increases coordination cost.

It may requires increasing time to communicate and coordinate with the service provider. Traditionally, the formal meeting cost of negotiating and monitoring the outsourcing contract are potentially wide ranging, indirect and substantial increasing, such as, additional releasing or transferring employees, in license transfer by software vendors and in re-negotiating contracts costs. So, the IT industry of profit motivates service provider might not be in the least interests of the outsourcing service receivers. Some IT service providers are in the business of maximizing their profit at any cost, this could run counter to a service receiver's interest.

Human resource outsourcing

1.1 Outsourcing or insourcing in human resource supply chain factor

To choosing of outsourcing or insourcing in human resource supply chain factor of the controlling service demanders needs to concern this issues: Should human resource activities be provided in house or should all or past of those activities be outsourced? The relationship between organizational structure and the HR function is an important variable. The individual activities that comprise HR systems include not only the employee life cycle from recruiting to termination, but also planning for organizational staffing needs and improving organizational effectiveness.

How organizations need to outsource HR function to not care employees knowledge and skill is a factor to influence any organizations choose to outsourcing non core employees when which have no any right employees to be promoted to do the position. For example, firms engage in HR outsourcing to reduce management access HR expertise, achieve workforce flexibility, focus managerial resources and keep up with changing workplace negotiations. Also, supporting the tend is the availability of common technology platform, which can reduce costs for organizations and risks. However, organizations are afraid of losing some control over delivery of outsourcing services and finding themselves dependent on the vendor or liable for the vendors actions where there are both benefits and challenges may be informed by the structure of the relationship between client firms and these organizations offering the outsourced activities to client firms.

What variables are impacted by HR outsourcing of staffing? Which include: administrative costs for labor expense, client firm to HR relations, HR regulatory competency requirement, knowledge of cost factors, e.g. billing and pay rates, vendor markups and margins, vendor management competency requirement, client and vendor relationship, communication is between client managers and staffing vendor, employee data-available, data quality control, data security, match with job requirement, employee quality, inter-vendor competition, mining of client talent by vendor , quality content for preferred staffing vendor, standardization of business process (intra-company), strategic focus of client firm, demands on client managers vendor competency and external economic environmental viability.

However, it has dynamic relationship between the client firms and staffing vendors. Moreover, the models of human resource supply chain, every has different set of advantages and disadvantages for the client firms. The models can be relate to the decision making process on outsourcing of human resources. As strategic services tactic decisions have an important impact or selecting the particular HR outsourcing model that a client firm adopter.

The another model is the balance of power and control over managing the control workers differ to decide what every worker individual skills or abilities outsourcing demand. Moreover, local contracting is also the predominant traditional model for outsourcing staffing with non-core employees. A client firm usually uses several staffing vendors to meet temporary staffing needs for seasonal functions, employee absences and special projects. The advantages of local contracting are high touch and high quality of service by staffing vendors, minimal bureaucracy, empowerment of hiring any high qualified employees to get the job done, and a relatively better fit between specific staffing vendors and functional needs.

4.1 The disadvantages of local contracting

The disadvantages of local contracting can increase costs from non-standardization of hiring practices and procedures across the client form, a significant amount of word of mouth and subjective quality issues, high local costs and client firm us subjected to the capabilities of the staffing vendors and contract employees. However, local HR contracting is the most flexible, high quality, but expense, inefficient and ineffective HR outsourcing model for the client firm. Another model is the working period to be decided to outsource HR contracting. In this situation, in the short term and on a day-to-day basis, the client firm aims to achieve on economy of scale with its staffing vendors. The total costs of temporary workers as well as internal costs for contracting with several different vendors are higher than if it needs one staffing vendors to meet all its needs. So, the client company can set the reasonable pricing that it pays for its temporary outsourcing staffs. Each staffing vendor secures a different rate range with each vendor as opposed as one contact. In the long term, it is benefiting, each specialized staffing vendor is able to fully work with each function needs temporary utilization is better than the average. Mismatches are fewer. Functional departments are able to receive a high quality / high touch service in any time period. Another model is the centralizing is when the department standardizes the staffing process to drive costs down of temporary workers. This tends to occur when a percentage of non-core employees reach a certain ratio of core employees. The advantages include more uniform standards in hiring process, billing rates and pay rates, departmental hiring managers can refocus their effort to choose outsourcing staffing, criteria may be established for a performed suppliers list and greater security for the staffing established vendors that offer higher quality services. The disadvantages include new departmental responsibilities in HR which decreases outsourcing efficiencies for the organizations daily administrative direction is rather than long term strategic direction. Usually lacking qualifications to fulfill the responsibilities, overall, centralizing of HR outsourcing is that firms can achieve more standardization which additional bureaucratic costs and the necessary non-core jobs do not get done as a need. Another model is purchasing HR, which manages staffing vendors from HR to the purchasing unit of an organizations. The goal is to continue cost reductions by increasing efficiencies. In conclusion, the main benefits of HR outsourcing include maintaining organizational control over the hiring process, application of purchasing capabilities for greater standardization in hiring processes pay rates and bill rates. So, any outsoucred HR organizations may be reduce hiring process cost.

4.2 Value supply chain outsourcing

Global outsourcing source strategy in a value supply chain advantages

What is global outsourcing source strategy in a departmental role? In a highly competitive global environment, many manufacturers are responded by setting and outsourcing relations for components and finished products with lower cost producers on a contractual electronic commerce department, (original equipment manufacturer basis). Outsourcing strategy is part of the value supply chain of corporate activated. Nowadays, global outsourcing increases organizational and technological capacity of firms and cooperating a network of remotely located external suppliers performing.

These understanding the important roles that product designers, engineers and production managers and purchasing manager etc. play in global sourcing strategy empowerment. Specially, electronic commerce is popular to supply chain. For example, Toyota car manufacturing company, owns unique capabilities by designing and manufacturing certain car components in-house , i.e. insourcing. Toyota also outsource manufacturing activities, Toyota adopts purchasing necessary, but no strategic inputs from independent component suppliers on obtaining a lower cost for these inputs. For example, products would be belts, tires and batteries to vehicle products that are not customized and do not differentiate its products from its competitors. Toyota's outsourcing strategy is car strategic inputs provide differentiation, e.g. engine, transmission etc. are sources from suppliers based on strategic partnership to gain to access to suppliers' capabilities and it is also a conceptualize global outsourcing sourcing strategy to Toyota car manufacturing company.

How value chain outsourcing affects firm level performance. Global outsourcing strategy means to identify which production units that will serve which particular markets and how components will be supplied for production and thus included a number of basic choices, companies can make in decision how to serve various markets. Either choice relates to the use of inputs, assembly or production within the country to serve a foreign market or decides to use of internal or external supplies of components or finished products. In this outsourcing source input situation, the term sourcing is needed to describe how multi-national companies mange in of components and finished products in serving foreign and domestic markets. Sourcing decision making is both contractual point of view, the sourcing of major components and products are occurred by multi-national companies. First is from parents or their foreign subsidiaries. Second is from independent suppliers on a contractual basis. The first type of sourcing is known as insourcing. Otherwise, the second type of sourcing is referred to outsourcing. How to achieve economies of scale by outsourcing or insourcing sourcing input strategy? Therefore, the two outsourcing strategies are multi-faceted and require careful examination.

The two economists (Abrahamson & Rosenkopf, 1993) indicated that In long term, outsourcing can help to reduce fixed investment in finance view point, in-house manufacturing facilities and thus lower the breakeven point, which subsequently helps boost an outsourcing company whose return on equity (ROE). Thus, if any one corporate performance is evaluated on the basis of its contribution to the company's ROE.

Also, in the short term or long term on resource inputs outsourcing view, early adopters of outsourcing strategy indeed experienced efficiency gains as they were able to reduce fixed investment in in-house manufacturing facilities and lows their ROE. But, later adopters may have different to gain institutions legitimacy or because of competition pressures in the industry, despite some inherent uncertainties about the long term costs and benefits of outsourcing strategy. It seems that outsourcing strategy was devised as any organization's policy makers to access trade linkages of benefits for short term or long term.

Outsourcing strategy is a systematic analysis of the economic, political and regulatory implications indicates potential benefits along with a number of potentially negative side effects to any organizations. Then, outsourcing strategy will be caused this question: How to assess the risks and benefits of outsourcing for organizational sectors and nations both? The decision to change outsourcing behavior to carry a business activity may have profound implications for outsourcer and outsource receiver both, but little impact of the sector level. The common occurrence of industry decisions to outsource most manufacturing, including sale of factories, it created a new sub-sector, contract manufacturing. Otherwise, at a national level and public sectors become less distinct to outsourcing strategy. Public policy on outsourcing has stimulated extensive debate, privatization social justice and value for money etc. challenges.

What is environmental uncertainty factor

What motivate outsourcing what is being outsourced risk and concerns?

Whether what motivate outsourcing, evidence of what is being outsourced risk and concerns? Outsourcing activities include: outsources manufacturing components and other value adding activities. Some focused on employment is outsourced another firm's employees carrying out tasks previously performed one's own employees. Outsourcing is an activity outside the organization's chosen core competencies. It seems outsourcing is a sub-contracting relationships between firms, all foreign production, hiring of workers in non-traditional jobs, such as control workers and temporary and part time workers.

What are the motivations for outsourcing reasons? Why outsourcing is needed to any organization. For example, it can enable firms to focus on core activities. The concept of focus originates in operation on a small, manageable, number of tasks at which the operation becomes excellent to specific technologies and as a risk of vertical integration advantages. Other benefits of outsourcing appear is literature on strategic management, operations management, purchasing and supply and innovations. Moreover, outsourcing can improve flexibility to meet changing business conditions, demands for products, services and technologies by creating smaller and more flexible clear evidence includes improved creditability image, greater workforce flexibility and avoiding being backed into specific assets and technologies are harder to measure. How outsourcing can improve company performance. For airline manufacturing industry example, Hill & Jones (1995) showed that the manufacture of a large portion of the Boeing 767 is Boeing's third largest commercial aircraft, which is outsourced to Japanese manufacturers, which include Fuji, Kawasaki and Mitsubish. As a result, only 10% of the value of the 767 Boeing is produced in-house. So, outsourcing is an attempt to enhance manufacturing air place industry competitiveness.

How can choose smarter outsourcing? Organizations hope to do sight options to save money, among themselves staff layoffs and a reduction of overhead costs, such as office space. Private companies have long outsourced in order to save time and money. During periods of economic growth, many organizations began to use outsourcing more frequently and staff workloads grew in proportion to increase budgets. Tasks such as conducting needs assessments, reviewing proposals, conducting site visits, monitoring and creating evaluations systems were increasingly given to outside contractors, consulting firms and independent consultants in the belief that external specialists could do the work more efficiently and effectively than company itself.

Nowadays, there is a growing stream of organizations need to research into the outsourcing of innovation activities within the innovation, management, marketing and economics disciplines. These organizations need to understand how with the outsourcing practice becoming more commonplace in their industry. However, their behaviors bring these two questions: Whether outsource or internalize innovation activities and the performance implications of this decision can support for both transaction cost and resource based arguments is examined with both theory bases showing substantial attention?

Whether outsourcing innovation activities can lead to faster product development and cost savings? On advantages hand, it is possible that outsourcing may lead to higher costs and slower new product development. Further the technological uncertainty may have conflicting impacts on the outsourcing decision that are not yet well understand. When outsourcing product development has reduced costs and has proved speed to market. On disadvantages hand, outsourcing has also reduce product development time delays and higher quality concerns. Why to cause performance implications of outsourced innovation activities in transaction in cost economics and the resource-based view point? When outsourcing product development has been to reduce costs and has improved speed to market, outsourcing product development is not unlike other make or buy decisions. So, make vs buy decision is similar to logistic and IT outsourcing. Internalization of product development will be preferred when transaction costs are excessive. Otherwise, the market i.e. outsourcing will be selected when transaction costs are low. Transaction costs can include adaption, safeguarding and measurement costs. Adaption costs represent efforts to adjust contract to change conditions and are a result of environmental uncertainty.

When a firm may have to revise on agreement with a partner company, this facing substantial penalties, due to an unstable market environments, the firm is likely to perform this function internally. Safeguarding costs characterize the costs of an outsourcing provider acting opportunities after investments have been made in the inter-firm relationship and are the result of transaction specific investment. Measurement costs include all expenses with confirming that contracts have been fulfilled passably. The contracting firm may face substantial costs to estimate quality for contractual services.

When the sum total of these transaction costs is substantial, internalization will be favored.

What is environmental uncertainty factor?

Environmental uncertainty refers to unanticipated changes in circumstances surrounding an exchange in market uncertain and technological uncertainty. Market uncertainty is the fluctuation and unpredictability of demand. With respect to innovation projects, market uncertainty may cause frequent changes to the development, complications and adding expense to external contracting. These changes may necessitate renegotiation or cancellation of innovation contracts, which will likely carry prohibitive penalties (a term) transaction costs. These transaction costs promote internalization under high levels of market uncertainty. Otherwise, technological uncertainty environments, selecting market governance allows firms the flexibility to end relationship should technical requirements shift. It seems that market and technological external change factor will influence to benefits to any organizations to choose outsourcing strategy. On the other side, outsourcing can bring this question: Whether the offshore outsourcing of information technology jobs choice is suitable to any IT organizations? Nowadays. The offshore outsourcing if IT jobs from the United States has been enabled by a powerful influence of global economic demographic and technological forces. In fact, many IT companies were drawn to offshoring outsourcing because of the need for programmers to fix the Y2K problem in the late 1990- year. It is shortages of US programmers.

Other factors driving this phenomenon include the wage gap between the US and developing countries, e.g. China and India, advances in technology, labor availability, expanding foreign markets and foreign government incentives. The spread of the offshoring phenomenon from low skill manufacturing to high wage white collar service industry jobs reduces the country's IT jobs critics, it represents the mobility for many US workers who saw post-secondary education as the route to a higher standard of living. The offshoring outsourcing of manufacturing and service jobs from the US to lower cost foreign nations become a national issue in a very short time. The impact of offshore outsource on the information technology sector gives outsourcing potential loss of millions of jobs at all wage levels and the critical contribution is the IT sector to US productivity growth. However, decisions about the locations of manufacturing or service facilities reflect market forces key factors include the size of local markets, capital availability and costs, labor availability skill levels and cost, logistic issues, reliability and infrastructure and IT in particular relationships with research institutions. All these factors will influence the choice of offshore outsource IT jobs strategy top any organizations.

Whether outsourcing can bring what benefit of work skills

Whether outsourcing will bring what kind of work skills. Many employers choose outsourcing to employ employees. This core of our work is identifying trends which will transform global society and the global marketplace. How it influences our nature of work form health care to technology, the work place and human identity. A decade ago, workers worried about jobs being outsourced overseas. Today companies, such as Odesk and Liveops can assemble teams " in the cloud" to dosales, customer support and many other tasks. It seems outsoucring can influence many high technological job of changes. Global connectivity, smart machines and new media are just some of the drivers reshaping how we thank about work, what constitutes work and the skills, we shall need to be productive contributors in the future. As computer technology in the cloud will be used popularly to society. A signal is typically a small or local innovation that has the potenial to grow in scale and geographic distribution. A signal can be a new product, a new practice, a new market strategy, a new policy or new technology, such as online cloud computing files storage service method. It is an innovative social science method to computer users. However, this new computer files storage method influences outsourcing service of needs increasing. It will have key drivers and skills areas that will be most relevant to the technological workforce of the future.

It is estimates that by 2025 year, the number of Americans over 60 age will increase by 70%. The challenge of an aging population will come. What it means to age, individuals will need to rearrange their approach to their career, family life and education to accommodate their life plan. Increasing, people will work long past 65 age in order to have adequate resources for retirement. Multiple careers will be commmplace and lifelong learning to prepare for occupational change will see major growth. To take advantage of this well experienced organizations will have to rethink the traditional career paths in organizations, creating more diversity and flexibility. As the high technological cloud computing storage method is invented. Any organizations can save their files to the central cloud computer storage system website to save or find their files from website more easily. It will reduce their computer department expenditure and staff salary. So, outsourcing computer file storage service demands will be influenced to increase to any organizations as well as organizations will reorganize their computer department job nature to shape the kinds of social, economic and political organizations which inhabit. Outsourcing is a good solve method to assist organizations to pay cheap salary to employ many retired high age workers by contract or temporary or part time method to reduce their computer department's number of employees and the retired labors only need to pay cheap salary to learn how to use internet to help whose employers to save their files to their outsourcing computer storage service provider's central computer storage system every day efficiently.

So, organizations do not need to employ many computer department staffs to avoid to pay much salaries to this computer department expenditure. They can choose outsourcing to pay cheap salaries to employ many retirement labors to assist them to do simple office storage job from internet channel efficiently and effectively. Hence, internet high technological innovation can influence office outsoucing of job duties increasing.

Whether domestic outsoucing in the America, what assesses trends and effects on job quality. Nowadays, US firms' use of contractors and independent contractors and its effect on job quality and inequality. Why firms choose contract out for certain functions and assess their predictions about likely impacts on job quality, stagnant wages, growing inquality and the deterioration of job quality are among the most important challenges facing the US economy today. Although any country's domestic outsourcing , firms' use of contractors, franchises and independent contractors any one of these factors is a potentially important influence to companies reduce compensation and shift economy risk to workers. However, the domestic outsoucing takes place on a much larger scale and effects many more workers than has been recognized ranging from low wage service workers, security guards, warehouse workers and hotel housekeepers to professionals and technical workers, such as programmers, health care technicians and accountants. These tends are part of structural change in the organization of production to influence quality of jobs and the nature of employment contract after outsourcing jobs are popular. The quality of jobs include wages, benefits, employee skills and training and mobility opportunities and job security as well as inequality across jobs. Domestic outsoucing concerns these issues: such as employment and labor law, the provision of health, pension and other workplace benefits. However, any companies choose outsourcing of employment reasons include, such as that it relates how management choices to pursue value added or cost focused strategies. Contracting out is difficult to define because a large part ot economic activity has always occurred through business-to-business transactions, as captured in macro-economic input-output models. Outsoucing job employment method can influence any one labor's individual quality of jobs. Usually, international companies choose the offshoring of work in global supply chains. Until recently, the domestic counterpart outsourcing employment method has grown supply chains to domestic or regional outsoucing employment.

What factors cause domestic outsourcing and whether firm decisions about what to retain in-house and what to outsource have changes over time. Some evidence suggests that firms have responded by focusing on their core competencies and outsourcing low value added tasks as well as higher value added specialized functions. Advanced technologies have facilitated this process by allowing firms to outsource entire functions ans more easily monitor contractors as well as employees who work, leading to new forms of networked production and rise of specialized outsouring employment firms. Domestic outsoucing influences the changes of job quality, benefits, hours, workload, job stability, schedule stability and occupational safety, health, incidence of wage theft and access to training and promotions. Predictions are less clear for job requiring professional or technicial or specialized skills or those that are outsourced to large and diversified outsourced contractors. Types of outsourced contracts include: suppliers or vendors of products, such as manufacturing inputs or services, such as business services or staffs service or staffing firms, franchisees and independent contract, such as freelancers, independent contracts or non demand platform outsourced workers. It is significant restructuring of domestic manufacturing supply chains will greater reliance on suppliers and subcontractors. In addition, the potential growth of on demand outsourcing work as well as other forms of job fragmentation. It causes this question: How outsourced workers are multiple forms of income generating work to achieve economic security and how outsourcing workers can build career across jobs and over time.

Firm in every sector of the economy contract with other firms as part of their production process, as do governmental entities. The functions that are outsourced vary widely. For example: human resources ans research and development functions, building services, recycling, regulation and compliance, accounting, credit card collection, call centres, mortage and check processing, information technology and data processing, logistics and transportation, machine maintenance, cable installation, food services, food processing, parts manufacturing and assembly, laundry and housekeeping etc. outsourced jobs causes.

Whether what business impact of outsourcing will be caused? Nowadays, IT outsourcing was clearly a part of an effective management strategy that the companies felt IT outsourcing strategy can bring to achieve positive results. Information technology outsourcing providing servicers will be predicted to provide services that is expected to raise over the next five years minimum. The companies demand clients expected benefits of IT outsourcing and determined that cost reduction, increased operation, efficiency and improved IT effectiveness. What are the impacts of outsourcing to influence better long-term improvement in the business performance? It is impossible to being benefits of significant reduction and lower growth in sellings, general and administrative expense to IT outsourcing company demand clients. Also, pre-existing corporate cultures are focused on business improvement to IT outsourcing company demand clietns. In the past researches, some economists indicated that points can be used to reflect the actual numbers increase or decrease in percent. However, their prior researches shows that prior to outsourcing, the annual growth in selling, general and administration expenses of eompanies in the study was already 4.2 points lower than sector medium. Moreover, within one to two years after IT outsourcing these companies improved even most.

Annual growth in selling and general administrative expenses for them was 9.9 points lower efford to assist any IT outsourcing will have selling and administrative expenses for long term. Also, almost two-third of the companies studied outperformed in increased growth in return on asset two to three years after IT outsourcing commenced. Prior to outsourcing, the annual ROA growth rate for companies in the study ws 7.5 points lower than the sector median. After outsourcing, however these companies experienced 8.6 points higher median a substantial change of 16.1 points. Also, nearly two to third of the companies studied grew earnings faster than their peers. Two to three years after IT outsourcing, companies experienced an annual rate of growth in earnings 11.8 points higher than the growth rate of the sector median. Thus, it seems IT outsourcing can assist the IT outsourcing demand clients to reduce expenditure and to raise income both as the same time. Then, it will cause these questions to IT outsourcing demand clients. Is outsourcing influencing in an economic downturn to finance sector in the short term? Is the finance sector's renewed change for outsourcing just a temporary cost-cutting measure? Will today's economic climate initiate long term financial and productivity gains?

Whether what are benefits and disadvantages of outsourcing finance sector IT. I shall demonstrate why outsourcing open source software support and maintenance can be a good choice to start. Firstly when company plans to budget cuts expenditures, IT outsourcing is often the first choice. For example in 2003 year, Zurich Financial services' sprawling IT department consisted of more than 7,500 employees. After posting a record loss of 3.4 billion the year before, Zurich decided to cut down on in those staff and outsource nearly half of its IT work. Outsourcing has successfully cut costs by 45 percent and cut the number of in house IT staff by 60 percent. Here are some of the benefits that companies enjoy when they outsource information technology functions to competent, reliable vendors.

In fact, it can be too expensive to maintain, company's own information technology, especially during a recession. Fortunately, many IT functions can be easily and efficiently outsourced, positively impacting individual company's bottom line. Employee costs are much higher than just salary and benefits, keeping employees happy, productive and busy takes time, effort and money. Although, many IT staffs will be dismissed, it will increase the unemployment ratio in societies. But, moving an IT service out of house means financial organizations don't have to worry about technology refresh costs in the future. It also cuts down on human resources requirements, specialist IT service provides which can provide the newest technologies and deliver quality service more than company itself in house information provides are the most effective to develop and implement and upgrade their clients' software or the launch on a new platform, due to the expert's time is wasted on day-to-day duties for whose other IT outsourcing demand clients. However, instead of IT outsourcing service outsourced offshoring in that service sector, how economic impact to influence the outsourced offshoring country. For example, United States continues to run an international trade surplus in services. Many Americans are particularly concerned about the loss of skilled, well paid jobs in such fields as computer programming and accounting etc. positions. These jobs seemed relatively secure at a time when many manufacturing jobs were being cost to import competition. Similarly, telephone call centers, once viewed as an esonomic development opportunity in some areas, increasingly are moving low wage countries, such as India and the Philippines. Thus, offshoring raises many questions for policymakers and general public. For example, which service jobs will be affected most by import competition. What are the likely effects of service-sector offshoring on U.S.A. output, employment and our standard of living, such as America? Is offshoring really a problem that requires restrictive government actions or are other kinds of policies more appropriate to give Americans or other countries the highest possible living standard?

The term of offshoring refers to the relocation of jobs and production to a foreign country. The relocated jobs and production could be at a foreign office of the same multinational company or at a separate company located abroad. In constrast, the term outsourcing doesn't necessary imply that jobs and production are relocated to another country. The major outsourcing service jobs include human resource, accounting and information technology etc. in-house service jobs in large organizations. However, the loss of service jobs and factory production is caused by offshoring is diffuclt to measure. It is also difficult to determine the impact of offshoring on total services employment in the United States or other countries. International trade in services covers a wide range of industries and activites. For example, travel and transportation includes travel expenditures, passenger fares and frieght and port services, royalties and license fees cover transactions including patents, copyrights, trademarks and other intangible proprietary rights to use, produce or distribute products.

Other private services include many of these industries, such as education, financial services insurance, telecommunications and other professional services etc. Some economists indicated that occupational employment statistics for the Unisted States provided additional evidence that past service sector offshoring had been small. About 14 million service jobs were at risk of offshoring in 2000 year, when about 96 million service jobs had a low risk of ofshoring. The decline in the at-risk service occupations from 2000 year to 2002 year was about 218,000 jobs or roughly 109,000 jobs annually, relatively small number that is consistent with the estimates of McCarthy or Zandi.

In percentage terms, employment in the at risk occupations fell at a faster rate from 2000 year to 2002 year than in the low risk occupations. This faster decline is consistent with offshoring activity, although the decline is consistent with other explanations as well, such as faster of technological change in industries employing the risk occupations or greater cyclical sensitivity in these industries. Because offshoring was not the only cause of job loss in the risk occupations, the number of jobs moved offshore was undoubtedly less than 109,000 jobs annually. However, the estimates may understate the total impact because domestic companies with expanding worldwide employment may have located may of their newly created jobs abroad even when they didn't reduce their US employment. Some of those foreign jobs might provide services to US customers and potentially foreign jobs might provide service to US . Conversely, the estimates may overstate the total job loss from offshoring of the foreign outsourcing of some support jobs prevents the loss of other domestic jobs by keeping US firms competitive in world markets. For example, cost reductions from offshoring IT jobs might help a US financial services company win foreign contracts, preserving many professionals and support jobs in the US.

Lower production costs in foreign countries are a major cause of service sector offering. Although, the costs of land and other resources may be cheaper abroad, but the main difference betweeb the US and developing countries is labor costs. There is a large gap in computer programmer wages between the US and other countries. Any organizational capital includes both physical capital, such as machinery and computers and human capital , such as skills and knowledge. The cost savings is come from offshoring also might be reduced if the firm needed to pay higher transportation and telecommunication costs or management spends more time on service quality and data security. Still, the much lower levels of wages ans benefits in developing countries suggests that many services can be produced abroad at lower cost. The in-house professional relocation of labor-intensive service activities, such as legal transcription services to countries with lower labor costs is consistent with economists' basic theory of international trade, comparative advantage. So, in-house outsourced professional service will be a corporative advantage, if the country's legal profession is poor level to compare with the another country. e.g. the skill in-house the legal professional labors of the developing country, such as China is poor educational level to compare with the developed country, such as US. So, if China large organizations chose to outsource themselves in-house legal service jobs to outsource offshoring to US legal professional lawyers to do. It can bring comparative advantage to China large outsourced in-house legal service organizations, due to these China outsourced large organizations can reduce to employ to pay too much salaries to these many in-house Chinese domestic lawyers and the US outsourced legal consultants whose can give more professional legal recommendation to serve to the China large organizations.

In conclusion, although offshoring strategy can increase unemployment chance for this disadvantge. But, all of outsourcing benefits weighs are more than the offsourcing disadvantages. However, outsourcing strategy can have these benefits to the outsourced service demanders. Such as outsourcing is no longer just about cost saving, it is also a strategic tool that may power the twenty first century global economy. Moreover, outsourcing can increase productivity and competitiveness, e.g. for every 1000 jobs British Airways sends to India , the airline saves $23 million, companies can devote a portion of their outsourcing savings to helping employees make job transitions, also leader can no longer afford to view outsourcing as a business tactic, it is now essential to remain competitive. On the world stage, workers now compete globally, so individuals must continually learn more to vie successfully with their peers worldwide, the average company only spends about 20% of the value of its outsourcing contracts to manage its relationship with the outsource provider. So, in the positive view point, outsourcing strategy can bring a potential primary driver of the global economy development. Although, outsourcing can also cause the raising of domestic unemployment chance. But companies may soon be more outsourced than in sourced, signifying a fundamental reorganization that will affect employees, managers, customers and executives. Customers' choice will increase product costs will drop and workers' roles will change. Finally, the most important, the developing country will earn comparative advantage from the developed country's employers' offshoring jobs provision. Thus, the developing country's unemployment rate will be reduced, then the global economy will be kept more balance fairly.

CHAPTER FOUR

Management science

Human development management science

High quality education and health systems aspect.

The current economic crisis has affected all aspects of life resulting in political instability, personal financial troubles and a growing number of business bankruptcies. How to use effective human development policy to prevent the economic crisis threats. I shall indicate that governments ought to consider how to apply human development strategy to prevent the economic recession crisis occurrence to threaten to influence whose social economic growth in these aspects.

On high quality education and health systems aspect. Different country's government ought to concern, due to it can support the productivity of an economy by providing healthy and highly trained individuals. Because of the country has good human development strategy, then it can use talent labors to assist its economic growth and good governance practices by governments easily. It seems that human development, good governance and economic growth has close relationship, so it can reduce the economic recession during times of crisis occurrence. It means that human development can influence economic growth. Economic development implies both the improvement of people's health education and general well being and the presence of positive economic indicaties, such as economic growth and low unemployment with economic development, people will have better education and healthcare and be more productive. Better human development nations tend to have lower crime rates and greater political strategy than less human development nations.

Does it bring positive consequence of human development to prevent economic recession? It will be an important resource to influence economic growth. How does this human development public policy solve economic crisis? Whether can government use of fiscal policy, such as human development to assist economic stabilization to promote growth and the increase of the capital income efficiency? A key issue relates to the effect of how to use public expenditure and its financing to spend human development on effects of fiscal policy by using a time series approach.

A general model that includes expenditure on education and health, which influences human capital, expenditure and health administration, public investment and transfers and consumption of public products four kinds of expenditure. The model can be used to explore and impact of human development expenditure used on long run per capita income. Debt and external and financing are also possible to be spent to human development expenditure in the general model. So, the public expenditure on the long run per capita income can be explored for low, lower, middle and upper-middle income countries policy that is needed to be esimated how to spend for each aspect of human development expenditure to assist to every country's economy development.

● What is time series perspective on economic growth to pursue for growth and human development strategies.

A time series perspective is explained on economic growth may be more useful to pursue for growth and human development strategies. A time series can allow to pursue time series studies for particular countries or country groups at particular stages of economic growth. It can allow for a more specific micro behavior of economic agents. In general, any country has three income groups, such as low income, lower-middle income and upper middle income groups. Also, any country may have these four types of public expenditure for human development which including: enhancing education and building up of human capital, public investment to finance general market and subsistence production, e.g. transportation system, such as roads, bridges, harbors, water supply, sanitation, health and care and education.

A 2005 year study had been carried by Dimonson, Marsh & Staunton, which performed an analysis is stock returns in 53 countries, going back to 1900 year for 17 countries, did not find evidence of a significant long term positive relationship between GDP growth rates and equity returns. Also the analysis from Schroders Economics team found that over the past sixty years, there has tended to be a positive relationship between GDP growth and equity market returns during the recovery, expansion and slowdown phases of the traditional business cycle. This relationship has traditionally broken down during the recession phase.

The Schroders economics team also indicated a traditional business cycle model, which has four stages. In the beginning, it is slowdown stage. It means output above trend, growth decelerating and inflation rising. Next is recession stage. It means output below trend, growth developing, inflation falling. Then, it is recovery stage. It means output below trend, growth decelerating, inflation falling. Finally, it is expansion stage, it means output above trend growth accelerating, inflation is rising. The economic team also suggested the traditional business cycle model: In the slowdown stage, GDP growth is positive, but falling, inflation is high and rising, so policy strategy is tight recommended in the recession stage, GDP growth is negative and falling, inflation is falling. So, policy strategy is loosening recommended. In the recovery stage, GDP growth is negative and rising, inflation is low and falling, so policy strategy is loose recommended. Finally, the expansion stage, GDP growth is positive and rising, inflation is rising, so policy strategy is tightening recommended.

It seems that governments ought concern the business cycle period to evaluate themselves country GDP growth to achieve the most effective policy to adopt to achieve different human development policies to invest to present economic recession crisis occurrence. Usually, in the recovery and expansion phases of the business cycle, the stock market tends to perform well as rising GDP and earnings growth drives positive excess returns on equity. In the slowdown phase, inflation is still high and monetary policy remains tight, resulting in s difficult environment for corporations. reducing earnings and stock valuations tends to result in negative excess returns for equities: declining GDP growth is therefore usually matched with poor equity performance. It also explained that during the recession phase, there is often GDP growth is falling, but the excess return on equity tends to be positive. Historically, falling inflation and an accompanying loosening of monetary policy is needed to rise re-rating.

Thus, it seems the business cycle and human development policy has close relationship. During in the slowdown stage, GDP growth is positive, but falling, inflation is high and rising, then the country's government ought spend less expenditures to human development because GDP growth is stable growth. Otherwise, during it is recession stage or recovery stage, it means output below trend, growth developing, inflation falling. Then the country's government ought spend more to invest to any human development needs to prepare to raise whose labor productivity and GDP growth. Finally, during the expansion stage, GDP growth is positive and rising, inflation is rising. Then the country's government can spend less expenditures to invest human development. Thus, any country's government ought concern what is whose country's business cycle stage to arrange to spend more or less expenditures to achieve its human development policy in different business cycle stages.

● What is quantitative evidence to review human resource policy

Regulatory management method

Nowadays, political scientists began to apply quantitative methods to classify and measure political interactions. In general, any countries' policies that maximize growth are optimal that cares solely about pure " capitalists". The greater, the inequality of wealth and income, the higher rate of taxation and the lower growth. It shows that inequality in land and income ownership is negatively with subsequent economic growth. Many economists have tried to explain lower growth rates and unemployment with a growing tax burden in many developed countries. Although, the impact of taxes on growth can be observed both from the aspect of efficiency and aspect of changes in equity that taxes introduce to economy. I shall indicate how to apply quantitative evidence to review policy to review human development strategy. In fact, economic or welfare outcomes to changes in regulatory policy has close relationship to be suggested outcome indicate to reduce risk face economic recession occurrence to any countries. Every country government ought design to gather quantitative data to prepare any policy implementation to support mutual learning and best practice in different societal and market conditions. The goal is to help countries to build better government systems and implement policies at both national and regional level that lead to sustainable economic and social development.

The critical public policy challenge is to ensure that the expected economic benefits from regulatory changes are both achieved and outweigh any economic cost imposed. I shall indicate evidence on the outcomes of regulatory policies to help policymakers how design regulatory measures that work better. This method is called "regulatory management". This regulatory management study suggests some conclusions to any policymakers as below:

● Firstly, poorly designed policy regulation can not raise economic activities and ultimately reduce economic growth.

● Secondly, it is impossible between a regulatory policy change and the impact on economic outcomes, such as economic growth is from statistic method easily.

● Thirdly, the reliance on economic recession analysis to investigate the relationship across countries between regulatory variables and economic outcomes may not be readily applicable to any countries and may not always be expressed in economic values. It is particularly useful in developing countries regulatory policy measures for recommendation to policymakers only.

● Fourthly, most quantitative studies deal with the costs of regulation and give little or no attention to quantifying the benefits of regulation. For the policymaker, it is important to compare the estimated costs of regulation. Any policy regulation is intended to correct market failures and assist to economic efficiency and growth. The public policy aims to reduce socially unacceptable income and wealth distributions or it can satisfy expectation that the public should have access to certain products and services, e.g. health care and education irrespective of ability to pay, such as merit products. Some of regulation, that governments need to concern, e.g. of property rights, company law, law of contract etc. and regulation can provide important economic and social, including environmental benefits.

Of course, those benefits need to be set against the costs. Because regulations are the operations of effective economies and societies to market rules, e.g. law of contract and protecting property rights and the rights of citizens. It seems regulatory management is important to influence any policies can be achieved effectively, due to one good regulation can supervise the leader's behavior and otherwise one bad regulation can not supervise the leader's behavior, even it can not assist the country economic growth for long term. So, any leader needs to concern how to use quantitative evidence to review huaman development policy if who hopes whose policy's regulations are achieved effectively.

Regulatory management method

At the same time, economic, environmental and welfare pressures raise the demand for regulation above minimum needed for operating a market economy to prepare to face the economic recession occurrence. So, evidence on the outcomes of regulatory policies should help policymakers design regulatory measures that work better. Similarly, evidence on the success or failure of regulation can be used for public accountability purposes.

Regulatory policy defines as the process by which government, when identifying a policy objectives, decides whether to use regulation as a policy instrument and proceeds to draft and adopt a regulation through evidence based decision making. The strategy shall commit governments to remain a regulatory management system, articulating regulatory policy goals, and the impacts of regulation on competitiveness and economic growth. For example, regulation, such as employment law or competition law, the regulation of employment law is applied to control any employers' behaviors to give the fair treatment to whose employees and to protect employees' benefits.

Besides the regulation of competition law is applied to control the fair competition in market. Why this regulations has direct relationship to economy growth. An identifiable economy theory of specific regulatory policies, e.g. administrative simplification and specific economic and welfare outcomes, e.g. high economic growth. The result is a series about the impact of regulatory management on economic indicators. There can be set out as a causal. Thus regulation can be supportive of market transactions and may result in significant economic, social and environmental benefits.

At the same time, ill-designed regulation can have appreciable economic costs, leading to the concept of regulatory burden. In particular, good regulation can reduce the chance of lower economic growth or GDP occurrence, damage investment and competitiveness. But, it has also weakness, such as regulatory costs may act as a barrier to entry into industry in the form of set up cost, e.g. installing equipment to meet health and safety laws and on going annual cost, e.g. preparing returns and facilities inspections.

However, regulatory can be unduly costly to comply with administrator and enforce, but it simplification can reduce the regulatory burden. For example, regulation may not only affect the behavior of those targeted by a rule (direct effects), but invoke behavioral change in the economy (indirect effects). Whether regulation can support governments to avoid or reduce the threats of economic recession occurrence, it depends on the leader's concern how to use quantitative evidence to review policy before who decides to implement which kinds of regulatory management methods.

In recent year, some countries had considered how to achieve policy field with a view to introducing better regulation. The aim is to ensure that regulation occurs only when it does improve social welfare and that regulatory changes do, so with the minimum net cost or maximum net benefit to society. For a policy making perspective, it is important to appreciate how and why a regulatory achievement can be expected to result in a particular impact.

Causal chain analysis is a technique for explaining the way in which a caused regulatory results in an economic impact. By helping to understand the how and why questions, regulatory impact, so causal chain analysis can provide policymakers, with relevant information on the consequences of their policy decisions. It seems that regulation can lead economic improvements, such as higher GDP growth, higher productivity, move business start ups. etc. Due to the causal chain analysis relates to each component separately. So, any decision maker hopes to achieve better regulation, who needs time to attempt to different regulations to achieve whose policies every year. Then, who can review why whose policy can not improve whose country's economic growth as well as to attempt to find reasons how to apply better regulatory to achieve better policy to improve its country's economic growth. It seems review regulatory policy which ought to concern to any decision maker, if who wanted to achieve better regulatory policy to raise economic and welfare gains every year.

In capitalism view, capitalism tends equal systematically, through not uniformly to reward business behaviour that is honest, fair civil and compassionate. When does irrational honesty behaviour influence social economy development? It concerns behavioral economy to individual decision maker whose individual psychology, social psychology into economics. It helps policy makers to incentive in market transactions and in response to policy interventions. So, policy advisers are already using the finding of behavioural economy to advantage to public policy, there is nothing about behavioural economy, but for a long time, it has tended to be concerned how the social economic development, particularly in macroeconomy. For example, policy makers concern of money in nominal rather than real terms in whose how to solve to unemployment. Also, policy makers neglect to recognize how economic motivations apart from those based on rational calculation usually. Most, probably of policy decision makers' decisions to will be drawn out over many days to come, who feels action rather than inaction to any decision immediately, and not as the outcome of a weighted average of probabiities. It seems that the policy decision maker's irrational honesty behaviour will influence how our social's economic development to be good or bad.

Tax management science
●
Tax policy influences, during polictical instability environment.

Whether it has relationship between political instability and national economic performance. By past history indicated that the depletion of resource during wars may be one reason why some countries fail to sustain adequate economic growth. However, because economic growth affects a population's well being, this question concerning how was related to growth is important from a policy perspective. So, civil wars can influence any country's economic growth because war can cause the falling changes in a country's physical and human capital as well as lacking technology supporting can reduce GDP per capita to be country during war occurs. For example, during war does noe occur, then trade liberalization, democracy, government stability and a legal system that strongly protects private property rights enhance growth.

During the political instability is occurring, whether tax policy can assist economic growth and social welfare growth. On of central questions in macroeconomics and public policy is how changes in tax policy affect economic activity and social welfare. Consequently, it is possible that sometimes, taxing leads to inefficiency in economy. Whether can taxes stimulate people to change their behavior. For example, the person could either work so hard as before introduction of taxes and reduce whose spending, or work more and spend less time at leisure, thus not needing to reduce spending substantially. However, the inefficiency is caused by taxes, will be presented with a simple supply and demand diagram. In other words, taxes have impact on the amount of supply and demand for products and services.

The purpose of understanding of the impact of taxes on welfare, the decrease in welfare of consumers and producers should be compared with the tax revenue by the country. Such an analysis will show that the decrease in consumers' and producers' welfare exceeds the tax revenue collected by the country. The loss of welfare that takes place after introduction of taxes (a part of which belongs to no one either to a consumer or producer, nor to the country) represents a weight loss or excess tax burden as a degree of inefficiency that taxes introduce to economy. However, full understanding of weight loss requires a detailed tax burden of analysis is needed to governments.

What determines the size of the heavy weight loss to tax? A higher price elasticity of demand curve, or a higher price elasticity of supply curve can lead to a higher weight loss to tax. The more elastic the curves are, the higher is the inefficiency that taxes introduce to the market. The fact is taxes introduce heavy weight loss to the economy because which stimulate people to change their behavior. Since elasticity of supply and demand is a measure of change in the behavior of consumers and producers in relation to change of prices , it also determines the rate of market distortion. The more elastic supply and demand curves, the higher is the heavy weight loss. Another important determinant of the size of heavy weight loss is the tax rate. When price elasticity of supply and demand is the same, heavy weight loss is low when taxes are low and it grows when which both grow. Indeed, heavy weight loss grows faster than most taxes: we can sat that the size of heavy weight loss provided that production costs are constant is equal to 1/2 (elasticity / product quantity), where it is tax rate. Elasticity is price elasticity of demands, product is price of Q is quantity of products.

Individual tax payable honest behavior influences economic growth

What is taxation of savings and investment relationship? Taxes can reduce economic growth by affecting savings and investment. The higher the proportion of income that is being saved and invested, the higher will be the future income level, In other words, through its impact on the amount of the income being saved or invested, taxation policy has a crucial effect on the future level of income per capita. The impact of taxes on saving of individuals and companies, investment in fixed capital and investment risk is briefed represented below: How impact of taxes on savings of individual? The gross savings in private sector and accumulated in households and companies.

However, a large past of the gross savings is used for covering depreciation and is needed for the existing capital. The net savings, consisting of savings to householders and earnings of companies, represent the real potential, available for new investments. If all householders would save the same proportion of income, then the impact of income tax on the total savings would be the same, regardless of the pattern of the distribution of tax burden to individuals. But, wealthy individuals shall save more than poor citizens. So, it is expected that the tax collected from higher tax brackets create more burden on savings than the ones collected from lower tax brackets.

Consequently, on individual tax behavior view, a more progressive income tax seems to be creating a heavier burden on savings than a less progressive tax system. So I suggest a less progressive income tax policy will encourage more savings of individuals. However, it is a only assumption, it has another factors to influence citizen's tax behavior: such as, a varies during a life cycle in youth and in old age, it is much lower saving than in middle are when income in highest and when people save for education of their children for a house or flat and for the old age to prepare retirement. So, tax policy is not considered by firms or policymakers in isolation from other aspects of site selection including benefits from public products which are needed to use by citizens, e.g. gardens, swimming pools, entertainment facilities etc. different public facilities.

Finally, I shall explain why individual tax payable honest behavior has moral consequences to cause economic growth. For citizens of all too many of the different countries, where poverty is still the normal. But the tangible improvements in the basic of life that make economic growth, so important whenever living standards are low, greater life expectancy, few diseases, less infant mortality and malnutrition have mostly been played out long before a country's per capita income reaches the levels enjoyed in today's advanced industralized economy.

In fact, immoral or dishonesty business or economic behaviours are caused by some people who pursue material well being and who aim to do benefit to themselves, but it will cause illegal money transactions to raise any overall country's economic or GDP growth. In fact, this business transactions are not legal. So, which can't cause GDP or economic growth to any country. Also, the illegal businesses can not contribute any benefits to any society, so which can not bring any economic benefits or welfares to any countries to satisfy any citizen'e needs ensurely. Even, in parts of the world where the need to improve nutrition and literacy and human life expectancy is urgent, there is often aspect to the recognition that achieving superior growth is a top priority. So, it seems dishonesty behaviours will not improve and raise low income level people whose life expectancy and life quality because this illegal businesses income is used to spend to the illegal businesses or immoral policy decision makers themselves benefits and who won't spend to social welfare.

It seems that these illegal businesss or immoral policies can not assist any economic growth and raise GDP growth rate as well as dishonesty or immoral economic activities can not bring any benefits to societies in our world, even these bad behaviours will bring harm to our societies. e.g. encouraging illegal drug sale to harm young people health and raising crimes rates; winning illegal gamble to earn illegal profit to increase high interest loan businesses and crimes or causing bad families relationship to raise social challenges.

What is the root of the irrational behavioural problem? I believe that is our conventional thinking about economic growth fails to reflect the breadth of what growth, or its absence, means for any society. There are some people's dishonest behaviours only weigh material positives against moral negatives. I believe this dishonest economic activites are seriously. In some cirsumstances dangerous incomplete, the value of arising standard of living lies individuals live, but in how it shapes the social, political and ultimately the moral character of a people.

Economic growth means a rising standard of living for the clear majority of citizens. So, dishonest economic behaviours can only give benefits to the individual and these irrational behaviours can not give welfare to overall societies. In fact, economic growth bears moral benefits as well. So, it seems dishonest behaviours can not raise moral benefit, then it can not also raise economic growth to any country. Moreover, dishonest behaviours are also caused to any country's political democracy. e.g. Many policy decision makers usually only consider self benefit, so who will neglect to consider social welfare benefits to whose citizen. Themselve benefit behaviours will be unfair to whose citizen. The importance of the connection between economic growth and social and political progress and the consequent concern for what will happen of living standards tail to improve, are not limited to the United States and other countries that already have high income and established democracies. So, economic growth or its absence often plays a significant role not only progress from dictatorship to democracy, but also the democracies by new dictatorships.

Also, for dishonest behaviours are caused by decision makers, such as the link between economic growth and social and political progress in the developing countries has yet other political implicatons as well. For example, the continuing absence of political demoracy and basic personal freedoms in China has deeply troubled many observers in the West. Until China gained admisson to the World trade Organization in 2002 year, these concerns regularly gave rise in the Uniter States to debate on whether to trade with China on a most favored nation basis. These concerns still cause questions about whether to give Chinese firms advantage advanced American oil company. Both sides in this debate share the same objective: to foster China's political liberalization. How to do so , however, remains the focus of intense disagreement. The improvement in nutrition, housing, sanitation and transportation has been dramatic, when the freedom of Chinese citizens to make economic choices, where to work, what to buy, when to start a business is already broader than it was with continued economic advance, the average Chinese standard of living is still only one eighth that in the United states, greater freedom to make political choices too, it will probably follow. So the economy is actually developing, like China won't have to wait until China can achieve Western level incomes before they experience significant political and social liberalization.

To conclude, if any country's policy makers who do not consider citizen welfare and who only consider self benefit, it will cause dishonest behaviours to influence social economic development to cause poor situation for long term. So, policy makers must need concern their behaviors are rational choice to make any economic decisions to let their citizen to give welfares for long term. Also any businessmen ought choose to do rational economic behaviours to benefits for societies and clients and governments in order to achieve economic growth to GDP to their countries if who hope whose businesses can be stable to compete for long term. So, policy decision makers and businesses ought consider rational honesty behaviour before who do any economic decision.

Educational management science

How does every country government teach its citizen to do social moral honest behavior which can brings economic growth? How honesty is influenced to economic positive relationship. The dishonesty behaviour includes: e.g. corruption is as an illegal payment to a public agent to obtain a benefit that may or may not be deserved, or the abuse of public office for private gains to consume, corruption probably amounts are to a large share of the gross national product in any countries. So, corruption worries policy makers and international organizations, who remains the adverse effects of corruption.

However, in the macroeconomic view, the academic literature is less definite about how bribes minimize the waiting costs associated with queuing in a equilibrium. Both of those waiting cost associated with queuing and inefficiency models equate bribes as allocating the true worth of the licenses or permit to the most worthy bidder in public sector.

Forbidding bribes that amounts to prohibiting the use of price mechanism in the public sector. In terms of economic growth, the only thing worse than a society over centralized, dishonest bureaucracy is over-centralized. So, the quality of government institutions, including the degree of corruption, affects investment and growth as much as other political economy variable. e.g. political freedom, civil liberties and political violence. Another example, some firms that pay more bribes also spend more time with bureaucrats in more corrupt countries and have a higher cost of capital, thus countering the view of corruption.

Some countries are likely fairer and regulation is less. How does corruption affect income inequality? In addition, capital market imperfection and government spending have been suggested as two channels for corruption to affect inequality and economic growth. Finally, to what extent can corruption explain the differences in inequality and economic growth? So, it seems corruption is associated with a smaller increase in income inequality and a larger drop in growth rates. Also, corruption raises income inequality to a lesser extent in countries to achieve higher government spending. So, it seems corruption dishonest behaviour has close relationship to influence any countries' GDP economic growth.

Corruption is understood as sale of government property for private gain. However, most economists view corruption as a major obstacle to development. It is seen as one of the causes of low income and is believed to play a critical role in poverty. Perhaps the most quoted example of this is speed money paid by business people to government officials to speed up bureaucraties procedures. At the macro level, there is evidence that corruption affects adversely many of the proxy causes of economic growth. e.g. investment in manufactured and human capital. Moreover, high levels of corruption tend to with a lack of political accountability and disrespect for property rights factors which themselves tend to be obstacles to economic growth.

More fundamentally, however, there is a sense in which the focus on growth in GDP per capita is misguided. Ultimately, development is about how to improvement in human welfare. However, corruption is developing a few with access systematic distort political and economic decisions which might be made systematically with conflict of interest at play. For example, different countries' banks which achieve different bank schemes to aim to avoid illegal money saving from drug trafficking to cause false economic growth in any countries. The anti-corruption strategy advocated to economic development, democratic reform a strong civil society with access to information and overseeing the state, and the presence of rule of law. The governance program facilities at the request of client governments, a series and surveys involving broad segments of society and national and local government performance.

The causes of its development and many and vary from one country to the next. It seems corruption dishonest behaviours can cause to seem as one country's false economy growth and even, global false economy growth after any illegal economic activities had been done from any illegal businessmen. So corruption is a global issue which is government all over the world. However, what is the causes and consequences of corruption? It is possible that corruption is the intentional with length relationship aimed at deriving some advantage from this behaviour for oneself or for related individuals. So, in micro-economic view, corruption cause is derived from some advantage from this behaviour for the person. Otherwise, in macro-economic view, corruption cause is also derived from some advantage this behaviour for the organization, even overall country's social benefit, e.g. illegal shares buying and selling trading activities, illegal bank saving transaction source from drug trafficking activities.

On citizen educational honest behavior aspect, many of the assumptions which are attempted to rationalize the process of educational development have been criticized or abandon. However, the education quality role of different educational regulation, the choice of financing methods, the examination and certification procedures or various other regulation and incentive structures will influence educational effect to satisfy public needs. Thus, citizen honest educational policy makers need to satisfy public needs. Moreover, educational policymakers also need to concern any new policy making environment which will seriously constrain their attempts to ensure the early discussion of planning considerations as part of the education policy making process. So, every country's environment factor will influence every educational policymaker's individual decision.

As defined, policy represents decisions that are designed to guide (including to constrain future decisions or to initiate and guide the implementation of previous decisions). It is this time bound nature of policy and of policy making that makes it is such a critical concern for the educational planner. However, the failure of the traditional planning models and the recognition of the lack of nationality that can occur in policy making there combined to create an atmosphere of pessimism among some educationalists.

To capture the details of the decision making process of any educational planning itself, an analytical framework is presented that goes beyond the initial decision point to examine both the preceding actions (contextual assessment, technical analysis and the generation, valuation and selection of policy options) and the subsequent activities (planning and conducting implementation, impact assessment and where appropriate, design). Thus, the framework covers the full policy planning process, but with a focus on the facilitating and constraining effects that policy decisions and how they were derived and have no the choices available to citizen honest educational planners.

There are two ways of value to educational planners. First, the methodology of the framework and conclusions of the any one of educational case studies should help in the analysis of current educational policies and decision making procedures (an analysis of policy). So, it is a present method to gather current data from current case studies to make the update conclusions to achieve any any of eductional policies. Otherwise, Second, the another framework can be applied to have evaluation of proposed policies and used to forecast policy outcomes and the probability of successful implementation, given the country of fiscal and management capacity, political commitment etc. So, this framwork is a futuer predict educational method to gather data how to get the recommedation to achieve the effiective quality of educational policy in the future.

Citizen honest behavioral sducational policy can be lower differ in terms of scope, complexity, decision environment, range of choices and decision criteria. Any educational policy decision deals with large scale policies and broad resource allocation will have these questions to need to answer. For example, on strategic view, how can we provide basic education at a reasonable cost to meet equity and efficiency objectives?

On multi program view, should resources be allocated to university level education? On program view, how would occupational training centre be designed and provided across the country? On issue specific view, should graduated of rural universities be allowed to transfer to any one of city area universities to study easily? On the psychological view, some researches indicated behavioral economics with emotions has close relationship to any policy making, such as educational policy. More recently, economists as well as psychologists who are specifically interested in decision making have begun to take greater concerning emotional influence.

So, it seems any policy decision making whose any one of final policy decisions which is influenced to achieve or not achieve from their emotion indirectly. Usually, then an economy is doing well, there is less incentive to encourage new entrepreneurial firms if the country's citizens and firms have enough jobs supply and have enough labor supply in the job market. It seems that good economic growth country will have this question why it needs to take a risk on something new. So, emotions have close link to our societies to influence any country's citizens real needs and entrepreneurs' business aim to develop any societies' economy to be grown. So, any countries' policies decision makers ought concern whose enterprises and citizens whose real needs, then who can attempt to choose what methods of policies to assist whose countries' economy development more effective.

National environment protection management

On natural environment protection policy, whether national environment protection policy can assist economic growth to the country. The natural environment is central to economic activity and growth, providing the resources, we need to produce products and services and absorbing and processing unwanted by-product in the form of pollution add waste. So, environment assets contribute to managing risks to economic and social activity helps to regulate flood risks, regulating the local climate both air quality and temperature and maintaining the supply of clean water and resources both.

Government's environment protection role is to send clear signals and set a long term policy framework in order to provide businesses with the certainty who need to make investments in low carbon and resource efficient technologies. It is also essential that government listens to and works with business, so that environment protection policies are designed in a way that avoids unnecessary burdens and removes potential barriers to success. So, the natural environment plays an important role in supporting economic activity. It contributes: directly, by providing resources and raw materials, such as water, timber and minerals that are required as inputs for the production of products and services and indirectly, through services provided by ecosystems including carbon water purification, managing flood risks and nutrient cycling.

The relationship between economic growth and the natural environment is complex. Several different drivers come into play, including the scale and composition of the economy, particularly the share of services in GDP as opposed to primary industries and manufacturing and changes in technology that have the potential to reduce the environmental impacts of production and consumption decisions when also driving economic growth.

In fact, economic growth involves the combinations of different types of capital to produce products and services these include; produced capital, such as machinery, buildings and roads; human capital, such as skills and knowledge, natural capital, e.g. raw materials are extract from the earth, carbon and services is provided by forests and social capital, such as institutions and ties within communities. So, government needs to concern that national resources can not be extracted too much to lead our natural capital is lacked to produce any products or to provide services in the future.

In particular, market failure in the provision and use of environmental resources mean that natural assets would be over-used in the absence of government intervention. These market failures arise from the public product characteristics of the natural environment, external costs and benefits, where the use of a resource by one party has impacts on others, difficulties in capturing the full benefits of business investment in environmental research and development, and information failure. Market failures may include water quality and to vehicle emissions to influence human's body health.

So I suggest that any countries' government needs to achieve these policies which concerns on environmental protection aspect to achieve its public spending and technology policy, such as below:

● On developing flood infrastructure hand, supporting low carbon technologies electric vehicles. Also on the information provision and other policies to address barriers to influence consumer's behavior change, such as product labelling policies and policies to increase take up of resource efficiency measures to provide environment protection. So, effective environmental policy is likely to require and the use of multiple instruments, each tackling to require part of the problem when avoiding duplication and unnecessary regulatory burdens. Also, pricing environmental inputs can correctly help any businessmen to manage how to use natural resources effectively.

● Environmental policy aims to reduce how the economy and the businesses are to adverse environmental events, by reducing environmental risk both. For example, not just investments that facilities emissions reductions to avoid dangerous climate change, but also those investments that help to economy adapt to climate impacts already locked in by past and current emissions. The natural environment plays a key role in our economy, as a direct input into production and through the many services it provides. Environmental resources, such as minerals and fossil fuels directly facilities the production of products and services. The environment provides other services that enable economic activity, such as carbon, filtering air and soil formation. It is also vital for against flood risk, and soil formation. It is also vital for our wellbeing, providing us with recreational opportunities, improving our health and much more. Human wellbeing in a complex and diverse concept, determined by a wide-range of factors including levels of income absolute and relative, health status, educational attainment, housing conditions and environmental quality.

● National capital contributes to economic output through two main channels: directly as an input to the process of economic activity, indirectly through its effect on the productivity of the other factors of production. However, natural capital is as a direct input to wealth creation, which can provide the raw materials for economic production of products the raw materials for economic production of products and services, it includes non renewable resources like, fossil fuels, minerals metal extracted from the natural environment to produce energy, machinery, consumer products, renewable resources, natural processes or own reproduction. Why do our governments need to concern environmental policy? The reasons include natural areas provide global life support functions, including climate regulation and regulation of the chemical composition of the atmosphere and oceans. When natural areas play a role in the maintenance of life essential services, it is difficult to evaluate and demonstrate the contribution that particular habitat types or areas make. Water regulation can reduce flood and storm protection and prevent damage. Natural processes can also provide water quality benefits, pollution includes the removal of nutrients and pollutants from water, filtering of dust from the air, and providing noise. Waste sink includes all non recycled waste is produced by economic activity. In the absorptive capacity of the atmosphere, the oceans and the soil protection, such as many wetland habitats, provides benefits by preventing soil loss. Nutrient cycling includes storage, processing and acquisition of nutrients essential for plant growth in ecological process and waste decomposition, naturally occurring micro-organisms provide benefits through their ability to break down organization matter and speed up the process of waste decomposition.

Capturing private investment management

As the global financial crisis has reminded as once again of the economic role of trust and confidence, social capital attributes which are difficult to influence any policy decision maker's ration decision making more easily. Referring to recent financial crisis, which is related to any psychological drivers of economy activity, we can not understand the economic developments of recent times without psychological insights which go beyond estabished notions of rationality in its economic sense. As people with weigh the costs and benefits of each possibility.

This above assumption is based on the expectation that individuals and firms will act in a consistent manner, with a reasonably well defined notion of what who like and what whose objectives are, and with a reasonable understanding of how to attain those objectives. In fact, behavioural economy is a complement to deductive processes based on those assumptions. In any discipline with practical applications, such as public policy, conclusion is reached by chains of deductive logic based on those assumptions require the test of falsifiability or refutability, or at least that they be supported by confirmatory evidence. However, a rational means the predictive validity of the rational model holds, but that doesn't mean achieving policy should ignore interventions. For example, most people rationally avoid self-harm, but there will be extreme tails of highly protective and of highly reckless behaviour: the latter may require specific protection. So, it seems it has relationship between global financial crisis and individual or organization's irrational behaviour.

How can government' capturing private investment assist economic growth? How can government's capturing private investment policy attract foreign direct investment or different countries? I believe that Increased levels of trade and foreign direct investment worldwide which has a cause or effect of relationship to the closer interdependence of world economies, they are a reality. What is the relationship among these private, public and civil society sectors? Every country contribution is to add to the public policy stream to understand how the main forces in society operate and cooperate in promoting foreign direct investment. Governments have always been concerned about how to position themselves in an increasingly competitive market for a limited supply of investment resources.

Why should a multi-national firm choose one country attraction ? e.g. tax breaks, profit repatriation, low domestic content requirement etc. How can one country strategically position itself against others? Is there an association between pro-social public policy and levels of global private investment? We are particularly interested in those economies in earlier stages of development, where pro-social policies are a rarer phenomenon, as they provide a testing for our hypotheses. What is the relationship between the ability of an host country to attract private investment and the quality of pubic policies affecting the life of its citizens? Are pro-social host government policies in host countries linked to higher inward flows of foreign direct investment to that country?

There has three country level macroeconomic indicators to represent different facets of size: Host country economy growth rate, host country population and host country's rate of inflation. GDP growth, the annual percent change of output in real terms percent, reflects the strength of local economy and the increase in the size of domestic market, opening the door to large sales and high profits. Thus, higher GDP growth should generally be attracted to larger foreign investment. Population is another indicator of market size. It attracted to foreign investment with both large populations and high GDP per capita. So, encouraging immigration and birth rate can attract more foreign investment. Inflation enters the regression as a proxy for macroeconomic stability and as a reflection of the internal or external shocks suffered by the economy during the period under study, which may attract potential inflation sign of internal economic instability and of the host government's inability to maintain consistent monetary policy. It will influence foreign investment confidence. So stable inflation of the host country can increase confidence to let more foreign investment.

How Capturing private investment policy can affect medium to long term economic growth. It is difficult to measure the factors and to determine causality with certainty, between fiscal policy and economic growth relationship. Fiscal reforms are needed to concern structural reforms, e.g. labor or trade and supportive macroeconomic policies. At the macro level, fiscal policy can help to ensure macroeconomic stability, an essential prerequisite for growth at the micro level, tax and expenditure policies can boost growth by altering work and investment incentives, promoting human capital accumulation and enhancing total factor productivity. For example, combining fiscal reforms, e.g. sealing up infrastructure investment when improving the public investment process can increase their effectiveness. Complementary reforms, such as liberalizing trade of fiscal reforms by promoting savings, stimulating investment and not lacking productivity gains, policy uncertainty and high levels of public debt large fiscal deficits reduce aggregate savings in the economy and may lead to inflation, high interest rates and balance of payments pressures, with negative growth consequences. Policymakers need to concern the durability and equity. For example, Netherland, an expenditure cut of 15% of GDP between 1982 year and 2000 year created room sector job-creation. At the same time, both countries managed to avert adverse consequence on income inequality. In advanced and emerging market economies, age related spending on public persons and health care accounts for a large share of government spending (40% and 30%, respectively, IMF, 2014 f). Otherwise, Poland shifted from a financially defined benefit system to an actuarially solvent defined contribution system, and Germany put its pension system on a more sound financial by linking pension benefits to the old age dependency ratio, tightening access to early retirement and rising the statutory retirement age. In health care, Germany and the Netherlands introduced a combination of macro and micro level reforms to contain cost and enhance efficiency, including price controls on pharmaceuticals, higher co-payment and contributions and budget.

leadership behavioral management

Can national leadership and economic growth has close relationship? Can leader individual behavior affect economic growth? Leaders have strongest effects in autocracies, where who appear to substantially influence both economic growth and the evolution of political institutions. I shall indicate to explain why substantial roles for individual leaders and national institutional change, which can further influence the growth environment. In the past, examinations of the fundamental causes of growth debate between institutions, culture and geography, which typically operate without reference to the actions of particular personalities. However, economists may imagine leaders indirectly as policymakers, leaders, themselves are rarely the subject of focus.

The constraints imposed on leaders from electoral pressures, opposition parties, independent legislatures and judiciaries all vary across countries. To the extent that the authority embedded in formal institutional rules and the authority embedded in individuals act as substitutes, the increasing visibility of institutional variation in explaining paths may indirectly motivate leaders' behaviors. Theories of economic growth that emphasize public products, e.g. education, health, public entertainment facilities, such as parks, swimming pools etc. Also, national policies include international trade, monetary policy and fiscal policy etc. or all suggest possibly important roles for a national leader. However, identifying a causative effect of leaders on economic growth is challenging. Even, if it has relationship between particular leaders and particular economic growth in particular economic environment. However, it may be that growth changes drive leadership changes, without a causative effect of leaders. Assumption that a leader quality is independently, it seems the leader has no influence on economic growth. An important additional assumption is that the leader effects are strongest in autocratic settings, especially in the absence of political parties or legislatures to support the leader's any personal view points to achieve any regulations to influence economic growth effectively. These results point to an important effect between institutions and leader individuals in understanding economic growth paths. However, it seems institutions can influence the impact of national leaders behaviors and that national leaders can also influence the path of institutions. If leaders can influence economic growth, then may further these questions are raised: Do leaders act to obstruct economic growth or do they actively promote it? In this view, leaders can be actively good for economic growth, e.g. by investing in public products, choosing pro-growth trade policies, or overcoming national scale coordination problems. However, related questions of how leaders influence growth are related to the role of national policies in explaining growth. If policies might be well matter, even if leaders do not, if national policies care the expression of broader social forces. So, it seems national policies can also influence economic growth, instead of the leader's personal quality. So, it can get this question and conclusion. When asking how do we make poor countries rich? The unexplained, non-deterministic past of economic growth variation becomes especially relevant and given the results about leadership, more within reach.

However, nation leader's behaviour can influence the country's economy development. Concerning irrational honesty whether this behavior can influence social economic development. I shall indicate those questions to attempt to be considered, such as: Can there be a growing scaraity without a growing shortage or a growing shortage with a growing scarcity? Can a decision be economic if there is no money in involved? Can there be surplus food in a society where people are hungry? For example, building ordinary and building luxury housing both involves using many of the same resources, such as bricks, pipes, and construction labour. How does the allocation of these resources between ordinary housing and luxury housing tend to change after rent control laws are passed?

When a government institution or program produces counter productive results, is that necessarily a sign of irrationality on the part of those who run that particular institution or program? Why do American manufacturers of computers or television sets tend to have them transported by others? When Chinese manufacturers tend to transport themselves? How did the movement of population from rural to urban America affect the economy of retail selling in the early twentieth century? Advertising even when it is successful, is often considered to be a benefit only to those who advertise, but of no benefit to consumers, who have to pay the cost of the advertisement in the higher price of the products who buy. Is it irrational economy behaviour to society? Why would luxury hotels be charging lower rates than economy hotels? Whether governments choose to protect competition or protect competitors which method is better? What have been some of the economic and social consequences of the substitution of machine power for human strength, as a result of industralization and the growing importance of knowledge, skills and experience in a high-technological economy? How can per capita income be increasing by 50 % over a period of years, when average family income and average householder income remain almost stable over those same year? Does inequality of income tend to be greater or less in long run than in the short run?

All above questions concern the social and economic influences won't be better if the policy decision makers or businessmen do any irrational honesty behaviours. It seems rational honesty behaviour is important to any policy decision makers or businessmen because whose rational or irrational behaviour can influence social economic development directly are driven to act by economic as well as social ethical and other reasons. So economists need to study of what motivates individual acts, especically regarding economic decisions, offers an intellectual challenge to the human sciences. So, if economists can predict to judge whether any policy decision makers or businessmen whose act is irrational or rational, then who can assist the country's economic development more easily.

Promoting honesty in negotiation can influence social economy growth in global. In a competitive and moral imperfect world, business people are often facing with serious ethical challenges. Usually, many businessmen feel justified in engaging in less than ideal conduct to protect their own interests. However, our commonplace that work to promote credibility, trust and honesty of behaviours can influence our social economy growth in long term. For example, deception in negotiation behaviour is immoral, due to success in business typically requires successful negotiations.

Given the high value placed on honesty, the incentives for deception in negotiation create a serious moral tension for business people. Not surprisingly, deception in negotiation is a widely discussed problem in business ethics. How many negotiators their views are essentially, who is regarded as a superior moral philosopher, would find them objectionable? For example, philosophical debates about the loss of civilian life in war would be better served by putting resources and intellectual energy into developing political, economic diplomatic and military strategies that resources and intellectual energy how to be chosen to use in military strategies aspect or political aspect or economic diplomatic aspect. The country's leader will influence the whole country's social economy development in long term. However, individual and social stability are difficult to maintain in a social setting in which there is serious conflict between ethics and personal welfares. Because irrational honesty behaviour is usually caused between the personal welfare and ethics choice.

Can behavioral economy be applied to develop policy and influence economic growth effectively? Such policies stress that changing the way choices are presented or changing the environment in which decisions are made, can substantially alter behavior. Ideas from behavioral economics have helped to develop the traditional economic choice framework, in which people are assumed to make choices that are rational, self interested and consistent. Some of the most important behavioral insights for tax and benefit policy include: Faced with complicated decisions, people may make choices, which are often approximately optimal, in that who maximize welfare, but might in some cases lead to poor choices. There is evidence that how choices are presented affects outcomes.

The environment in which decisions are made would provide cues to make particular choices or made could provide cues to make particular choices, or some aspects of the choice problem may be more or less influence to consumers. When any policy relates to income and spending, or it is label money for another can affect what people choose to do with it. Individuals appear to care not just about their own outcomes, but also about those of others. This might be because people derive value from fairness and cooperation. These motivations could give intrinsic incentive to make particular choices. It is possible that providing extrinsic incentives, such as taxes, fines or rewards could be crowded our desirable behavior.

Consumers may have to exercise costly self control to make certain choices, such as eating health foods or giving up smoking. Commitment devices to help overcome self control problems are therefore values, for example, raising the cost of tempting choices, increasing cigarette taxes, say: when making choices with uncertain outcomes, people will do a number of behavioral features. Such as, attaching subjective decision weights to each outcome and these may differ from objective measures of probability. Usually, outcomes are measured against a reference point, relative to the reference point are felt more strongly than equivalent gains. When welfare increases and ever bigger gains falls, as the welfare cost is from ever bigger losses, then people will appear to be risk seekers when welfare cost comes to cause social loss. How people value the future changes with the passage of time. Usually people hope to earn immediate rewards in present than distant rewards in the future. This means that people make plans who find it hard to achieve. People may also make choices under the assumption that their preferences won't change in the future. So, for policymakers those biases have important implications for why behavior change interventions may be necessary.

Behavioral insights provide new reasons to intervene, issues of self control, for example, making failure, where outcomes are come from the perspective of either individuals or society or both usually. As a common failure is the case of externalities, when individual choices generate costs or benefits for others. Since, these are not taken into account in private decision making, which are come from a social perspective, there is too much or too little of the activity.

In this case, taxes or subsidies can help private and social incentives. So, behavioral economical concept can be suggested these important insights for externalities, such as private decisions are closer to the social optimum, reducing the need for correcting taxes or subsidies. It seems that taxes or subsidies will affect to change people's behaviors if social preferences are important. Externalities can arise not just because of how someone affects the well being of others, but also through how decisions made today affect the individual in the future. This is known as an internality. Taxes or subsidies policies both can influence people's present behaviors to be changed and future behaviors will be influenced to be changed from whose present behaviors in societies. Thus, policymakers can not neglect this policy of method to attempt to solve any social challenge nowadays.

Finally, I shall explain why national leader's behavior can assist policy development. Behavioral economy is a science, includes psychology, economics, finance and sociology to understand human behavior and decision making. Behavioral economics recognizes that constraints in time and mental resources prevent us from optimally evaluating every decision. To deal with our limitations, so we rely on mental decision to judge our face of uncertainty, but we can be leaded to predictably irrational behaviors from behavioral economical concept.

As government agencies enact laws and regulations that are focused in the society. They often rely on restrictions, incentives or public information campaigns in order to change citizen behavior. When well intentioned, those traditional approaches can be accepted. For example, regulations that can be supported to financial advisers disclose conflicts of interest have led to achieve any final results. Disclosures can increase pressures on advisees to comply with the advice provided and in some cases increase greater perceptions of trust rather than the evaluation of biased advice. Similarly, tax incentives can increase retirement savings rates which have had limited impact. Researchers studying the impact of concluded that such policies are an expensive way of encouraging new savings.

On the one hand, governments ought engage their citizens to do any action, whose action is influenced by behavioral economics to discover how behavioral economics can be provided powerful insights into human motivation and behavior. As different countries' government experiments are more from academic laboratories to the real world. So, it is a kind of method to be applied to assist any countries' governments how to use effective policy to improve people's lives. For example, designing what is the best reasonable taxes, subsidies, incentives or educational campaigns level at the rate, donations and retirement savings rates as well as healthy food product label consumption of selection etc. strategic policies which are related how to apply behavioral economy to analyze or experiment to gain the better choice among of them.

On the another hand, Economic agents ought attempt to spend time to gather data to choose to do the best decision, but not perfectly national ones. Also economic research should be used reasonable assumptions about agents' cognitive actives. So, economic models should take predictions that are consistent with micro-level data on decisions, including experimental evidence. Moreover, economists ought spend much time to learn from psychologists. Behavioral economists now routinely combine experimental data, field data and theory to construct their arguments. As behavioral economic continues to gain acceptance, behavioral economists will increasingly find themselves participating in policy discussions. As policy has the ability to do good or to create great mislead, depending on who, leader is in charge of making the rules. Indeed in some cases the findings of behavioral economists suggest that active policies may be quite harmful. Successful policy analysis should be concerned the motives of private actors, e.g. consumers and firms and the public or governmental actors need to design formulate and enforce policy with cooperation to regulators, bureaucrats, politicians.

So, policy analysis must also be carefully concerned the institutional environment in which these private and public actors interact, e.g. , market, elections and bureaucracies. However, any bad decision making is caused from bounded rationality, slow learning, framing and lack of self control with those effects in mind, one might conclude that government can easily improve consumers' welfare by paternalistically helping consumers make better decisions. Such paternalistic policies can improve consumer welfare by enhancing an individual's maximizing whose own welfare. So, this stands in contrast to most public policies, which address externalities or public products problems that arise because of interactions among economic agents.

To conclude, national leader and whose psychology which can influence whether he can do the reasonable policy and which have close relationship, As if the national leader had health psychology, then who will have more possible to achieve good behavior to perform to decide how to achieve any the best public policies to raise growth to make welfare to whose citizens. So any policymakers ought need to concern how to listen to behavioral scientists to let them to give any recommendation how to improve or review or revise whose psychological challenges to let them have more effort to decide how to choose to do the right decision effectively. Because the relationship between psychology and behavioral science has more generally to influence public policy which is particularly painful and frustrating of the success for any similar policy recommendations. Hence, economics and psychology indeed can provide policymakers with vital tools to develop the best policy to solve any social challenges.

Consequently, it seems the leader's psychology will influence whose behavioral performance to be decided to choose to do the more correct policy to influence economic development more easily. It also means that one leader's psychology is an important factor to influence any social economic development directly for long term. So who can not neglect to concern whether whose psychological mind is right or wrong to already to make any decisions to plan any policies before whose any polices are implemented. Because the leader's psychology will influence whose behavior is more correct to decide to decide how to do any policies effectively.

Reference

Dimson, Marsh & Staunton, London Business School (2005) In The Global Investment Returns Year Book, ABN Amro.

Fiscal Policy And Long Term Growth, International Monetary Fund, IMF policy papers, Washington, D.C. Available from April, 2015, http://www.imf.org/external/pp/ppindex.aspx.

Reference

Abrahamson, E., & Rosenkopf., (1993). Institutional and competitive bandwagons: Using mathematical modeling and a tool to explore innovation diffusion. Academy of management review, 18(3), 487-517.

Hill, C.W.L. & Jones, G.R. 1995. Strategic management, An integrated approach. Boston: Houghtom Mif In.

CHAPTER FIVE

Facility management influences airport and logistic employee performance

● Facility management assists employees reduce
maintenance service expenditure

Facility management provides a variety of non core operations and maintenance services to support any organizations' operation. For logistic organization example, it is possible to provide effective maintenance service to warehouse in order to reduce warehouse facilities to be damaged to bring to spend to buy any new equipment facilities expenditure. So, when the logistic company's warehouse facilities can be maintenance to be the best quality. Then, they can be used these warehouses' machines facilities again. Their performance can assist workers to manufacture any products to keep the most efficiently an raising the best production performance in whole manufacturing process. Then, this logistic company's facility management department can bring to avoid purchase any new machine facilities expenditure spending. One to these warehouses' production machine facilities are kept in the best production performance environment even in long term production need.

I shall indicates airport and warehouse facilities how to influence employees performances as below:

(1) How can comfortable warehouse facilities influence workers' efficiencies in logistic industry ?

The logistic industry's facility management department can create cost savings and efficiency of the warehouse's workplaces. It's machines facilities (production machines) are dealt with the maintenance management of the physical assets maintenance service. FM (facilities management) has been being applied to industrial facilities in logistic and warehouse industry long term as well as maintenance plays a significant role to ensure the full service and the warehousing system, including both building components and equipment in warehouse.

Maintenance service is needed to bring a certain level of availability and reliability of a warehouse facilities system and its components and its ability perform to a standard level of quality. So , it seems that logistic industry's warehouse asset cost reducing. It depends on whether it has one facility management department to provide maintenance service to itself warehouse workplace's production machine facilities and warehouse building itself in order to let workers t feel the manufacturing machines can bring good manufacturing performance to assist them to produce any products in one safe warehouse workplace environment. Hence, the performance measurement of warehouse maintenance issue will be valued to be consider to every warehouse manager and facility manager in logistic industry.

In logistic industry, (FM) works at two level on the one hand, it provides a safe and efficient working environment, which is essential to influence warehouse workers whether how they perform to do their manufacturing tasks or logistic goods delivery tasks in warehouse. When they feel the warehouse is safe environment to work. They will not need to consider anywhere has risk to cause they die by accident in warehouse. Hence, they can concentrate on doing their every tasks . On the other hand, it can involve strategic issues, such as property (warehouse workplace and management, strategy property decision and warehouse facility, e.g. manufacturing machine, facility maintenance and checking planning and maintenance planning development.

However, reducing the operating expense issue will be the main aim when the logistic company feels that it has need to set up one in-house facility management department to carry on any maintenance service for its warehouses' any workplace property and manufacturing machines facilities. So, when the logistic company decides to implement one facility management department, it needs to ensure its facility management department can bring the minimum level of keeping manufacturing performance and efficiency to its warehouses' any manufacturing machines and warehouses' property to avoid to be damaged in short term, such as loss of business due to failure in service, provision of project to customer satisfaction, provision of safe environment, effective utilisation of workplace space, e.g. warehouse effectiveness and communication between the workers and the logistic managers in the warehouse workplace , due to the warehouse's space is not enough maintenance service reliability to the logistic company's warehouse, responsiveness of the warehouse's worker individual negative emotion problem, due to he/she often feels need to work in one unsafe warehouse working environment. Hence, it seems that poor or unsafe warehouse working environment can influence workers feel negative emotion to work to bring low efficiency (inefficiency) or under productive performance in warehouse. It has relationship to influence they to bring psychological negative emotion feeling to work when the organization lacks one effective warehouse management repairing service to be provided to the warehouse's facilities and properties' maintenance needs in order to avoid ineffective measurement and misleading of performance.

Hence, the logistic company's facilities management department often needs to be reviewed whether its maintenance service level is passed to achieve the lowest repair (maintenance) service standard to its warehouse itself property and manufacturing machine or warehouse delivery tool facilities or warehouse lamps' light whether is enough to let workers to see anything clearly to avoid accident occurrence or see anything to work clearly or the warehouse space areas are enough to let they can have enough space to walk or communicate to their team supervisors or deliver any goods more easily in the short distance between the worker's sending goods location and the delivering goods destination in order to avoid because the lacking enough space to cause the accident occurrence , due to the space is not enough to let they deliver their goods to any locations in warehouse.

Hence, it seems logistic company's (FM) department can contribute to the organization's mission, such as avoiding warehouse accident occurrence, inefficiency, not enough and unavailability of the facility for future needs when the warehouse lacks enough space areas to bring poor performance of facility and dangerous warehouse itself property in warehouse, e.g. safe and reliable operations of material handling equipment and maintenance of warehouse facilities, grounds, security system, utilities, plumbing, heating , enough lighting system, air conditioning, warming heater, fire protection, security system alarm etc. facilities in warehouse.

Hence, it seems that if the logistic company expected to reduce to spend lot of excessive manufacturing machine purchase expenditure, lose of workers' life or bring workplace accidents , due to poor warehouse workplace environment, even bringing lawsuit compensation claim loss , due to the worker individual accident or death is caused from the poor warehouse facilities, or bring negative emotion to let the workers feel they are working in unsafe warehouse workplace environment. Then, it ought choose to set up on facility management department in order to provide enough maintenance service to its warehouse to avoid these non essential expenditure causing , due to these poor warehouse facilities factors.

Hence any logistic company ought choose to set up one itself in -house facility management department, it be better than outsourcing its all facilities service to one facility management (maintenance service provider) to help it to deal any kinds of maintenance service in warehouse. Because it is long term maintenance need to its warehouse's any machines and warehouse itself properties. If it chose to find one outsourcing facilitiy management maintenance service provider to replace its in-house facility management department to deal all related facilities maintenance tasks in warehouse. Then, it is possible that it needs to pay long time facilities maintenance service fee to its outsourcing facility management maintenance service provider more than itself facility management maintenance service provision department.

(2) Can facility management influence tourism industry's human resource management influence to improve productivity in airline, travel agent, hotel tourism sectors?

In tourism industry, measuring productivity froma HRM prespective is extremely difficult and has proven to be a limitation within the tourism sector. Due to the customers are not tangible. For example, how can the travel agent measure its travel consultant individual service performance to evaluate whether the travelling customer feels or does not feel satisfactory loyalty from his/her service? How can the airline measure its pilot , airline front-line travelling passenger service attendant indiviual service performance to evaluate whether his/her travelling passenger feels or does not feel satisfactory to whose service performance? Whether airport facility management can influence airline counter service staffs performance ?

However, the complaint number whether it is more or less to the airline or travel agent's service behavior , it does not represent whose service attitude or behavior or performance is poor absolutely because there are many travelling consumers whose complaints are unreasonable , although they feel satisfactory to the airline attendent or airline front -line service staffs individual service performance, but if they feel unhappy to be caused by the airline or travel agent service staff. They will still compain their performance. For this suitation example , it is possible that the travelling passenger is delayed to catch the airplance to fly, due to the country's sudden worse weather influnce, he/she will complain the airline fron-line counter travelling customer service staffs, it concerns when the air plane will arrive the airport, if the airline counter service staff's feedback is that the airplane needs long time arrival. Then, the travelling passengers will complain to the airline counter service staffs in angry. But in fact, the air plane delays to arrive the airport, the airline counter service staffs ought not need responsibilitie to explain the reason why they can not assist the delayed air plane to arrive the country in easier. Furthermore, thy will be complained unreasonably. Hence, it is difficult to measure tourism sector's service staffs ' performance, also the complaint exact number is not one judgement factor to measure their service performance absolutely.

I assume any tourism industry's front -line service airline staffs, they must attempt to serve their travelling passenger in positive service attitude and behavior. So, any tourism industy, how to improve their front -line service staff performance in order to let they to know how to deal unreasonable complaints in sudden unpredictive suitation. Their training materials or contents my include: Teaching them how to provide positive feedback to treat any travelling passenger individual difficult problems or unreasonable complaints in order to reduce their psychological pressure to unknown how to treat these passenger individual related problems when they are facing in airports or travelling agent workplaces. The travelling agent or airline travelling service organizations can attempt to collect measures of employee performance from customers , for example, comment cards in hotel rooms, airplane, travel agent's workplace, mystery shoppers etc. more focus shouls be pleased on this form of evaluation. In order to evaluate the actually place value on the customer ratings to every employee. The all every day, the form of evaluation concerning the actually value on the customer ratings , will be gathered to strategic , it has how many customers feel good or bad ratings to every employee individual performance when every one's tasks are finishing. Due to one month, it can make statistic report to calculate how much performance marks to give to every employee in order to evaluate whether every one's performance is satisfactory to be accempted to the lowest level. If the employee's marks rating is low, his/her department manager can arrange a time and day to meet him/her to discuss whether which aspects of problems who feels in order to give recommendation how to improve his/her service attitude to let customer to give higher marks rating to him/her next time.

Hence tourism industry's service sector organizations need to have one training department to arrange courses how to improve employee service performance in order to let customer to give higher marks rating to very one as well as finding methods how to excite every front line service employee individual loyalty , they can increase their confidence to know how to deal sudden unreasonable complaints in effective and efficient positive attitude.

In conclusion, how to improve employee service performance issue will be any tourism service organization's HRM concerning problem. Airports need to arrange how to implement efficient and comfortable and available convenient airport facilities to let any airline service counter staffs feel enjoyable to serve their passengers. They need to know how to find the most effective methods to solve how improvement of front line employee individual performance problem in order to raise the airline or travel agent's quality of service to let itself further customers to feel its service performance is better than others. So, facility management has indirect relationship to influence airport airline service staffs performances.

In conclusion, to decide whether the company ought need or not need facilities maintenance service or either set up in-house facility management department or outsource one facility management maintenance service provider. It depends on whether its organization has how many facilities are used in its workplace, how many staffs are working the workplace, how much size of its workplace, its workplace is office or warehouse or factory, how long time of its facilities' useful time etc. factors , then it can decide whether it needs or does not need one facility maintenance service department or outsourcing facility maintenance service provider to help it to deal any facilities management problem in its organization.

● Facility management role in
organization

When one company feels that it has need facility management service. It can choose to set up either in-house facility management department or seek one outsourcing facility management service provider to help it to arrange any facility management service need. However, this facility management role is only one for the organization. It concerns this question: What facility management maintenance function can bring the benefits to the organization?

It can define that all services required for the management of building and real estate to maintain and increase their value, the means of providing maintenance support, project management and user management during the building life cycle, the integration of multi-disciplinary activities within the built environment and the management of their impact upon people and the workplace. In traditional, (FM) services may include building fabric maintenance, decoration and refurbishment, plant, plumbing and drainage maintenance, air conditioning maintenance, lift and escalator maintenance , fire safety alarm and fire fighting system maintenance, minor project management. All these are hard services. Otherwise, cleaning , security, handyman services, waste disposal, recycling, pes control, grounds maintenance, internal plants. All these are soft services. Additional services, might also include: pace planning, things moving management, business risk assessment, business continuity planning, benchmarking, space management, facilities contract outsourcing service arrangement, information systems, telephony, travel booking facility utility management, meeting room arrangement services, catering services, vehicle fleet management, printing service, postal services, archiving , concierge services, reception services, health and safety advice, environmental management.

All of these services will be every organization's in-house facility soft or hard services needs. So, it explains why some large organizations feel need one effective facility management department to help them to arrange how to implement facility services efficiently in order to achieve cost reducing, raising efficiency and performance improvement aims because one effective facility management control system can influence employee individual productive effort to be raised or reduced indirectly.

However, (FM) can be selected either setting up one in-house (FM) department or outsourcing its services to one facility management service provider to help the organization to solve any kinds of facilities maintain service problems. One on-house (FM) department is a team, it needs employees to deliver all (FM) services. Some specialist services are needed to be outsourced, when the service is on expertise in the company. The no expertise services will be outsourced to simple service contracts, e.g. lift and escalator (FM) department will have direct labour, but it can outsource some specialist to help it to do some complex facilities management service. So, the team leader can of can manage whose team staffs, such as maintenance technicians run low risk operations . Otherwise, the outsourcing facility management service provider needs to help it to operate high risk operations or maintenance vital plant facility management service. Anyway, it can set up in-house (FM) department to arrange specialist direct labour and outsourced (FM) services to more than one facility management service providers to do different kinds of (FM) services. One of these outsourcing (FM) service provider, who can arrange sub-contractors to assist it to finish any (FM) services of it's outsourcing (FM) services are more complex to compare the other sub-contractors (third parties).

● What is a facility manager's role to provide quality service to satisfy its user needs?

We need to know how quality can be defined in facility management and why it should be defined by the customer? How facility managers can find out customer (user) needs? What are the difficulties in finding out users' needs and in delivering quality services? Whether improving quality always means requiring higher cost?

In general, facility manager's major responsibilities may include these major functional areas: longer range and annual facility planning, facility financial forecasting, real estate acquisition and/or disposal, work specification, installation and space management, architectural and engineering planning and design, new construction and/or renovation, maintenance and operations management, maintenance and operation management, telecommunications integration, security and general administrative services. When the facility manager had implemented any one of these FM services for those user. How does he/she provide excellent (FM) service quality ot let whose users to feel satisfactory?

In fact, quality issues can not be considered without customer-oriented perspective service quality involves a comparison of expectation with performance. (FM) service quality is a measure of how well to service level delivered matches customer expectation. So, these issues are (FM) service user's general measurement level requirement. The (FM) manager needs to achieve these the minimum performance measurement level to satisfy whose (FM) user's needs.

However, (FM) service quality has three characteristics: Intangibility, heterogeneity, inseparability. But in fact, (FM) service delivered may be through tangible physical aspects, e.g. factory plant workplace building, machine equipment maintenance, intangible (FM) services, e.g. managing space moving in plant to let staffs to work, managing outsourcing cleaners to clean factory equipment. However, all (FM) service performance often varies, due to the behavior of service personnel. Hence, a well developed job specification and training can help to improve the consistence of services of (FM). Any (FM) production and consumption of many services may are inseparable and they are usually interactions between the (FM) client and the contact person from the service provider.

Hence, it seems that service quality is considered as hard to evaluate. In (FM) service quality, it includes physical quality and interactive non-physical service quality. Physical quality is tangibles: The appearance of the physical facilities, equipment, personnel and communication materials. Non-physical services quality means reliability: The ability to perform the promised service dependably and accurately; responsiveness means the willingness to help customers and provide prompot service to let user to feel; assurance mans the competence of the system in its credibility in providing a courteous and secure service and empathy means the approachability, ease of access and effort taken to understand customers' needs.

Hence, a good performance of (FM) manager , he/she ought satisfy the user's tangible and non-tangible both service quality needs. I recommend that he/she can attempt to predict what are the (FM) customer expects in each (FM) service needs. Then, it can make decision what aspect(s) will be the (FM) users major (FM) service need and what aspect(S) won't be the (FM) users major (FM) service need. Then, he/she can make more accurate decision to arrange time, human resource , cost spending amount arrangement whether when it ought concentrate on finishing the (FM) major service tasks as well as whether how he/she ought finish the major (FM) service tasks to be more easily, e.g. how to arrange staffs number to finish, how many the minimum staffs number is needed to be arrange the major (FM) service tasks, time arrangement is important factor, because it can influence whether he/she ought finish the major (FM) service tasks today or tomorrow or later in order to have enough time to finish other non-major (FM) service tasks. Instead of time management, staff number arrangement is also important factor , if he/she arranged the excessive staffs number to do the (FM) major services tasks, then it is possible that it will have shortage of staffs number to finish the non-major (FM) service tasks on the day. So, avoiding either major or non-major (FM) services can not finish on the day. The (FM) manager needs to predict when the major (FM) services and the non-major (FM) services which are necessary to be finished in order to have enough time and staffs to assist him/her to finish every day major and non-major (FM) service effectively. Then, the achievement of his/her (FM) major and non-major tangible and non-tangible services , it will have more chance to be performed efficiently by his/her managed staffs.

In conclusion, in any organizations , (FM) manager needs have good predictable effort to evaluate whether when his/her managed team need to finish the major and/or non-major (FM) tasks as well as whether how he/she ought arrange the accurate time and staff number to finish any major and/or non-major (FM) service tasks on the day. Then, his/her leading of (FM) service team can be managed to work more efficiently in order to satisfy her/his (FM) service user's needs.

Facility management how influences
public service transport service performance

● How (FM) space moving management brings employees efficiencies
There are interesting questions: How (FM) can bring value-add to avoid loss or earn more profit to the organization? Can it influence employees to raise performance and improve efficiency ? Some organizations' (FM) service need which is necessary in order to let employees can raise productivity.

It is based on these assumptions: I assume the organizations have completely either outsourced or in-house their (FM) facility management departments will gain more effect on added value than they have no (FM) function as well as organizations have a strong coordination with the (FM) department will gain more added value than organizations with a weak coordination. Organizations in the profit aim can gain more added value than organizations in the not for profit aim sectors.

In fact, any organization is difficult to confirm it has relationship between improving performance, raising efficiency and owning (FM) function in its organization. (FM) could have to do with the attraction of easy but incomplete indicators of efficiency rather than the necessarily and less direct measures if the effectiveness and the relevance of space moving useful management, e.g. whether building has the enough space to let employees to move to work easy in order to raise efficiency, whether the building has excessive furniture and equipment number and they are putted on wrong places to be caused employees move difficulty in the building in order to influence productive performance.

However, how to arrange space moving management to equipment, e.g. copying machines, faxes, productive machines, they are putted on the locations where have enough space to let employees to move to another locations. For example, the building floor has more than 50 employees, but its space is not enough to let these 50 employees to move to any locations to let them to feel easily often. Then, it is possible to cause they feel nervous pressure and they can feel difficult to work , when they are working in a small office space or factory space or warehouse space. Then, the consequence will be under-predictive efficiency or poor performance to any one of these 50 employees in this office or factory or warehouse.

" Facility management is responsible for coordinating all efforts related to planning, designing, and managing buildings and their systems, equipment, and furniture to enhance. The organizations abilty to compete successfully in a rapidly changing world." (F.Becker)

The author explains equipment, workplace internal space designing, furniture space putting location arrangement will have possible to influence employee individual productive performance or efficiency to be raised or reduced in the workplace. Hence, it seems that, in the value chain (FM) belongs to the activity part of the firm. To make the facilities cooperation with each office or factory or warehouse using space moving facility management. Facility space moving management must be linked strategically, tactically and operationally to other support activity to add value to the organization's office or factory or warehouse space moving management arrangement more effectively.

Thus, how to arrangement space moving management issue it will have possible to influence the organization's employee individual productive performance and efficiency in whose workplace. It seems that (FM) space moving management arrangement have indirect relationship to influence the organization's employee individual performance and efficiency , due to they need often to work in the workplace, if they feel moving difficulty , or excessive equipment , furniture number is putting into the small office, factory or warehouse locations, or they feel the office or factory or warehouse has excessive (a lot of) staffs number to work in the small space of office or factory or warehouse. Then, they can not concentrate nervous on finishing every tasks in possible. In long term, their efficiencies will be poor or inefficiencies or their performance won't be improved or causing poor performance in possible.

Instead of the not enough space moving and excessive staffs number factor, it will bring another question: Can enough information systems equipment cause a more efficient and improved performance to the organization staffs in the workplace?

I assume that the office has 100 employees and it has only ten copying machines. So it means that ten employees use one copying machine. Hence, it brings this question: Is it enough to provide only ten copying machines to average ten employees to use? It depends on other factors, e.g. whether any one of these 100 employees needs to print how many documents per day , whether the five copying machines' locations are far away to separate different locations or they are stored in one printing room in the office, whether the day has how many staffs are absent, whether the day has how many printing machine(s) is/ are broken to need to be repaired. Hence, these unpredictable external environment factors will influence whether the five copying machines number is enough to let these 100 employees to use in the office every day. Hence, facility manager ought need to spend to observe average their copying behaviors every day in order to make data record. Many employees need to use copy machines to print documents, average how many document's page number, they need to print, how much average time spending to print their documents, average how many staff absent number on the day. Even, if the all five copying machines are stored in the printing room, calculating the staffs number whether how many staffs need more than five minutes to walk to the printing room to print their documents many staffs need to spend five minute to walk to the printing room, and they have other urgent tasks to wait to finish. It is possible to influence their efficiency, due to they often need to spend more than five minutes to walk to the printing room to print documents. If there are many staffs need to often to print documents, but their printing task will have many time, e.g. 20 separate printing tasks. Then, they need to spend at least (20x5) 100 minutes to spend time to walk to the printing room to print their documents. It must influence that they should not finish the other urgent tasks on the day. If there are many staffs to spend much time to walk to the printing room in the least 20 separate printing time or more on that day. All the facility manager needs to evaluate whether all the five copy machines are stored in the printing room whether it is the best location decision or they ought need be separated to put on different office locations in their workplaces, even he/she ought need to evaluate whether it is enough copying machines number, when the office has only 5 copying machines. He/she ought need to buy more copying machines number to satisfy any one of these 100 employee individual copying task need.

In conclusion, effective office or factory or warehouse space moving facility management will be one part task of (FM) function. If the office or factory or warehouse can have accurate equipment, machine , furniture number to avoid excessive or shortage number problem to cause employees often feel moving difficult problem in their workplace when they need to move to another location to work in office or warehouse or factory as well as whether the staff needs often spend time to wait the another employee to use the copying machine to print whose document or fax machine to deliver whose document. Then, it is not that fax or printing machines number is not enough to provide the employees to use in the office or warehouse or factory workplace.

Hence, (FM) includes space moving facility management to equipment , machines, furniture number as well as choosing anywhere is(are) the suitable location (s) arrangement to putting or storing these facilities in workplace as well as decision of the staff number and the workplace area size whether it has excessive staffs number to cause these staffs need to work in the small area size of office or warehouse or factory workplace. So, the organization ought need to decide whether it needs to reduce the office's staffs number to let them to work in another more suitable locations in another workplace. Hence, all these facilities space moving management and staffs and workplace size issues will be (FM) manager's consideration issues, because these external environment factors will influence employee individual efficiency and performance to be poor to cause low valued to its organization in long term in possible .

● Predictive the choosing right
data asset and (FM) analytics
solutions to boost public
transportation service quality

Can gather the choosing right data public transportation service station facilities asset and analytics, it can give recommendation to help any organization to boost service quality? (FM) analytics data can be applied to public transportation service industry to be supported how and why the train, train, ferry , ship, air plane, underground train public transportation tools' time arrival and leaving information notice board and automated ticket paying machines facilities are putting on or stored any where locations in order to boost passengers to feel their facilities locations are convenient to let them to buy tickets and see the arrival and leaving time for the next public transportation tool from the information notice electronic board machine. So, it seems that these public transportation tools' station facilities locations can influence passengers to feel the public transportation service company how to consider to its passenger's buying ticket needs and next public transportation tool's arrival and leaving time information needs in order to boost its passengers use service quality and let them to feel better service reliable performance in any train, tram, ferry , ship, underground tram, airplane stations.

As these public transportation service organizations need to learn data analytics represent an opportunity for its ticket paying machine equipment facilities as well as the next transportation tool arrival and leaving time information notice board electronic equipment facilities anywhere the locations are the most suitable to put on or store these equipment to let passengers to walk to the ticket paying machines to buy the ticket to catch the train, tram, underground train, ferry, airplane, taxi, ship more easily. So, they do not need to spend more time to find these facilities locations and spend more time to queue to wait to buy ticket to catch the public transportation tool in stations conveniently. Instead of where is the seeking ticket paying machine location, where is the next public transportation tool arrival and leaving information notice time , these both issues will be any public transportation tool's passenger's main needs.

Hence, how to spend time to seek where the next public transportation tool's arrival and leaving time information electronic notice machine location and where the ticket paying machine location , these both factors will influence any passengers' positive or negative emotion causing. For example, if the passenger feels difficult to find the ticket paying machine in the large area size train station or /and he/she feels difficult to find the train time arrival and leaving information to let him/her to know when the next train will arrive the station. Due to he/she feels difficult to find the train ticket paying machine, he/she needs to spend much time to find any one ticket paying machine in the train station. Then, it will influence him/her to choose another public transportation tool to replace the train public transportation tool, e.g. he/she can choose to catch tram, underground train, taxi, bus, ferry, taxi, ship to replace train. So, it seems ticket paying machine and time arrival and leaving information notice electronic equipment 's location putting or stored choice will be one factor to influence the passenger to choose another kind of public transportation tool to replace train at the moment. When, he/she feels that he/she arrives the destination in the most short time. Then, the public transportation service organization (FM) manager has responsibility to evaluate whether there are enough ticket paying machines number to let passengers do not need to spend more time to queue to buy tickets to catch the public transportation tool in short time as well as there are enough time arrival and leaving for next transportation tool to let passengers to know. It will be their concerning issues when they arrive the public transportation service tool's station.

Hence, predictive passenger individual walking behavior can help the public transportation service organization to choose whether where are the most convenient and attractive locations to let the ticket paying machines and the arrival and leaving time information electronic board machines to be putted on or stored in the suitable station positions in order to let many passengers can find these essential facilities in stations very easily. So, gathering data concerns passenger walking behavior in the public transportation service any stations, which can help the facility manager to make more accurate evaluation to attempt to predict whether where the locations are common places to let passengers to choose to walk daily or where the locations are not common places to let passenger to choose not to walk daily in general. Then, he/she can apply these data of different locations in the stations to evaluate whether anywhere they will have many passengers to choose to walk or whether anywhere they won't have many passengers to choose to walk in order to make more accurate decision whether anywhere are the most suitable locations to let the ticket paying machines and the time arrival and leaving information electronic board equipment to be putter on or stored in order to let them to feel it is so easier to let them to find.

Anyway, calculating each station's passenger number per day issue is important to predict whether where , there are many passengers choose to walk or where, there are not many passengers choose to walk in these different public transportation service stations in order to evaluate whether where the stations' different ought put on paying ticket machines or time arrival and leaving information electronic boards in order to let they feel very easy to buy tickets and seeing the next arrival and leaving time information for the kind of public transportation service tool conveniently in the different stations. Moreover, if the station has no enough ticket paying machines number to be supplied to let passengers need to spend more than ten minute time to wait to buy ticket to catch the kind of public transportation service tool in every queue every day. Then it will cause them to choose another kind of public transportation tool to catch go to working place or entertainment place to replace it to on that day. Then, it will cause these passengers who often do not like to queue in the kind of public transportation service tool's any stations, who will not choose to go to anywhere of this kind of public transportation service tool's any stations again. Hence, in long term this kind of public transportation service tool will lose many passengers. Thus, calculating each station's busy time of passengers number , which can predict when it is the busy time and it can make more accurate decision whether the station has need to increase enough ticket paying machines number in order to bring enough supply number to satisfy passengers' ticket purchase need in the busy time.

In conclusion, gathering above all stations' public transportation service equipment facilities number, storing positions data and every station's passenger walking behavior data, they are necessary to any public transportation tool service industry, because these equipment number and storing locations will influence them to make decisions to choose another kind of public transportation tool to replace it's transportation service if they often feel difficult to find these facilities in its different stations. Thus, it is part of task to facility manager's responsibility if the public transportation service organization expects it won't lose many passengers , due to these external environment factor influence and it also implies cheap ticket price does not guarantee the passengers will choose to catch this kind of public transportation service tool to go to anywhere.

● The relationship between facility management and productive efficiency

It is one interesting question: Can facility management function bring benefits to raise productive efficiency to organizations? I shall indicate some cases to attempt to explain this possible occurrence chance as below:

● Facility management benefit to office workplace

In private organizations, when the firm has facility management department, whether it can bring efficient administration to influence clerks to work efficiently in office, e.g. reducing administrative time or shorten time to work in administrative processes, in order to achieve minimizing clerk number labor cost. How to design office facilities to let office staffs to feel comfortable to work and reducing their pressure to work. It seems that office working environment will influence office staff individual performance. If the office working environment could improve efficiency and creativity of services to satisfy office workers' comfortable working environment needs. It will reduce every administration manager's working pressure when he/she needs often to find methods to attempt to encourage whose administrative clerks to avoid to waste working time to do some non-major administration tasks.

Hence, how to design or allocate or arrange office any facilities' stored locations or whether how many equipment number is the enough to store in the locations, which will influence office employees' working attitude in order to raise or reduce their administration tasks efficiency indirectly, e.g. the office is clean or dirty, whether office reception has enough information telephone switchboard operation facilities, whether every clerk's table has enough computers number to supply to every to use, whether internet speed is fast or slow in order to let any employees can send and receive email to communicate or download any document from internet in short time, whether data processing and computer system maintenance service supply is enough to be repaired to employees' computers immediately when their computers are broken to wait repair, whether website editing facilities operation whether is enough to link to office every staffs in order to let any office staffs can apply internet to do their tasks conveniently in short time. Hence, all of these general office equipment facilities whether they are enough supplied and their stored positions anywhere are the suitable to assist any clerks to work conveniently, they will influence every office employee's administrative and productive efficiency indirectly as well as all faxes, copying machines, computers, whether internet linking maintenance service time is short or long to prepare to any office employees to use conveniently any time, these different issues will also influence every employee individual efficiency in office. Hence, it concludes that office working environment, facilities supply number, facilities maintenance service and facilities location storing both factors will influence employee individual administrative productive efficiency in office.

● facility management benefits to service working environment

Can effective facility management improve service working environment to raise employee individual work performance? It is a concern about the quality of service to its customer question. The term" standards and goals" are often used to measure staff individual service performance whether he/she can serve to customers to let them to feel this staff's service performance or attitude is good or bad.

Is the service workplace working environment facilities enough, it will influence customer service staff individual performance.

For shopping center service industry case example, for this situation, e.g. shopping center's facilities are enough or are placed to the suitable locations in order to let the shopping center's customers to feel comfortable to shopping when they enter this shopping center as well as whether the shopping center's facilities can influence the customer service staffs to serve whose shopping customers easily or difficult, due to whether the shopping center's facilities whether are adequate supplied or their locations are the best suitable positions to influence their service performance to let them to feel easier or comfortable to serve their customers in any large size shopping centers. For example, whether the lamps' lighting energy is enough to let the shoppers to feel safe to walk to visit any shops when there are many shoppers were walking to cause crowd and they feel difficult to walk to avoid any body contact to any one in busy time when the shopping center has no enough lights to let them to see anywhere in the shopping center's dark environment. Then it will influence customer service staffs to feel difficult to find any shopping center customers, e.g. when two shopping center customers are fighting in one location where is far away to the shopping customer service staffs and securities in the shopping center, because the shopping center is large and it has no enough light to let the customer service staffs and securities to find their frighting location to deal their fighting behavior and other shopping center's shoppers will feel very dangerous to walk their fighting location to avoid to close them. Then, it will has possible to cause death or hurt to any one of these two fighting shoppers ,even other shoppers' life. Because the shopping center's securities and customer service staffs who need to spend much time to find their fighting location, it will delay they can bring the policemen to their fighting location when they arrive this shopping center's destination in short time in order to solve their fighting behavior to influence all shoppers' life in this shopping center. Hence, the shopping center whether it has enough lamps number and the lamps' light whether is enough, these lighting facilities will influence any shopping center customer service staffs and securities who can spend less time to arrive any locations to deal any urgent matters.

For another situation in shopping center, if the shopping center has no enough paying telephone service facilities to supply shoppers to phone to anyone when they feel need to phone to any in the shopping center.

Then, it will lead to some shoppers decide to find where the shopping center's reception's telephone to supply to them to phone call to anyone. If they are ten shoppers are waiting to use the shopping center's reception telephone to phone call to their friend or family within one minute. Thus, it will influence the reception customer service staffs feel difficult to arrange how to distribute the only one telephone to these ten shoppers to use to phone call their friend or family when they are queuing within their one minute waiting time in the shopping center's reception. If these ten shoppers can not use the reception telephone to phone call anyone. hen, they will feel dissatisfactory and complain to the reception service staffs politely. So, lacking enough facilities in the shopping center's any where, it will possible to influence their shopping centers' shoppers to feel all shopping center's service staff individual performance to be poor. It means that if the shopping center expects to improve customer satisfaction to its customer service staff's behavioral performance, it meets have enough facilities to be supplied in the shopping center to let its shoppers to feel it is one comfortable and safe shopping center. In conclusion, shopping center's facilities will have possible to influence shoppers' feeling to evaluate its customer service staffs to evaluate whether their service attitudes are good or poor indirectly.

● Can facility management improve productivity

The productivity means resources (input) is therefore the amount of products or services (output), which is produced by them. Hence, higher (improved) productivity means that more is produced with the same expectation of resource, i.e. at the same cost is terms of land materials, machine, time or labor. Alternatively, it means same amount is produced at less labor cost in term of land, material, machine, time for labor that is utilized. So, it brings this question: How can facility management improve productivity? I shall explain as these several aspects, it is possible to be improved productivity from (FM) successfully.

Improved productivity of farm land: If the farming land has better facility management to bring advantages by using better seed, better facilities of cultivation and most fertilizer. It is in the agricultural sense is increased (improved). So, facility management can bring benefits to any land resource to raise productivity in possible. It implies that the productivity of land used for better facility management of industrial purposes is said to have been increased if the output of products or service within that area of industrial land is increased output aim.

Improved productivity of material: If the factory has improved better equipment by facility management method to assist skillful workers to raise the manufacture cloth number, then the productivity of the cloth number is improved by (FM) method.

Improved productivity of labour: When the factory has good manufacturing equipment facilities to be supplied to improve methods of work to product more producing number per hour, then (FM) improved productivity of worker. Hence, in any workplaces, when organization has good facilities, it will influence employees to raise productivities in possible, because they need often to improved equipment facilities manufacture products to achieve higher production number aim.

● Can facility management raise bank employee productivity

Bank workplace environment is busy, the bank counter service staffs need to contact many bank clients to help them to serve or withdraw money from bank's counters. Whether does the quality of environment in bank workplace will influence the determination level of employee's motivation, subsequent performance productivity in bank working environment. For example, if the bank's staffs need work under inconvenient conditions , it will bring low performance and face occupational health diseases causing high absenteeism and turnover.

In general, bank size is usually small, it will have many bank clients enter bank to contact counter staffs to need them to help them to save or withdraw money. So, it will bring air pollution the crowd queue in every bank counter challenge when the bank has many people are queue waiting in counters to queue. So, bank working condition problem relates to environmental and physical factors which will influence every bank counter staff individual working performance to serve bank clients satisfactory. However, bank staffs need to deal many documents concern every client personal data every day. So, they need to spend much time to use computer and painting machines. This is particularly true for these employees who spend most of the day operating a computer terminal in bank workplace. As more and more computers are being installed in workplaces, an increasing number of business has been adopting designs for bank offices installment. So, bank needs have effective facilities management design because of demand of bank staffs for more human comfort.

An good equipment facility management for bank staffs to use conveniently, it is assumed that better workplace environment can motives bank employees and produces better productivity. Hence, bank office environment can be described in terms of physical and behavioral components to influence bank staffs to work inefficiently. To achieve high level of bank employee productivity, bank organizations must ensure that the physical environment in conductive to bank different department organizational needs, facilitating interaction and privacy, formality and informality, functional and disciplinarily, e.g. house loan or private loan departments, counter service department, visa card application department.

Thus, in a high safe privacy facility management working environment will let different department bank staffs feel safe to worry about privacy loss in possible. So, the improving bank facility to bring safe and high privacy to avoid bank client individual loss in working environment issue, the facility management can be results to bring these benefits, such as in a reduction in a number of complaints and absenteeism and an increase in productivity.

● Can (FM) create value to organization?

(FM) can reduce managing facilities as a strategic resource to add value to the organization and its overall performance, e.g. saving the energy in building and take care of shuttle buses and parking facilities space management for , on economic efficiency and effectiveness, or good price and value for the organization.

If the organization expects to apply (FM) process to save energy, it depends on possible input factors, i.e. interventions in the accommodation facilities services. So, it seems that the organization expects to save its energy consumption in its building. It needs have good space management facilities between parking its shuttle buses in its property's car park.

Why does space facility management is important to influence efficiency and productivity. For one school's building example, when the school decides none of the two gymnasiums student sport entertainment centers to be built in order to reduce financial cost and higher benefits. Remarkably, the use of space with the school overall strategic goals , such as creating spaces that better can support the teaching, motivate students and teachers, attract more students and increase the utilisation of existing space to accommodate an increasing number of students.

If it hopes to make high quality teaching facilities on student's choice where to study. The school will need to choose to build either one comfortable and new design facility teaching accommodation or build two gymnasium sport entertainment centers in its limited land space either for students' learning or sport aim. Due to it feels new teaching accommodation can make more attractive to increase students numbers to choose it to study more than building two new gym sport centers to let them do sport in school.

Hence, space choice (FC) management strategy will be one important considerable issue, when the organization has limited land space resources to make choose to build any constructions in order to increase many clients number. Such as the school organization has limited storage land resource to let it to build either two gymnasium sport entertainment centers or one new teaching accommodation in order to attract many students to choose it to learn. Hence, it needs to gather data to make more accurate evaluation to decide how to apply its space facility to choose to build these both kinds of buildings in order to achieve the attractive student learning choice aim, so whether the two sport entertainment activity centers or one new teaching accommodation choice, it needs to gather information to decide whether the school ought to choose to build which kind of building in order to achieve the increase of student number aim, so space facility management will be this school's land shortage problem.

● The relationship between facility
management and consumer
behavior

How and why shop facility management can influence consumer individual shopping behavior? If it is possible, what shop facility management factors can influence their consumption decision when they enter the shop to plan to buy anything. I shall indicate some shop case studied to explain whether how and why every shop's facility management can influence consumer individual consumption desire when any one consumer enters any shops.

● Shop's low ceiling height location (FM) influence consumer behavior
Can the shop's ceiling height influence shoppers' shopping behavior? Can the shop's variation in ceiling height can influence how consumers process information to decide to make purchase decision in the shops, e.g. for this situation, when the consumer enters the shop, he/she feels the ceiling height is low and it has a lamp will contact his/her head in possible. So, he/she chooses to move far away from the low ceiling location in the shop. It is possible that shop's ceiling low height and the lamp locates at the ceiling low height position will influence many customers' choices to leave the low

ceiling height and lamp location, then the shop's low ceiling height will have possible to influenced many customers to choose to find the another shop to buy the similar kind of products , due to the lamp locates in the low ceiling height, so this lamp and low ceiling height will be possible factor to influence any shoppers who won't choose to walk to this dangerous location in the shop. If the shop's all spaces are ceiling height and it has many lamps are located at the low ceiling height spaces. Then, it will be serious to cause many shoppers do not want to spend too much time to choose any products in the shop because they feel dangerous to walk to the any low ceiling height lamps' locations in the shop.

Hence, hoe to design the different concept may be activated by the showroom ceiling if it were relatively high, as it tends to be in mall stores, versus low, as it is in most strip mall shops and outlet centers. Relatively high ceilings may bring safe shopping emotion to let any consumers to feel thoughts related to freedom, whereas lower ceilings may let consumers to feel dangerous to walk the locations in any shops. Hence it seems any shops ought not neglect whether their ceiling height is tall and the lamps ought avoid to locate in any low ceiling height locations in order to influence consumers number to be decreased.

● Can house facility management influence consumer individual purchase intention?

When one new property is built, whether the property consumers will consider how the new property is facility to influence their purchase intention to the property will the new property's (FM) influence buyers in real estate markets' preferences choice and living interest. Any new property's internal characteristics of the house unit itself , such as rooms available, when example, of external are location, accessibility to utilities services and facilities will have possible to influence the property buyer's final property purchase decision, so it seems that even the property price is cheap, it is not represent the property buyer will choose to buy the property, if he/she feels the property's facility management is poorer to compare other similar kinds of properties.

So, it can help real estate analysts better explain and predict the behavior of decision makers in real estate markets. Property consumers will search for property information, concerns the property's quality, price distinctiveness, ability, facility management, service of the property's external environment to decide whether the property is high value to choose to buy to compare other kinds of properties.

However, the external environmental forces, such as limited resources, e.g. time or financial will influence whose property consumption choice and living the property's satisfaction feeling (represent) a feedback from post-property purchase reflection used to inform subsequent decisions. The process of the property buyer's leaving experience will serve to influence the extent to which the property consumer how to consider future next time property purchases decision and new information methods. Hence, when one property consumer chooses to buy a house, it refers house features are house internal attributes , such as quality of building, the design as well as internal and external design, which are important factors for a property consumer when he/she needs to select and purchases one house.

The other (FM) factors which can influence the property consumers' needs, include living space as features, such as the size of kitchen, bathroom, bedroom, living bath and other rooms available in the house. The environment of housing area is also important factor, e.g. the condition of the hood, attractiveness of the area, quality of houses, type of houses, type of houses, density of housing, wooded area or free coverage, slope of the attractive views, open space, non-residential uses in the areas vacant sites, traffic noise, level of owner-occupation in , level of education in level of income in, security from crime, quality of schools, religious of , transportation , shopping center, sport entertainment can be supplied to close to the house area. All these human related issue of the property's location will also influence the property buyer's living location selection. Hence, above (FM) influence property consumer purchase behavior, it is based on the relationship behavior. The consumer's house purchase intention and house features, living space, environment and distance to recreation center, supermarket, library etc. public facilities variable (FM) factors.

In conclusion, the house internal space facility management and external environment facility management factors will influence property consumer individual house purchase intention.

● The effects of in-store shelf design facility management factor influences consumer behavior

Can every store retailer's shelf design influence supermarket and large retail stores shoppers' behaviors when they visit the stores? However, currently many stores tend to build on traditional and repetitive design for their store shelf layout, it brings results in outdated store layouts.

Another important store shelf layout design aspect, retailer should consider carefully is the allocation of products on shelves. So, it seems that efficient shelf space allocation management does not only minimize the economic threats of empty product shelves, it can also lead to higher consumer satisfaction, a better customer relationship.

Why does supermarket shelves design is important? Any retail tore will sell product category within a shelf. They can use the same nominal category , e.g. crisps next to light crisps, same food product shelf. Anyway, a goal-based shelf display can contain several product, that determine a common consumer goal, e.g. fair trade. Hence, these two categorical product structuring methods are also described in terms of how to put product, or food on shelf benefit and attribute -based product categories.

These shelf design food or product storing method will have more influence consumers to choose to buy the supermarket or retail store food or products more easily , due to products, or food put on their shelf very convenient and systematic to attract consumers' shopping consideration to the supermarket or retail store.

● Music (FM) environment influence consumer consumption desire

Is it possible that shop music (FM) environment can raise consumer purchase desire? In one shop or supermarket, it can provide soft music (FM) equipment to let consumers can listen soft music or songs in the supermarket or retail shop when the are staying to spend more time shopping and whether soft music facility can be expected to raise customer individual value-added options to the music facility shop in the supermarket or retail shop.

Can the music facilities prolong consumers to stay in the store? It is possible that tempo soft music can influence consumers to stay longer time in restaurants and supermarkets and retail shops. It is possible that the different types of music (FM) in any supermarket, restaurant, retail shop owning music listening facility shopping environment. It will have possible to influence consumers to prolong staying in their shops. For example, one wine selling retail shop has classical music (FM) listening equipment to let consumers to listen when they enter the wine shop, it is possible to cause consumers to choose to buy more expensive wine products. Some researchers indicate when the wine shop owns classical music facility to let all consumers can list classical music when they walk in the wine ship, it can evoke the wine consumers to choose to buy purchasing higher prices wine products in the long term classical music listening environment. Otherwise, in a fitness sport center, musical fir and excite or popular music (FM) environment can attract fitness sport players' emotion to play and kind of fitness sport facility longer time. Also, in one supermarket, the soft music facilities listening environment can persuade or attract food consumers to spend more time in the mall consuming food or beverage also purchase other products more easily, due to they will listen soft music to be influenced to choose to prolong staying time in the supermarket. It seems that it has relationship between retail shop's music facility environment and consumer's emotion will be influenced by these different kinds of soft music or songs to raise consumption desire in the supermarket, if some consumers like to prolong to stay longer consuming time in the owning music facility environment's retail shop.

In fact, some researchers indicate the owning background music facility selling environment's ship , it can affect consumer decision making, memory, concentration consumption desire. So, classical , jazz soft music facility ought be installed in restaurants, retail shops, restaurants' environment. Otherwise, popular , exciting, noise, pop music facility ought be installed in fitness sport centers, theme park entertainment parks business places in order to influence fitness sport players or theme park entertainers to prolong playing or entertaining time to feel real sport or entertainment theme park playing machine facility's entertainment enjoyable feeling as well as attracting restaurant or supermarket or retail shop's consumers to prolong their staying time to make consumption decisions. Hence, it seems that music facility environment can raise consumers' consumption desire in possible.

● University bookstore atmospheric factors how to influence student's purchase book behavior?

Any university bookstore how to do international control and structuring of book internal environment to raise students' purchase book desires in university itself school's bookstore, it will be one popular question to any universities. Hence, whether the university bookstore internal (FM) factors include: lighting, music, colors, scents, temperature, layout and general cleanliness as well as university external factors include: the university bookstore shape/size, windows, university parking facility for students availability and location, which can play an influential role of the university bookstore image in order to influence the university itself students to choose to buy books from themselves bookstore or university outside bookstores.

Whether the university student needs to spend how long individual learning time and how much learning nervous to spend time to choose any kinds of book in the universiity bookstore or outside bookstores, this issue , he/she will consider. Because he/she does want to expect spend much time and nervous to choose to buy books in any bookstore. If the university's bookstore physical location and internal (FM) image can let its target student customers to feel it's all book products are stored in any attractive internal book shelves places, e.g. the cheapest and the most expensive different subjects of text books are stored in one system method to bring the positive image of value and quality in order to let university target student customers can find their books' choice location to spend less time to search any books to read in the unviersiity bookstore easily.

However, due to learning time is shortage to every university student of the university's book shelves can display all text books in the attractive right locations in the university bookstore as well as the university's bookstore ought has an adequate space to let university students to walk to anywhere and find any subjects of text books and compare their book sale prices in the bookstore's any shelves' locations easily when they walk to the subject of book shelf location, then they can make accurate decision either to buy the right kind of subject book or not buy it to read in the short time. They will feel their book choice purchase decision making process won't influence their learning time in themselves universiity. Then, the university students will be influenced by themselves university's bookstore's attractive external university facilities in the university's any teaching places and the university's bookstore internal attractive environment facility image which can influence the students to make final choices to buy their liking books to read from their university's itself bookstore. Hence, the university's bookstore internal and external building environment (FM) design factors will influence its students whether choose to buy from themselves bookstore or another outside general bookstore.

● How and why does retail atmospheric environment influence consumers behavior in retail shop?

Any shop's internal facility management design can influence atmospheric environment to influence consumer individual shopping desire, e.g. colour, lighting, music, crowding, design and layout factors, which internal shop (FM) environment can influence the first time shopping visiting client ' cognitive process how to feel the shop store image. Such as if the store's (FM) environment can bring enjoyable and fun and happy image to let them to feel shopping's enjoyment.

In conclusion, when consumers will like to stay longer time in the store. Due to the store's internal (FM) atmospheric environment can attract them to stay longer time in the store. Then, the customer's shopping value will raise and it can bring purchasing intention and shopping satisfaction. How can (FM) influence retail atmospheric physical (FM) environment ? Can (FM) bring indirect relationship to influence how the consumer individual causes positive or negative purchase intention when he/she has influence to prolong staying desire in the store, when the shop has good (FM) , it will bring long time to make consumption chance in the shop.

● Facility management influences
consumer satisfactory service
level

Can facility management (FM) quality influence consumer satisfactory service feeling? Any organization's facility management can improve the effectiveness of the maintenance organization. It can provide improved operational and maintenance functions to maintain the physical environment to support the overall mission. However, any organization will consider whether it improves its facilities, it will raise consumer satisfactory feeling when it provides the service to them, e.g. education service industry, when students need to often to attend any school's classrooms or lecture halls, computer rooms, libraries, all these facilities will be student's learning environment. If these school facilities can be maintenance to let students to feel comfortable to enjoy to study in their schools' any learning locations. Then, it has possible that to bring their enjoyable learning feeling in theirs schools.

● How school's facility management influences student's learning satisfactory feeling.

However, in education industry case, the school's facility management has those criteria can be used to measure effectiveness. Student individual response time between the student's request for computer use service in school computer rooms, library reading service in school library , classroom computer facilities and tables, chairs etc. furniture supplies service and the facility management supply number and available to useful time. If the student believes that the response time is too long when he/she feels need to use any school facilities, the actual number of seconds or minutes, he/she needs to wait how long time to queue to use his/her school's any facilities in library, classroom, computer room. So, the student's queue waiting time to use any his/her school's facilities, it can measure the school's facility management effectiveness.

● Scheduling of preventive maintenance activities.

It schedules of any maintenance activities are not arranged effectively to the school. Then, it will influence students' poor learning facility service to their school. For their situation, when the school's first floor has two men toilets are damaged. They are needed to be required. However, it is one week period, the first floor 100 students can not use the first floor men toilets. Hence, in this week, all 100 students need to go to other floors toilets to often use. They will feel busy and time is not enough when they need to attend to any classrooms to listen the first floor classrooms teachers' lesson. If he/she arrives the first floor classroom too late, due to he/she needs to go to another floor male toilets to queue to use. Then, he/she will feel angry and worries about whose absent or late attending classroom behavior when the lesson's teacher has attended early in the first floor classroom , and he teacher will need him/her to explain why he/she will go to this classroom lately, if his/her explanation won't be accepted to attend to the first floor classroom too late in the week. So, arrangement maintenance schedule to any school's facilities issue is importnt to influence student's satisfactory feeling to the school. Also, lacking of preventive maintenance activities will bring results in unscheduled shutdown of critical equipment can have an unrecoverable impact on the school's good learning environment providing to student's mission.

In fact, however in any organizations, such as school, ship, office etc. organizations, achieving balance of effectiveness and efficient difficulties and takes time and effort on the part of management and staff. It is not enough to establish an optimal relationship between these two parts. It has another factor that organizations need to consider costs. In today's budget tightening environment, decreasing expenses requires accepting a lower level of efficiency and effectiveness. The goal is to determine the point at which decreasing efficiency and effectiveness is no longer acceptable before that point is reached.

It brings this question : How to apply facility management knowledge to rise efficiency and effectiveness in order to improve quality standard of service to satisfy consumers' needs in short time? Such as school's facilities service case. What factors can influence student's level of satisfaction with regards to higher educational facilities services? It seems that any school's facilities will influence its students how to satisfy its education service indirectly. Because they need often to go to school to learn. So, any school's facilities, e.g. classrooms, computer rooms, libraries, toilets, lecture halls, canteens, sport and entertainment centers, research laboratories, school car parks, student enquiry counters, all these places to the school's any students will attend. So, how raise schools' facilities improvement to satisfy students' learning needs in the school's any locations which will have help to influence it student individual satisfaction level to the school's service, instead of every teacher individual teaching performance service to the school's students.

For any service organizations , such as hotels, restaurant, financial institutions, retail stores and hospitals etc. The physical environment can influence how customers' evaluation of their service. Due to service has intangible nature, so customers will rely on evaluate service quality.

Any higher education institutions are education service providing organizations. They need have comfortable and enjoyable educational environment to be provided to the students to attend the school's any places in order to meet whose learning expectations and studying experience needs. So, the school's facility management will be one factor to influence student's learning satisfaction when they expect to attend the school's any locations or places to let them to feel the school's learning environment have good facility management feeling.

In fact, if the school has comfortable classrooms or lecture halls educational environment to let its students to feel, it will bring assistance to raise their learning satisfactory feeling. So, comfortable learning facility management environment is one kind of school's facility service characteristics, it includes intangibility, perishability, inseparability and variability. So, they are every student individual learning feeling when they are attending to the school's any learning locations. So, school's facility management service feeling will influence whether they expect to choose this school to study. If the school's facility management learning environment is more comfortable and teaching facilities are better to compare other schools' facilities. Then, it will have possible to attract many students to choose this school to study. Such as any educational organizations, instead of the teachers (lecturers and professors) whose educational level is influence students number. The university's building environment will influence students' learning feeling, when they attend in the university. The facilities include laboratories, lecture theatres an offices, but also residential accommodations, catering facilities, sports and recreations centers because university students need have university life feeling to let them to fell the university can give welfare services , e.g. medical services, career guidance, sport entertainment, residential accommodation etc. service, instead of educational learning service in classrooms and lecture theatres. Hence, university's diversification facilities services are needed to satisfy university students to choose it to study, instead of university teacher's educational performance. When one student can enroll the university to study from secondary education institution. The admitted student will usually consider two aspects to decide to choose the university to study. One aspect is the academic programs, of sequence of courses choices and the another aspect is the university's facilities whether they can satisfy their university life need, e.g. library, dorms, bookstore, food canteen , gym's sport entertainment, education technological facilities in the classrooms and lecture theatres to let the students to feel the university's teaching facilities are achieved his/her learning demand.

So, these two factors (teaching and learning and facilities) are linked to each other to influence student's total school learning experience and attitude towards a particular institution and this is termed as value chain in the student's learning process in the university. Hence, student individual evaluation variables will include teaching staff, teaching method, enrolment and facility enough supply actual service need.

However, the university's facilities, such as any residential accommodation, canteen, library , classroom, lecture theatre, sport gym, entertainment center will be their useful facilities need to satisfy their learning, entertainment and eating ,even living need in residential accommodation in the school's learning life experience every day. If one student chooses to live in the university residential accommodation . All of his/her learning and eating and living time and spending will be calculated to the university's any facilities to let him/her to feel it can provide enough facilities to let him/her to enjoy.

Hence, the facility management factor, such as overall campus environment, library, laboratory, classroom, lecturer theatre size and facility supply of on campus accommodation, welfare right service, parking areas, cafeteria , sport center etc. They will be every students facilities service needs from the university supplies choice. So, any university ought not neglect how to improve itself university's space area facilities to achieve satisfy their needs after they choose this university to study. Hence, any university's facility management will influence how the student's satisfactory learning service feeling when he/she chooses the university to study.

In conclusion, better facility management will attract more students to choose the university to study. Otherwise, worse facility management will not attract more students to choose to study the school. Hence, it seems that the school's facility management factor has relationship to influence student's satisfactory feeling, instead of teacher individual teaching performance factor to the school.

● Property facility management influences householder buying behavior
One new property's low price is attractive factor to influence property buyer individual preference choice. Does the new individual's facility management factor influence the property buyer's preference choice decision, if the property buyer feels its facility management is better than other similar properties, even it's price is higher than other properties. I shall indicate some cases to analyze this possibility as below:

Some properties' facility management service quality has possible to create true value for any property buyers when they consider the calculation ingredients to make decision whether to new property has higher value to choose to buy. The factors may include: price, natural environment, transportation tools convenient available, shopping centers supplies, the neighour quality, and the property's internal facility management etc. factors.

In fact, car or house purchase buyers, they have similar behaviors. It is that car's buyers will consider the car's machines whether they are safe to drive on roads, instead price, manufacture loyalty factors. It is possible that the car's machines quality factor will be preference to any car buyers when they make preference decisions to choose which brand its cars are the suitable. However, if the car's brand is famous and its appearance beautiful and price is cheap. But the car consumer feels its machine qualities are unsafe to let the driver to drive on road. Then, the car's poor machine quality factor will influence the car buyer's decisions to choose to buy this car. It can influence the car buyer individual car purchase decision.

The car buyer's behavior is similar to property buyer's behavior. Although, the new property price is cheap, good neigh ours are living near to the new property's location, shopping centers and transportation tools are available to near to this new property's area. But if the property buyers' feels its facility management is poor quality to compare other similar properties. Then, the poor quality of facility management factor will have possible to influence the property buyers whose final buying decision to choose to buy this new property. It brings this question: How and why can the facility management poor quality factor influence property consumers' preference choice?

In general, all property consumers won't know whether the new property's facility management is good or bad quality , they need to spend time to visit to the new property in order to observe whether its internal facility is satisfactory to his/her acceptable level. In simple, their purchase decision will regard to how to allocate household budget, how the household's economic resources are influenced, e.g. for travelling, visits to restaurants, comparing the different similar types of property product groups, e.g. apartments or houses or houses of a givn size data. For example, if one property's room(s) size is (re) small to compare other kind similar product type of room(s) size. Although the prior property's price is cheaper to compare to the later properties. But, if some property buyers hoped the property has large room(s) size, then the later larger room(s) size which will be possible to some property buyer's preference choice. Even, their property price is more expensive to compare the smaller room(s) size of properties. Thus, the property's room size which will be one major factor to influence property buyers' purchase decision. room's size had relationship to facility management issue. Moreover, if the room's quality and design is attractive, then it will bring more attractive to persuade some property buyers to choose to buy them to live in preference.

Hence, whether the new property is good durable product feeling which will influence householder's choice. If the householder feels the new property has long term durable life to avoid to spend much maintenance expense when they have been living in the new property for a long term period. They will believe it has better facility management, quality to let them to live longer time and the most importance is that they do not need to spend any maintenance expense , due to the property 's any internal facilities are damaged easily.

The external factors may include: culture, reference groups, family, social class and demography of lifestyle as well as internal factors may include: feelings, past property buying and living experience , property knowledge, motivation of the property buyer individual psychology. These both factors can influence any property buyer individual decision making process to do final house purchase behavior. However, internal factors, such as: property knowledge of facility management and property living experience, e.g. how to evaluate to choose to buy the property , due to the property buyer's past living experience for the past property's facilities whether its facilities can satisfy its property buyers' comfortable living needs. This internal factor will be more important to influence any property buyer's property purchase final decision. If he/she feels whose prior old property's facilities are satisfactory. Then, he/she will compare this new property and old property's facilities to decide whether this new property is value to buy. So, the old property's facility will be the measurement standard to compare his/her next new property purchase choice. So, the property purchaser will compare these new and old property's property facilities product knowledge to similarities among property alternative which will influence his/her final decision to choose to buy the new property to live.

It seems that property low price factor must not guarantee to attractive many property buyers' choice. Otherwise, it is assumed that many property buyers like rent or buy to live the property for themselves for long term intention. There are less property buyers expect to sell the first property to earn profit intention. So, they will usually consider whether the property is long term durable product to avoid to pay maintenance expense when they had been living in the property in long term.

Some factors that taking consideration are proximity to the specific location, housing prices, developer's brand, the payment scheme, reference group, which are not the main factors to influence any property buyer individual choice. Because property buyer's need is that the property has good facilities to supply to them to live, e.g. good heater equipment can provide hot water to them to bath in winter or good air conditioners can provide cold temperature to let them to feel cool comfortable feeling in summer in their homes. Good electric tools facilities , when they have need to use electricity in safe environment at home, e.g. car park accessibility facility , level of security facility , surface area facility and housing types, bedroom, bathroom facilities, quality of housing manufacturing raw material, house design , house durable guarantee, speed of complaint responsiveness, specification accuracy, confirmation of building plan service, showing legal file property purchase process service, finance instalments process assistance, speed of responsiveness, officers' skills of presentation. All of above these concern property facility management issues will influence any property buyers' final choice to decide whether the property is value to buy. So, facility management will influence property purchaser individual final decision in possible.

● Hotel facilities influence hotel consumer choice

Travellers choose hotel to live. They will consider price, room comfortable feeling, hotel location , gum sport or entertainment service facility supplies , hotel room booking service etc. factors to decide whether the hotel can achieve every traveller individual minimum living need. However, whether hotel facilities factor will be the main factor to influence travellers' living needs. How and why do travellers consider hotel facilities whether are enough supply or facilities of quality to satisfy their demand to cause their living choice to the hotel final decision.

Usually, hotel's customers won't plan to live too long time, e.g. more than three months in the hotel. Because they are travelling aim. It will bring this question: Does hotel facilities quality consider to influence their hotel living choice if the traveller is short-term traveller to the country? However , some travellers who have effort to spend money to live high class hotels, even their journey is short trip. Hence it seems that short trip , hotel living reason can not influence the high class hotel travellers' living comfortable demand to the high class hotel room. Hence , the high class hotel room's facility management quality is also needed high performance. Even, when they need to eat breakfast, lunch , dinner in the high class hotel canteens or playing any sport equipment, or gum equipment or wathching movie in the hotel's small cinema room . They must need high class hotel can supply more entertainment, restaurant , sport facilities to satisfy their comfortable needs in the high class hotel. Moreover, they must consider safety issue when they are living in the high class hotel. So, thy must demand the hotel have enough five fright equipment in their rooms, or corridors and the stairs to let them can leave the dangerous locations to arrive the most safe locations immediately when the hotel has fire accident occurrence in any where . So, it ensures that the high class hotel's customers must ensure the high class hotel's facilities can satisfy their any one of above these needs before they decide to live this high class hotel.

In fact, high class hotel's room price must be more expensive to compare the low class hotel. So, it explains why high class hotel's consumers will need the hotel has safe and good quality of facilities to let them to feel it is one reasonable price, safe , good service and good facilities' high class hotel to live. Usually, when the traveller arrives the country to travel, the travelers chooses the hotel to live, it is whose first time visit in common. So, he/she ought consider that the hotel environment seems it is good or bad to let the traveller to select to live. If the hotel's facility environment is new and beauty and design colorful to let the first time travellers to feel. Then, it is possible that good facilities environment can influence the first time travellers to select to live, even the hotel's room price is more expensive to compare other similar hotels in the travelling living places. Hence, it explains why hotel facilities can influence traveller individual room booking choice. When he/she is the first time to visit the hotel to select whether to live or not.

● How and why facility management can influence workplace productivity to bring customer satisfaction

Facility management is one part of manufacturers or retailers as their productivity in workplace as their input and functionalistics within physical environment. In fact, facility management in workplace may include: site selection, property disposal, site acquisition, workplace space allocation, space inventory, space forecasting facility management, interior furniture change planning, interior furniture installation, moving maintenance, inventory, design evaluation, employment satisfaction evaluation plan, external maintenance and breakdown maintenance, preventive maintenance, landscape maintenance, energy space facility management, hazardous waste disposal, capital , operating furniture budgeting. So, it seems that one workplace considered whether the workplace's facility is enough to let employees to work in order to raise efficiency and improve productive performance more easily. Then, it will bring this question:

● How and why workplace facility management can influence consumer individual satisfaction?

Strategic FM delivery is essential for business survival. I shall explain why for delivery is important to influence customer satisfaction. In business process view point, an effective and meaningful service to their customer , i.e. the user. For logistic industry, the product's delivery time will influence when the product can be sent to the user's arrival destination. If the product is delayed to sent to the user's home or office or any location destination. The reason is because the logistic product sender has no efficient facility management (FM) arrangement in its warehouse . Then, its warehouse lacks efficient (FM), which will cause users to feel its delivery service is poor and they will complain its delivery service staffs. Then, they will find another delivery service company to replace its service. So, it explains that logistic industry's warehouse (FM) service arrangement can raise efficient time to send any products to their customers in order to let they feel satisfactory service. For example, Amazon online logistic company's warehouse has applied artificial intelligence robotic tools to assist warehouse workers to arrange the different kinds of products to deliver to the right shelves . Then, the warehouse robotics will follow their right product shelves locations to follow the right products to deliver to US domestic or overseas product buyers in the short time and it can avoid the wrong products to deliver to the wrong buyers' risk. Also, the (AI) delivery tools can raise time efficiency to assist Amazon warehouse workers to reduce their work load, and tried to work in large warehouse environment. Although, its warehouse's area is large, the (AI) tools facility can help them to deliver the different products to different shelves in the right locations , e.g. exact product number and the kinds of product to be delivered to the right country' client's shelf location in the warehouse. Also, it implies FM is very important to influence Amazon warehouse delivery efficiency and avoiding delivery wrong occurrence chance. For example, the shelf location belongs to US domestic customers, or the shelf location belongs to Japan customers, or the shelf location belongs to Hong Kong customers, or any other Asia or Western countries' different customers' locations. The warehouse's facility needs have different countries' shelves enough space to put and it also need enough space to let the (AI) tools, robotic delivery workers and human workers both to walk to different shelves locations easily and the different countries' shelves number needs to be calculated accurate. For example, it has how many client number will buy Amazon's the kind product per day. If it has above 5,000 to 10,000 China clients to buy the kind of product. Then, it will need to make judgement how many shelves are placed in the warehouse. So, it can avoid to lack enough shelves to put any different kinds of products to prepare to delivery to China clients in efficient time and it won't avoid to delay to deliver to their homes or offices or any locations in China.

Hence, such as Amazon logistic case, it explains why warehouse's space shelves number and area or locations facility management can influence workers or (AI) delivery tools how to move convenient and avoiding the delivery to the customer's wrong destination chance occurrence and shortening time to deliver products to its clients efficiently. Then, due to the delivering time is shorten and the wrong delivery destination's occurrence chance is also reduced , even it can avoid to deliver the product to wrong client's destination occurrence. Then, the logistic firm's clients will feel more satisfactory to its product sale delivery service and their complaints will be avoided. Hence, it explains effective warehouse (FM) space management service arrangement is essential to any logistic businesses nowadays.

● Facility management brings departmental benefits

Why do organizations need have facility management (FM) service? As above examples indicate that (FM) can improve workplace environment facilities, e.g. warehouse environment to let workers to raise efficiencies or improve performances, even it can influence consumers to raise satisfactory to it's services indirectly, also it can help organizations' equipment to be used long term to cause old and are needed to spend expenditure to maintenance or change new equipment in order to improve better quality . So , it can assist organizations to avoid to spend more expenditure for new equipment purchase or maintenance. All these issues will be facility management service's benefits to an organizations, which can concern raising customers' service satisfaction, raising efficiency or improving productive performance, raising productivity, reducing equipment or property maintenance or new alternation much of expenditure spending, office or warehouse or any workplace space planning arrangement .

However, every organization will need a facility manager or manage whose team effectively . When a facility manager begins to apply FM techniques to solve business problems. The case for FM is made. It is a simple matter of demonstrating a qualified return on the investment required. Every organization's success, FM operation of three key activities: they include: needing a proper understanding of the organization's needs, wants, drivers and goals and knowing when needs to review its changing circumstances, developing an effective facilities solution o support the organization's needs, wants , property drives and contribute to achieve its goals both short term and long term, achievement of reliable delivery of that solution in a managed, measured manner.

So, it bring one question: What are the influential factors to be followed the right direction to FM manager's strategic FM operational decision? The influencing factors may include: ownership, governance sector, complexity and perhaps of most significant, the size of the organization's property portfolio.

In fact, major occupiers feel FM service need, they are large corporate organizations and public service organizations. Their aims usually are to raise. The most marginal improvement in efficiency or effectiveness, these aims are the great significance. Major property occupiers will already have a facilities department or individuals performing the FM function with another department like property, finance or human resource, sale and marketing's facilities.

Usually these FM need occupiers who will encounter this problem: How can apply FM service systems and processes to be developed to improve reliable service delivery making use of the economies of scale, not suffering because of the size of the problem. This question will be facility manager individual concerning question: How to apply (FM) technique to solve the improvement reliable service delivery making use of the economics of scale problem for whose organization?

In reality much of external facilities management benefits to organizations, instead of raising efficiency, improving performance, raising productivity, reducing maintenance expenditure, e.g. energy saving, reducing natural resource waste, increasing local employment, improving supply chain management are all elements of the FM contribution to every organization's need. Hence are the work life balance argument and provision of an effective and safe working environment that supports why some organizations feel need (FM) service to support their organizational development.

Moreover, on cost benefit of space saving efficient view point, space service cost reduction is a key driver for all organizations and the medium, or large sized players will benefit directly from a well coordinated facilities strategy. For example, application FM technique to help warehouse or office space area to save 50% space vacancy to let employees can move easily or putting enough furniture or equipment or many stocks can be putted in warehouses . So, paying more rent expenditure to rent or purchasing another new warehouse or office to satisfy workers or employees' working environment to be better need. If the organization has effective (FM) technique, then it has enough space vacancy to supply to the increase stocks number to be putted inside in warehouse and it can let workers to move safety in available to let staffs to move easily and equipment have enough space to be stored in the limited warehouse space problem.

For greater space savings benefits will bring either long term renting or buying of increasing offices or warehouse number expenditure problem to any organizations, when the organizations' cost or renting or buying accommodation probably accounting for 60 to 70% of total occupancy cost . So a strategic program to release space or the prevent the acquisition of moves can be the most significant consideration to any facility manager, with between 40% and 60% of the workplaces are unoccupied in most offices or warehouses at any given moment in time.

Hence, how to apply (FM) technique to save space occupied areas for employment moving or stocks or equipment saving need in offices or warehouses. This issue will be any facility managers' seeking methods to solve problem. However, the important major advantage of facility management to organizations is that the application of management principle to keep the organization's property assets with the aim of maximizing their potentials. Thus, any organizations' facilities have become important, due to the property facilities' worth will increase if the organization's facility management technique can protect the organization's facilities have good performance. Then, the organization's maintenance expenditure will reduce and it won't need to spend expenditure to buy any new facilities to replace old facilities , due to they often damage factor when they are used old.

In conclusion, it explains why effective FM combines resources and activities can raise work environment improvement, which is essential to the raising employee performance aim. For hotel living service case example, this industry must need have good facility management service because hotels must need to fully equipped in term and facilities for effectiveness to satisfy hotel living clients' demand , hotels ought need good facilities asset management style lead to effectiveness in service delivery, there are benefit derivable from the adoption of facilities management from which other hotels can learn from for their effective operations. Hence, it explains why effective FM can bring benefits to hotels' properties to be more comfortable, beautiful appearances to attract many hotel customers to choose to live the hotel. Because hotel's building industrial kitchens, rooms facilities, equipment , halls of categories, restaurant facilities, gum sport entertainment centers' facilities, fans, elevators, lifts, electrical installation, escalators, baking equipment, recreational facilities, including golf courses which will be important factors to influence hotel clients' comfortable living feeling, if the hotel can keep its all facilities in the best living environment often. Then, it can raise chance to attract many hotel customers to choose it to live. So , hotel industry has absolute need to implement effective FM strategy to keep its properties more attractive to satisfy its clients' living needs.

Instead of hotel industry, logistic transportation industry also needs effective facilities management in warehouse, because of the logistic company's warehouse 's facilities are good, then it will assist to raise employee individual efficiency in the safe and system shelve stored facilities in workplace environment and improving performance.

Consequently, it will bring the shorten time to deliver any products to clients to avoide the delaying time delivery in order to let customers to feel more satisfactory to their services. In simple, it seems that some industries need have effective facilities management techniques to help them to bring long term customer satisfactory feeling, worker individual efficiency raising and performance improvement benefits. Hence, it seems facility management techniques' demand will be increased to some industries in popular in the future because it has help to raise employee individual efficiency , productive performance and client individual satisfactory level consequently.

Facility management how influences employee Psychology to raise productive efficiency

● How to impact of workplace
management on well-being and
productivity

In facility management strategy, design can lead promotion, the value of offices that are enriched, particularly including warehouses, shopping centers to raise their market value. Moreover, effective organizations, such as raising powering workers when giving the effective design of office space. I assume that a good design of an interior office workspace environment seems a psychological department to influence staff individual emotion to bring positive power in order to raising productive efficient influence, such as in a commercial city office. So, it brings this question: How workspace management strategy can impact on staff's working behaviors in office.

In fact, office tasks general include various forms of productivity, e.g. information processing, information management and any clerical tasks by computerization. Hence, office productivity concerns how to influence each office white color worker applies computers to work in office. The office space can impact on white color workers' performances in these several aspects: feeling of psychological comfort, organizational physical comfort and job satisfaction and productivity, efficiency. So, it seems that office workspace design strategy can influence white color workers' working behavior and attitude and performance indirectly.

The office space management includes: how to removal from the workspace of everything except the materials required to do the job at hand, how tight managerial control of the workspace, and how to implement standardization of managerial practice and workspace design. So, these key ideas will influence how each white color worker's efficiency and productivity in office working environment.

For this office space design situation, a large unseparated small space size's space design can accommodate more people and so brings itself to economies of scale. As a result, space occupancy can be centrally managed with minimal disruptive interference from office workers. Indeed, many businesses now adopt a clean and fresh air office working policy because they have more employees than they have spaces at which they can work. This desks are either taken on a first -come first -served basis. (hot desking) or can be booked in advance. So , when a company has many employees need to work in a small space working environment. It must concern how to let staffs to feel more comfortable in order to reduce high psychological pressure to work in this uncomfortable working environment. Hence, it explains why workspace design can impact on office workers' performance in some offices. All these issues are assumed that empowering workers to manage and have input into the design of their own workspace, then the effective office or any working places space management will enhance wellbeing to bring workers' positive emotions and improving productivity. I also assume the space working environment design have relationship of these depend variable factors to influence office worker individual productive efficiency. The variable factors may include psychological comfort, organizational comfortable, job satisfaction, physical comfort and productivity.

However, office furniture , facilities will influence office white color workers' performance ,e.g. the room size whether is big or small for manage office worker, a high backed, comfortable leather chair is needed for office staffs to sit down to let more comfortable, the door and most of the walls need glass, the office room environment needs have sea-grass rug beneath the desk covering the immediate working area, the office also needs have plants and pictures, mail boxes, telephone and computer facility is needed. When one staff needs to send email or phone call or send letters or deliver documents conveniently. These office elements are essential in order to increase physical well-being and feeling of satisfaction to white-color workers. Hence, geren office and office working space design management is needed in order to influence white color workers' productive efficiency in long term.

● Effective workspace design can influence communication to raise productivity

Office white-color workers often need communication between their managers, supervisors, and themselves. Office communication extends from the way that a user experiences a service. An effective office communication can bring these benefits; Providing positive influence on decision making by presenting a strong point of view and developing mutual understanding, delivering efficient decisions and solutions by providing accurate , timely and relevant information, enabling mutually benefit solutions, building health relationships by encouraging trust and understanding between the high level, middle level and low level staffs.

Effective office communication needs to clearly communicate its nature and purpose. Good communication ensures that all service staffs are sending out the same messages. Communication is also important for ensuring the service understands what users requires and why he/she talks about understanding users' needs and communication receiver can have effective communication skill to understand what he/she needs the another to do and the another knows he/she ought how to work by his/her task demand. Then, it will shorten much time. If the office has 100 staffs need to often communicate. However, if the office has good space management arrangement to let every staff can communicate easily and walks to anywhere to find the right staff to communicate conveniently. Then, they can spend less time to waste on communication issue. Then, their productive efficiency will be also influence to raise.

● Health and safe work environment influences productivity

Is a health and safe work environment can raise employees' work productive efficiencies indirectly? How and why it can influence employees' productive performance? Some occupations' working environments are easier to occur occupational accidents and diseases risks when the workers are working in the high health and safe risk's working environment. Hence, health and safety issues at these high life risk workplaces can be considered as a key to influence employees' overall performance. The idea that health and safety management program have positive impacts on productivity.

When one worker needs to work in this high risk of health and safe workplace. He/she will consider whether how his/her work behavior will bring suffer serious injuries for shorter or longer time from work related causes in possible. So, he/she will work carefully in order to avoid injuries occurrence chance. It is possible to influence whose work performance, low productive efficiency in order to avoid any occupational accident occurrences in the dangerous workplace.

If the employee feels danger when he/she needs to stay in the warehouses stable location to work often. Then his/her absenteeism day number will have increase, due to he/she feels that workplace accidents and occupational illnesses and can lead to permanent occupational disability, when he/she needs to attend the stable dangerous workplace to work in the warehouse. Hence, he/she will choose to apply holiday often in order to avoid injuries chance increasing when he/she needs to stay in the stable workplace location in the warehouse. It explains why companies increase need qualified, motivated and efficient workers who are able willing to contribute activity to technical and organizational innovations. So, healthy workers working in healthy working conditions are thus an important precondition for organization to work smoothly and productively. Hence, a health and safety workplace environment can bring these benefits to organizations as below:

It can prevent among workers of learning work, due to health problems caused by their working conditions, the protection of workers in their employment from risks resulting from factors adverse to health. The placing and maintenance of the worker in an occupational, environment adapted to his/her physiological and psychological, capabilities, mental , physical and social conditions of workplace and adequacy of health and safety measures are needed to any employees in order to bring positive impact not only on safety and health performance, but also productivity. However, identifying and quantifying these effects will difficult to be measured as well as the quality of a working environment has a strong influence on productive efficiency.

For one aviation air plane manufacturing factory, where workplace can environment will have high risk to occur occupational related accidents to cause employees' injuries. Hence, employees will be consider themselves safety when they need to work in high accident occurrence workplace. The bad consequence will influence such as absenteeism day number increases, leaving this kind of aviation air plane job of employees number increases, low productive efficiencies, due to there are many proficient experienced employees who choose leave this kind of high accident risk occupation. Consequently, any high accident occurrence risk workplace environment , employers need have good safe and health strategy to let their employees have confidence to work in this kind of high risk accident occurrence workplace if they expect low productive efficiencies effect is caused by high accident occurrence risk workplace factor.

● Employee personal
empowerment factor influences
performance

Is empowerment one good method to raise employee himself/herself effort in order to improve productive efficiency in organizations. Empowerment often consists of support groups, e.g. management's effective leading or trainer's training, course educational opportunities. Employee self-management education may impact to improve himself/herself job performance, e.g. increased self-empowerment, self-management skills and job treatment satisfaction.

Only organization's empowerment strategy can lead every employee to through improvements in the employee individual decision making efficacy, improvement task performance behavior by reviewing whether what are the employee himself/herself errors when he/she encounters any job difficulties, after he/she reviewed his/her task error and his/her manager feels his/her performance can be improved. Then, it can enhance satisfaction with the employee and his/her manage relationship and better access and raising efficient performance in possible . Hence, empowerment can let every employee to discover whether what task related difficulties he/she faces or encounters every day. When his/her manager give ideas to let him/her to know how he/she ought review his/her task error in a supportive education working environment, it aims to let the low performance or low inefficient employees to increase confidence to continue work in the organization. So, the employee turnover number will decrease , if the inefficient employees can feel that they can attempt to solve their task-related difficulties successfully by themselves. So, empowerment can increase social support, leadership and advocacy development , it has resulted in greater employee individual performance psychological empowerment, autonomy and authority to let every employee to feel to achieve to improve themselves efficiencies more effectively in any organizations.

For hospital organizational efficiency measurement empowerment influence case, how empowerment can influence hospital's efficiency raising? Efficiency is one of the most important indicators of hospital performance evaluation. Why do some hospitals' efficiencies poor? It is possible that mis management of resources, lacking health plan packages, e.g. coverage of basic health insurance, poor quality of care service, more payment demand for out-of pocket payment , quality of primary healthcare , healthcare providers neglect to concern potentially about service efficiency issues.

In fact, low hospital efficiency is the major problem to influence patients number to choose the hospital's medical service, e.g. when the hospital often needs patients to queue to wait for doctor's care medical service. They need to wait on hour at least or more when the hospital has many patients are waiting for its medical service. Then, it will influence them to choose another hospital to replace it , if the hospital 's medical fee is cheaper and it does not need patients to spend long time to queue to wait its medical service. So, service efficiency is important to influence patients consumers' positive or negative feeling to choose the hospital's medical service. Even, the hospital's doctors are famous or they own many medical working experience, if patients often need long time to queue to wait its medical service . Then, it will cause its patients number to be reduced .

These are variable factors to influence the hospital's inefficiency. They may include old speed hospital information system and medical record documents based on inefficient input and output variables. Input variables may include the number of hospital admissions, the number of nurses and the number of available beds. The output variable may include average of length of stay and bed turnover interval inefficient paper document record in the patient record administrative department.

However, to evaluate the hospital efficiency indicators may include technical, scale and managerial efficiency the out-based data development analysis approach and the variable returns to scales assumption was used. Based on the out-input based approach (maximizing the factors of medical service production), to increase efficiency the organization should be increased outputs.

Hence, when the hospital has good efficient evaluation method to measure every staff's performance , e.g. ward administrative clerk, patient registration clerk etc. Then, it can base on an put-put based approach and assuming a variable return to scale, there is capacity to improve technical efficiency and managerial efficiency in these any hospital different administrative units without an increase in costs and use of same amount of resources in relation to technical efficiency and managerial efficiency and scale efficiency of hospital's administrative labour individual task.

In conclusion, factors, such as modification of managerial practices, use of modern technologies tailored to the cultural, political and formulation of clinical guidelines to standardize the medical processes in order to reduce medical errors and increase the empowerment of health care buyers (insurance organizations), length of stay, management hospitals by specialist managers, administrative requirement, full time hospital physicians, limiting the authority of decision makers in relation to the recruitment of staff in accordance with the needs of the hospital and optimal allocation of beds, conducting economic evaluations and the type of hospitals ownership had an impact on the hospital efficiency significantly. By increasing the number of beds the hospitals efficiency decreases. Otherwise, optimizing the bed size can increase hospital efficiency.

However, the important factor to raise hospital overall staffs efficiencies empowerment is needed to let every hospital staff to review whether why and how himself/herself error is caused and he/she needs to review his/her errors to avoid to be caused from any negligence again in order to avoid patients' complaints again or reduce the patients' complaint number aims. So, empowerment of staff himself/herself error review factor is one major raising efficient good method.

● How organizational facility environment factor influences new and old employees long term performance

In psychological view ,in any organization's environments, they depend on the types of social and physical environment factors to influence employee personal behavior how to be caused. How and why does the employee select to do whose behavior? If the organization's physical and social environment is better, then it may influence its employees select to work hard. It is possible to bring productive efficient raising consequence.

In fact, when one new employee enters the new organization to work, he/she needs to learn how to adapt to cooperate with the organization's old employees to work together. So, it explains how and why organization's physical and social environment can influence the new employee individual motivation of behavior to work. In regarding new employee individual behavior by new employer's culture expectations as well as new employees need to adapt of actions that are likely to productive positive outcomes and generally discard those that bring unrewarding or puniishing outcomes by new employer's treatment.

However, anticipated material and organization environment co-operation outcomes between the new employee and the organization old employees' cooperation, which are not the only kind of incentives that influence the new employee behavior of the new employee actions were performed only on behalf of anticipated external rewards and punishment from the new employer. In actuality, the new employee concerns considerable self-direction in the face of the new employer's organization's old employees competing influences. However, when the new employee has adopted an intension and an action plan. When, he/she works in the new organization for a period, he/she can't simply not back and visit for the appropriate performances to appear.

The new employee's new job goal will be motivated by enlisting self-evaluative engagement in activities rather than directly. By making self-evaluation conditional on matching personal new job standards, the new employee will give direction to his/her new job pursuits and create self-inventions to sustain his/her efforts for new job goal attainment. The new employee will select to do new task behavior to give him/her self-satisfaction and a sense of pride and self worth for the new job chance.

Efficacy beliefs also play a key role in shaping the new employees' behavior to do their tasks by influencing the types of new organization's activities and working environments, the new employees choose to set into any factor that influences the employee's choice behavior can affect the direction of employee personal career development in the new organization. This is because the organizational working environment influences operating in the employee how to select working environments continue to work. Thus, by choosing and shaping the new organization's working environments, new employee can have a hand in what they expect.

In conclusion , when a new employee chooses the new organization to work. He/she must need to adapt the organization's new working environment. If he/she feels difficult to adapt or accept to the organization's new working environment, then he/she will be influenced to work inefficient or poor productive performance , due to he/she feels unhappy to work the new organization's working environment and the new organization's manager will dissatisfy his/her performance and complain or give verbal warning to dismiss him/her. Then, it will bring the poor consequence to let the organization's inefficient productive performance effect. If many new employees feel difficult to adapt to work in the new organization. Then, inefficient productive performance will be influenced to keep a long term. So, it implies that the organization will need to change its organizational culture in order to let many new employees can adapt and accept this new organizational culture to work happily if the organization expects new employees work to raise productive efficiency successfully.

● Raising efficient and effective
interview psychological methods
In human resource department, interviewing and selecting the most right applicants to do different kinds of positions, it is one part of HRM function. If the interviewer need to spend more time to interview to decide whom is the most right applicant to do the position in one day, e.g. 50 at least , even more applicants number as well as he/she can also make the more accurate personal selection decision to choose the most right applicant to do the position after the interview day. Then, the interviewing process needs to be avoided to spend more time to choose the most suitable applicant to do the position within the day. It is difficult to judge whether whom ought be the most right applicant to do the position, if there are more than 50 applicants , they are needed to be interview in the day. The consequence will bring HR department can spend extra time to do the interview task, but it can have enough staffs and time and resource to do other urgent or important task at the interview day. It will bring this question: How to apply psychological method to raise interviewer's efficiency to shorten to spend extra time to do interviewing tasks ? I shall explain some psychological methods to attempt to let interviewers have more confidence to select the most right applicant in short time as below:

1. Behavioral interview skill
The interviewer can apply the actual behavioral interview method to let the interviewee to answer how he/she deals the matters, he/she feels that it is the best decision in order to judge and analyze whether whom applicant is the most suitable to be selected, e.g. describing the situation, he/she needs or the task that he/she needs to accomplish. The situation may be from a previous job, any relevant event, describing the action he/she took and be sure to keep the focus on him/her , e.g. discussing a group project or effort in the team; explaining what results he/she achieved, what happen? How did the event and what dis the applicant accomplishes? What did the applicant learn?

In the behavioral-based interview. the interviewer can need the applicant to attempt to explain examples clearly in order to judge whose analytical skill whether he/she is the suitable applicant to do the position. The interviewer may ask the applicant to identify some examples from whose post experience where he/she demonstrated top behaviors and skills that employers typically seek. To judge whether his/her examples should be totally positive, such as accomplishments or meeting goals, the other half should be situations that started at negatively , but either ended positively or he/she made the best of the outcome.

This behavioral interview test aims to review whether the applicant's every example answer, he/she can provide an appropriate description of how he/she demonstrated the desired behaviors. In the behavioral interview, the interviewer can attempt to judge whether the applicant has good imagine effort to mind any relatively small set of examples to respond to a number of different behavioral questions to satisfy the right example are applied to the right situations in the limited interview time. Hence, behavioral interview can let the interviewer to make more accurate analysis to judge whether whom applicant(s) has (have) good analytical effort to solve any work-related situational problems in the most reasonable way or attitude in order to select whom is the most right applicant to do the position.

2. E-mail interviewing in qualitative research

E-mail interviewing is another good interview method to select right applicant to do the managerial level position. E-mail interviewing can be in many cases a viable alternative to face-to-face telephone interviewing. Internet-based qualitative research methods may include online personal interview and virtual focus groups. However, it brings two questions: What opportunities and challenges does online in depth interviewing present for collectively qualitative data? How can in depth e-mail interviews be conducted effectively?

The applicant targets may be the top-level manager, advertising executive , sales manager, human resource manager etc. management position applicants. They need to answer any complex or difficult interviewing question by email in the limited time, e.g. how to solve one case study problem , how to give recommendation to solve the situation problem. The interview participants may be recruited by tool/method of psychological test questions, the interview questions may be interview guide in a single e-mail and follow yp, length of email data collection period may be up to 10 weeks, the number of e-mail or follow up exchanges may be several number. The electronic formal and require little editing or formation before the applicants are processed for analysis all e-mail interviewing questions. So, they need to answer any managerial case study problem in limited time. It is one good managerial interview test method to evaluate whether whom applicant has the best analysis effort in order to the managerial position, because they need to find the best solutions to give recommendations to attempt to solve any situational problems in any un predictive case study problems. For example, when the applicant or a focus group of discussion applicants whom need to spend the maximum half hours to give recommendations to discuss to solve one complex or difficult case study problem either between the interviewer and the another interviewee applicant or between the group of five to ten interviewees (job applicants) themselves. Thus, after the interviewer sent the one case study question to let the applicants to know by every email channel. The interviewer needs to judger whether whom one applicant or one of the focus group applicants their recommendations are the most reasonable to solve the case study managerial situational problem within half hour to one hour. Then, the interviewer can make more accurate judgement to select whether whom has the best analytical effort to do the managerial position.

3. The effectiveness of motivational interviewing for young or older adult applicants selection process

How can apply case management skills to be effective to prepare any interview motivation? How to do the most effective and efficient to meet the objectives of the interview? Some interview techniques used may vary the based on the individuals involved in the interview. For an interview with the young age applicant more require a different approach than an interview with a senior adult applicant. The following are one pointers to assist with preparing for the interview as below:

Knowing the purpose of the interview and what needs to be accomplished . What is the expected outcome? Gathering all forms that need to be completed or signed having the interview and making list of questions that need to be asked, knowing the key facts and topics to be discussed, during the interview. Gathering factual information that may be helpful. Opening mind is needed in the whole interview process. Making an appointment for the interview and arranging sufficient time to set fully participate in the interview. Taking notes during the interview, let the participants know in general terms the reason notes are being made and how they will be used, opening ended questions invite the applicant to provide more information usually begin with other words who, what, where, how, asking one question at a time and keeping wording simple and specific, defining any terms that may be unfamiliar to the applicant , giving the interviewing participants in the interview an opportunity to ask their one questions or to clarify anything that was discussed, closing the interview with a review of the information discussed and facts gathered, reviewing any follow-up that is to be done by the case manager or others involved in the interview.

In an efficient and effective interview, the interviewer needs have good body and spoken word communication to the interviewee or the position applicant. Because a good communication can reduce waste time or avoid the extended longer interview time if the interviewer can make good communication to impact good message to let the applicant to understand what is the mean to his/her interview question. What he/she wants to know, the total impact of a message includes ,e.g. 7 % verbal (words), 38% vocal /volume, pitch, rhythm etc. and 55% body movements (mostly facial expression). The interviewer's body and verbal behavior can make more clear message to let the interviewee(job applicant) to understand what answers are he/she wants to know mostly. Hence, an efficient and effective interview can let the interviewer to control and manage the whole interview to evaluate whether whom the applicants' answers or feedbacks are more reasonable to be acceptable to be better to compare other applicants to apply the position more accurately.

● What is efficient achievement of technological inputs factor in construction industry

What is organizational efficient raising actual mean? I shall indicate construction industry case to explain technological factor is the major factor to assist construction organization to raise efficiency. For construction industry example, improved productivity could be attributed to advances in and increased usage of information technologies, increased competition, due to globalization and changes in workplace and organizational structures.

For construction efficiency, the construction process can reduce waste in coordinating labor and in managing, moving and installing materials, loss avoidance. It can achieve efficient aim. The construction productive efficient concept can be defined efficiency improvements as ways to cut waste and labor. So, one construction organizational efficient achievement means that it implemented through the capital facilities sector, these activities would significantly advance construction efficiency and improve the quality, timeliness, cost effectiveness of projects in construction processes.

On construction industry technological factor influence hand, it can influence that construction productivity how well, how quality, and at what cost buildings and infrastructure can be constructured, directly affects prices for homes and consumer products and the robustness of the national economy. Construction productivity will also affect the outcomes of national efforts to renew existing infrastructure systems; to build new infrastructure for power from renewable to renew existing infrastructure systems; to build new infrastructure for power from renewable resources to develop high-performance " green building" and to remain competitive in the global market. If the construction organization expected to achieve effficient aim. It ought consider how to change in building design, construction and renovation and in building materials and materials recycling, will be essential to the success of national efforts to minimize environmental impacts, reduce overall energy use, and reduce greenhouse gas emissions.

However, construction industry analysts differ on whether construction industry productivity is improved by efficiency outcome. They indicate construction efficiency needs to reduce 25-50 percent waste in coordinating labour and in managing, moving and installing materials. This is the most minimum standard efficient achievement level to any construction organizations.

What are the factors influence efficiency to any construction organizations? An efficient construction task process is made possible by a range of information technological tools and applications, including computer-aided design and drafting, three and four dimensional visualization and modeling programs, laser scanning, cost-estimating and scheduling tools and materials tracking. So, high technological tool will assist to raise efficient construction process to any construction organizations. It can help them to shorten time and avoid materials waste and control cost effective estimation for any construction projects.

Effective use of interoperate technologies requires effective team cooperative processes and effective planning up front and this it can help overcome obstacles to efficiency created by process fragmentation. Interoperable technologies can also help to improve the quality and speed of any construction project related decision making, integrate processes, managing supply chains, sequence work flows, improve data accuracy and reduce the time spent on data entry, reduce design and engineering conflicts and the subsequent need for rework, improve the life-cycle management of buildings and infrastructure.

All of these factors will influence whether the construction organization can implement efficiency in success. For example, interoperable techcholgies include legal issues, data-storage capacities and the need for " intelligent " search applications to sort quickly through thousands of data elements and make real-time information available for on-site decision making. How to improve job-site efficiency through more effective interfacing of people, processes, materials ,equipment, and information. The job site for a large construction project is a dynamic place, involving numerous contractors, subcontractors, trades people and labors, all of whom must require equipment, materials and supplies to complete their tasks. So, they need to know how to manage activities and demands to achieve the maximum efficiency from the limited available resources. Time, money, and resources will have possible to be wasted when projects are poorly managed, causing workers to have to wait around for tools and work crews are not on-site at appropriate time or when supplies and equipment are stored in complexity or difficulty, requiring that they can be moved multiple time (time waste).

How to improve job site safety and improve the quality of projects, significantly cut waste? The use of automated equipment, e.g. for excavation and earthmoving operations, pip installation, concrete placement, and information technologies, e.g. radio-frequency identification tags for tracking materials personal digital assistants for capturing field data. These high technological tool can help any construction projects to raise efficiency to process improvements and the provision for real -time information for improved management at the job site.

Moreover, on mannal research and development tools hand, instead of data technological tools hand, any construction organizations also need to consider how to take a variety of forms: How to test field on a job site? How to arrange lecture shows in efficient way, seminrs, training and conference, and scientific laboratories time, human resource available arrangement, spending expenditure budget to finish. Moreover, effective performance mearements are enablers of innovation and of corrective actions throughout a construction project's life cycle. They can help any construction companies or organizations understand how processes led to success or failure, improvements or inefficiencies and how to use that knowledge to improve construction products , processes and outcomes of active projects.

The nature of construction projects, the industry itself, any construction organizations ought consider the construction working environment how to influence construction workers' emotions. For example, when the construction site is high levels, of noise, dust and airborne particles, adverse weather conditions,and other factors that can cause injuries and thereby reduce efficiency and productivity. New types of equipment can make an active physically easier to perform, easier to control, move precise , and safer for construction workers. Similarly, changes in materials can reduce the weight of construction components, make them easier to handle, move and install. Manufacturing building components off-site providers need more control conditions and allow for improved quality and precision in the fabrication of the component, One study that examined the relationship between changes in material technology and construction productivity based on 100 construction a related tasks, the study found that labor productivity for the same activity increased by 30 % at least when higher materials were used and labour productivity also improved when construction activites were performed using materials that were easier to install or were pre-fabricated. So, it seems material heavy can influence construction worker individual productive efficiency in site, if the material is higher , then the construction worker's productivity will be influenced to improve (Goodrum et al. 2009).

Thus, the factors influence construction organization's efficiency. It focuses on whether the construction firm applies how advanced construction technologies to assist its construction workers to work as well as whether its construction environment can let workers to feel safe to avoid life danger or accident occurrence. When the workers do not worry about whose life safety as well as they can apply advanced construction technology to assist them to work. Then, their productive efficiencies ought need to be improved easily. Thus, facility management and advanced technology will be the main factor to raise construction workers' efficiencies.

Psychosocial and medical interventions for mental and physical health facility management strategy

The business case for implementation science is clear: As healthcare systems work under increasingly dynamic and resource-constrained conditions, evidence-based strategies are essential in order to ensure that research investments maximize healthcare value and improve public health. Implementation science plays a critical role in supporting these efforts. This case concerns how management scinece solves psychosocial and medical interventions for mental and physical health facilities management challenges.

Implementation science is "the scientific study of methods to promote the systematic uptake of research findings and other EBPs into routine practice, and, hence, to improve the quality and effectiveness of health services." Implementation science is distinct from, but shares characteristics with, both quality improvement and dissemination methods. Implementation studies can be either assess naturalistic variability or measure change in response to planned intervention. Implementation studies typically employ mixed quantitative-qualitative designs, identifying factors that impact uptake across multiple levels, including patient, provider, clinic, facility, organization, and often the broader community and policy environment. Accordingly, implementation science requires a solid grounding in theory and the involvement of trans-disciplinary research teams.

Facility management, or FM, is a broad discipline that includes a variety of industries, from food to technology, manufacturing to e-commerce and beyond. But, though the core of each business may be completely different from even its closest competition, successful facility management practices are easily interchangeable from enterprise to enterprise. As a matter of fact, it is one of the only job titles that can be found in, basically, any small to large organizations, including public entities, like schools and hospitals, to private buBut, reciprocal tendencies aside, facility management procedures and techniques must be highly-specialized for the business in which they are being used. Because the discipline covers complex specifics, including business continuity planning and even fire safety, it's key that your organization offers a holistic outlook on its facility management procedures.sinesses, like those that manage their inventory in warehouses. The discipline of facility management encompasses – and why poor management could easily lead to an organization's demise:

Safety – It's the facility management team's job to ensure the safety of all of the employees and customers occupying the property. This responsibility spans all possible environmental health and safety issues, particularly ones that concern the building and its equipment, specifically. Failure to do so can mean serious business in the form of fines, lost business, or even prosecution if it was deemed that the manager or business' negligence caused casualties or permanent environmental damage. Fire, for example, is usually right at the top of the radars of facility managers because it's a preventable tragedy that, when prepared for sufficiently, can save lives and valuable inventory. A thorough facility management team can protect its company best by guaranteeing that all parts of the facility are up-to-code, its employees are trained well, and all permits and certificates are completely valid. This function entails everything from safe and efficient lighting to flooring choices.

Security – In regards to importance, second to safety is facility security, yet another important piece of the puzzle in which the facility management team must answer to. Though larger companies or ones with particularly pricey inventory or equipment might make the wise choice to outsource its security needs in the form of a private firm, it's still the role of the facility manager to ensure that the firm performs competently. Technology advancements like biometrics and wearables are making it possible to maintain strict access control for high-security areas, but it's up to facility managers to stay on top of these developments and make smart security technology investments. In addition to general safety, it's also important that the facility management team has the technological know-how to safeguard and maintain its priciest hardware. This role is a key one as it doubly affirms that assets are protected just as closely as the safety of the community.

Maintenance and Inspections – No matter the focus of the organization, one of the most heedless things that a facility management team can do is slack off on its building maintenance duties. Every part of the building, including installed machinery such as HVAC systems, must be maintained by the facility management team. Because some facilities contain countless elements that need regular maintenance, establishing and following strict maintenance schedules helps to ensure that all moving and permanent parts of the facility stay up-to-date and working well into the future. Along with general maintenance, inspections are also something that facility management teams must always be ready for. They can prepare the business by conducting internal inspections, as needed, for the many formal regulatory inspections they might incur annually. Of course, the team must also take into account any time the facility undergoes a major change in hardware, level of inventory, or capacity – and, they must also keep their eyes on all changes in laws that could affect their current procedures.

Business Continuity Planning – Part of leading an effective facility management team means planning for "worst case scenarios." This means that each team must sit down with the powers that be to come up with a plan in case disaster strikes and the business can't afford to shut down operations. For example, let's say that a community college endures a major fire and the authorities have deemed the entire main building a total loss. The community college is currently in the middle of a semester which it can't cut short – this is a situation where prior business continuity planning is key. If this were done in the aforementioned scenario, the facility management team would have already come up with alternate locations to hold classes and operate the organization's administrative duties. In addition to the new venue, the team would have already made a solid plan for the temporary facility's security, maintenance, and hardware needs.

Daily Operational Duties – In addition to serving as the safety and security liaisons for the facility, it's also important that facility management teams are organized to handle the inherent day-to-day challenges that might arise. Depending on how the given organization is structured, this can mean anything from mending a leaky roof in the women's restroom to even fixing a jammed fax machine.

I shall discuss how to apply facilities management strategy to assist hospial organization how to raise its medical health care service to let patients to feel more comfortable and care for medical care in any hospitals as below:

Hospitals and health systems that engage in cost management are looking to reshape and reduce costs, and there are eight main strategies that can lead to effective cost management opportunities, cost management, at its core, involves two components: improving the planning and execution of current operations and attacking overhead costs and other costs that are "flying below the radar." Here are the eight strategies to reduce hosptial cost as below:

1. Understand the organization's readiness for cost management. Conducting a cost management assessment that details a hospital system's thinking, alignment, operational planning, overhead management and other moving parts could determine if a hospital is actually ready to begin a large cost management initiative.

2. Define cost-reduction goals based on the organization's capital shortfall. Revenue streams are not what they used to be for hospitals and health systems, and all cost-reduction goals should aim to close the capital shortfall as much as possible. "The goals quantify the performance levels necessary to fund the organization's strategies and maintain its competitive financial performance," according to the report.

3. Use internal and external benchmarks to identify possible sources of savings. Reviewing historical trends and applying global and departmental benchmarks and peer department comparisons can give a clearer picture of where possible savings could be.

4. Supplement benchmark data with other data analytics. Benchmarking data, while necessary and helpful, cannot map a cost management strategy alone. Using several data analyses, with input from medical staff and department managers, can hone in on cost-reduction opportunities.

5. Understand and focus on the key drivers of staffing and productivity problems. Inadequate plans, poor execution of staffing plans, unclear staffing roles, use of overtime and other staffing and productivity issues drive higher labor costs, which generally constitute more than half of a hospital or health system's operating expenses.

6. Drill down on staffing methods. Changing staffing methods could certainly keep costs in check, but it could also enhance the relationship between staff members and patient demand. For example, improved staffing in the operating room or emergency department will account for

variations in patient volume but will still keep a strong semblance of patient contact.

7. Streamline overhead functions. Eliminating redundancies in human resources, accounting, revenue cycle, information technology, marketing, legal, materials management and other hospital functions can both improve operational flow and "yield large savings," according to the report.

8. Ensure cost-reduction targets are integrated with organizational plans and budgets. Inserting the cost management initiatives into the hospital's strategic financial plan, annual budget and operating plan can allow management to monitor progress and report results to the entire organization.

However, above these cost management is accounting method to reduce cost in hospital organization human resource side, such as reducing staffs or staff number, reducing electricity fee. But, it does not represent the actual successful to implement the actual cost reducing, but it won't influence the patients' comfortable and enjoyable feeling. So, how to implement facility managment to bring actual cost reduce and avoid patients feel medical services are worse and lack of enough nurses or doctors number care need. I shall explain how to implement the new kind of facility management strategy to reduce cost and raise patients comfortable and care feeling in the same time to medical organizations as below:

● What is the new model of healthcare facility management

A growing number of healthcare organizations are moving to an integrated real estate model in an effort to better manage costs, respond to regulatory requirements, and support changes in patient care delivery. As healthcare organizations seek solutions to the challenges presented by today's evolving marketplace, it's clear that the cost and performance of their facilities will have a significant impact. Whether it's the need to drive cost reduction, respond to regulatory requirements or support changes in patient care delivery models, the effectiveness of an organization's facilities management program plays a critical role in their ability to provide high-quality, cost-effective patient care.

As healthcare leaders realize the importance of an effective real estate platform, many are finding that transformative changes are needed in order to realize outcomes that cannot be achieved under traditional facility management models.

● What is the tradition facilities management model to hospitals

Historically, facility management services have been provided on a campus by campus basis or separated into acute care and outpatient programs. In many cases, these programs have been limited to plant operations, which are segregated as an individual support service and function in a silo environment. Due primarily to organic growth or mergers and acquisitions, healthcare systems often find themselves managing their facilities in a bifurcated manner, with individual hospitals operating more or less autonomously. While many organizations have identified the goal of standardizing real estate operations across their system, it's common to find that these initiatives have been in the planning stage for some time. As a result, the inability to proactively manage facility costs and performance at the system level continues to be an obstacle to progress. Although facility management teams may have a "best-in-class" process at an individual hospital, a lack of resources or resistance to change may prevent that process from being consistently implemented across the system. As each individual campus makes incremental process improvements, they move further and further away from a comprehensive real estate solution. Recognizing that future success will require a systemwide approach to facilities management, continuing with the status quo model increases the cost of change in the future and forfeits the savings that can only be achieved through a centralized real estate platform.

The lack of a comprehensive real estate delivery model also inhibits an organization's ability to effectively develop essential programs at the system level. Services which are critical for long-term success, such as work order management, energy management, benchmarking, and standardization, are often pursued on a campus by campus basis. These initiatives require the dedication of significant time and resources to collect and reconcile data before creating and implementing the new program. So, successful facility management to any health care or hospital organizations. It must help them to bring cost reducing benefits.

With disparate facilities management systems at each campus, the process must then be repeated across the system. When evaluating the benefits to be gained through individual campus initiatives, consideration must be given to the cost of replicating the process as compared to the cost and time to market to create one process for the entire real estate portfolio. The lack of a consistent facilities management program also creates challenges related to business planning at the system level. A common example may be seen in the capital planning process, as the prioritization of projects breaks down due to a lack of reliable comparison data and the absence of analytics based on performance and cost projections. The process then becomes politically driven, rather than following a disciplined approach based on projected need and justified by consistent business case analyses.

A similar result is frequently displayed when organizations attempt to implement segregated processes related to space allocation to any hospitals or medical care organizations. The practice of assigning space based on availability is common, but it creates higher occupancy costs and difficulties in forecasting future demand and associated expenses. This reduces the accuracy of the business cases that drive the decision making process. Hence, one excellent facility management medical organization , it ought can reduce cost , but it can also let patients feel more large area occupancy patients rooms or any occupancy area to toilets, bath rooms , cooking rooms in any hospitals locations. It aims to let patients to feel comfortable and enjoy to live in the hospital. Without a comprehensive approach to facilities management, the space allocation process becomes reactive and can lead to the unnecessary construction of new space, when the reality may be that a solution is achievable within the organization's existing real estate.

● Approach to reducing costs

The challenges caused by the lack of a systemwide facility management platform are exacerbated by the traditional approach to reducing costs, which is to cut staffing levels. In the absence of a comprehensive facility management program, these staffing cuts are often a reactive response to an immediate need to reduce costs rather than a component of a long term plan. As the ability to focus on preventive maintenance decreases, the organization's risk increases and employee satisfaction and performance decreases. At some point, doing more with less is counterproductive and a new approach is needed. In order to achieve significant improvement, the status quo model must be transformed as part of a centralized delivery model to optimize the performance of facilities and create financially sustainable real estate practices. A comprehensive facility management plan will provide alternative paths to achieving cost reductions, as well as processes to ensure the continued support of patient care.

● The path to a solution

In order to achieve lasting results, healthcare organizations should embark on a process to consolidate their existing facility management services into a systemwide, best-in-class real estate platform. With the volume of changes impacting the healthcare market, having best-in-class facility management will be critical to long-term success. All aspects of facility services should be included as a baseline delivery model, with adjustments made in policies and processes to address different facility types. This system-based approach to planning and analytics provides a substantial competitive advantage. Given the time involved in developing and fully implementing real estate plans, organizations that pursue integrated facility management models will have an advantage over their competitors who continue operating as they have in the past.

A systemwide real estate program, including facility management, project management, facility activation services, property management, strategic real estate planning, real estate accounting and market-based transaction management allows organizations to successfully implement proactive initiatives such as ambulatory prototyping, site selection, labor analytics and workplace environment optimization. Once the assessment is complete, it will be possible to produce a gap analysis to identify opportunities to reduce costs and improve processes and performance. These opportunities can then be evaluated by weighing the cost to implement new system based programs against the expected savings or operational benefits. Each opportunity should be validated as part of a consistent decision process, allowing prioritization based on an organization's overall business plan and appetite for change.

Once the facility management program is on its way to best-in-class status, it should be integrated with all other real estate services to fully optimize performance. Ideally, this transformational process will follow concurrent and coordinated schedules across all real estate services, with the objective of developing supportive and complimentary processes among all teams. As the delivery of patient care evolves, the delivery of real estate services must transform to keep pace. The solution is to transition to an integrated systemwide real estate model, drawing on examples of successful platforms and driving improvements based on quantifiable data and objectives.

As part of an integrated platform, these programs allow organizations to fundamentally change the way real estate is managed, dramatically reducing year over year expenses and enabling the accurate prediction of future space requirements and the reliable forecasting of associated long term financial obligations. When truly integrated, the real estate platform will provide cost-effective management of assets and contribute significant value to many internal departments, including strategy and business development, clinic systems, finance, compliance, and procurement. The benefits of an integrated real estate platform cannot be achieved without completing a comprehensive transformation of the traditional model.

On conclusion, in order to achieve that goal, healthcare organizations should pursue the transformation of their real estate platform by taking the first steps towards a best-in-class facility management program. Successful healthcare organizations of the future will have integrated real estate services, with facilities that operate at peak efficiency and are proactively managed to respond to and support changes in the delivery of patient care.

Reference

Becker, F. (1990). " Facility management : a cutting edge field?" property management 8 (2): 25-28.

Bernard, M.B. & Bruce, J. A. (1994) Improving organizational effectiveness through transformational leadership: US. Sage publications, Inc. pp. 11-13.

Fiona, M.W. (2004). organizational behavior and work , a critical introduction, 2 ed. : New York, US, Oxford university press, pp.79 .

Jac, F.E.& John , R.M. (2014) predictive analytics for HRM:US Pearson Education pp.13-16

Stephen, P.R. & Timothy, A.J. (2018). Essentials of organizational behavior, 14 ed.: US. Pearson Education, Inc. pp.108-110.

Strategy Plan Implement

● Economy and management factors
  Economic factors influence
to meet strategic management?

What economic factors will influence any organizations to achieve their strategic plans successfully? Why does one firm cut prices when another firm buys out competitors? Why does one firm diversify into new industries, when another firm spins off subsidiaries to focus on its core ? Why do some strategic rise when others all? These organizations' activities will be influenced to choose to implement by economic factor influences.

These are central concern of both strategic management theorists and strategic management draw on diverse ideas as well as which have relationship to be influenced by unpredictable economic factors . So, organizations need to concern what external environment economic situation is. Such as development or decline (recession), then to decide how to adopt the most effective strategic plan to achieve the aim of effectiveness and efficiency more successfully. So, it seems that external economic environment factors can influence why organizations need an efficient and effective strategic plan to do more better.

Firstly, In organizational internal need hand , strategic management theorists need to view whose firm from different standpoints. Each strategist explores efficiency from the perspective of whose firm, developing theories of why one strategy is more successful then another, given product, service and industry characteristics.

Sociologists focus on efficiency from the perspective of the corporate environment itself, who neglect the exernal economic environment factor can influence the organization leaders how to implement their strategic plans. Developing theories about the context in which one strategy becomes defined as efficiency an effectiveness.

Secondly, In economic factor influences organizational strategic plan hand. Strategic management theorists need to begin with very different methodological imperatives. Strategists seek to develop adequate theories of why certain strategies are optional or at least efficient, based typically on insights from successful firms. Sociologists seek to explain variance in behavior across large populations of firms and over time, to research why potential causes for any economic situation.

These differences derive in part from their different goals, strategic management is oriented to develop concepts for cooperate leaders, whereas, economic sociology is oriented to explain the trends why to cause corporate behavior. For example, why does IKEA furniture business need to let any visitors who attempt to sit down to have comfortable feeling? Why does Apple brand computer business need to design and innovate any new model of notebooks and mobile computers.

In external economic environment influence, strategic theorists presume that firm behavior is driven principally by competitive pressure and quest for effectiveness and efficiency. Analysts tend to give great power to market factors and little power to historical, political and social factors. So, organization leaders need to concern how competitive pressures may lead whose firms to alter whose strategies, but the new strategies who choose are shaped by public policy, limitation, power and historical happen.

I shall indicate this question concerns why organizations need strategy plans. Why do firms diversify? In another view point to ask this question. Why is it efficient for some firms to diversify, and for which firms to diversify and for which firms is efficient and effective? Why do firms choose diversification? Why does a particular firm choose at a particular time? Economic sociologists usually ask this management challenges, who find organization challenges to give solution in economic view point. But for strategic management theorists, this problem concerns an argument based in efficiency. Question is such as: Can organizations make diversification efficient if which lack one efficent and effective strategy plan?

For economic sociologists, this problem is to explain the social processes behind the rise of a new business practice. Does it ensure to need diversification tend if the organization lacks an efficient and effective strategic plan to evaluate ? It's possible that diversification strategy can let multi-product firms are more profitable to campaign single product firms.

In the past, the diversification trend is during the 1980 year. What does cause this? On economic first view point, Davis et al. (1991) cite the inefficiencies inherent in diversification. Can strategy plan cause efficiency effect? On economic second view point , Davis also showed most firms make a mix of good and bad decisions, such that a disastrous strategy in product, which may be altered by a good one in marketing, or in human resources. On economic third view point, he also indicated firms seek to copy their profitable pears may have difficulty figuring out what to copy and may have difficulty copying it. However, sociologists certainly see managers as striving for efficiency . But managerial decisions , which are focus on how sociological processes to led managers to choose from an alternatives.

How to feel strategic thinking? Strategy took on a military significance and represented the action of commanding or leading armies in times of war, i.e. a military campaign. It meant a way of prevailing over the adversary, a tool of victory in war and why was it applied to other contexts and fields of human relationships: Political, economics, business, among others.

Into a field of knowledge in management, strategic management, with content, concepts and practice reasoning can be applied to any businesses. Management uses this old military concept to associate the activities of an organization's manager. Since it represents an important tools for business management in a competitive marketplace. The main objective of strategy involves preparing the organization to deploy the skills qualifications and internal resources of the enterprise.

So, it seems that strategic plan is similar to military campaign. If one country's soldier team lacks one efficient and effective military strategic plan to prepare to war, it is possible that the soldier team will fail, due to the soldier team lack one team leaders who can lead them how to organize whose team to co-operate efficiently. So, one organization will be failure to compete its competitors if which lacks one efficient strategic plan to prepare to organize which teams to co-operate to work from top level to middle level and down level in its organizational structure.

According to Obembe (2010) indicated knowledge management in an organization is begun by identifying the knowledge that individuals bring in from outside the company. In this case, the development of organizational strategy depends on understanding the perceptions of their managers on what strategy and strategic management actually is. The identification of perceptions of future managers on the concept is used in contributing significantly to organizational management practice. This enables the organizational knowledge on the field of strategy can hardly be managed should each manager understand the concept differently. So, if organization can have one efficient strategic plan, then it will raise ability to learn knowledge management skill to solve any human resource, strategic management etc. challenges more easily.

For example, Walt Disney entertainment theme park, which had innovated one efficient knowledge management strategy to reduce visitors' complains and dissatisfaction, such as designing fast ticket queue system, which can reduce visitors' queue time. Although, admission fee is more expensive to compare to normal ticket buyers. But who can choose not to need to wait long time to queue to play more than one kind entertainment facility to play. If who can come back the prior entertainment facility queue within one hour, who do not need to queue again to play the prior entertainment facility. So, who can reduce queue time to chose to play any prior queue entertainment facilities within one hour coming back, who will feel more satisfactory to spend loss queue working time to play different entertainment facilities. Also, when any visitors feel need to enquire how to go to anywhere , who can find cleaners to enquire how to go anywhere conveniently and easily. Because the cleaners will give map to indicate any location to let who to know. So, any visitors do not need to spend much to find to any visible map noticeboard to find location. Cleaners can tell to them how to go to any anywhere to let them know more clearly. So, knowledge management is one kind of strategic thinking to solve customer individual psychological dissatisfactory feeling. The Disney leaders need to continue to discover to seek any weakness points to solve customer psychological satisfactory feeling or need from daily observation in Disney entertainment park.

Strategy is a business logic, rational and sequential to the most dynamic that understand this process as associated with culture and learning factors, political and power relations. Thus, there are two major problems affecting the understanding of what the concept of strategy really means that confusion is between strategy and effectiveness tools as well as confusion is between strategy and strategic planning. The rook of the problem seems to be the lack of a full understanding as to what strategy really is.

Organizational strategy can mean different in scale and complexity, which can mean policies, objectives, tactics, goals, programs, among others. However, the concept of strategy has been used indiscriminately in the field of management, meaning anything from a precisely formulated course of action, a positioning in a particular environment, through to the entire personality and existential rational behind a company's existence. Strategy is not only one way of dealing in a competitive environment or market, as treated by much of the literature and its popular use, as it can't only summarize the ideas, proposals, guidelines. This fact has an explanation. Strategy in organizations , as a field of study is much newer than its current practice, and its knowledge remains under construction.

Some strategic professionals think strategy is such as: what matters are for the effectiveness of the organization, the external point of view, which stresses the relevance of the objectives against the environment, in terms of internal stresses, balanced communication between members of the organization and a willingness to contribute towards actions and the achievement of common objectives, analyzing the present situation and changing at whenever necessary to find what one's resources are or what which should be.

It is the determinant of the basic long-term goals of a firm and the allocation of resources necessary for carrying out these goals, it is a rule for making decision to be determined by product/market scope growth, competitive advantage and synergy. So, it is a thinking to any leaders to be prepared to make any decisions and develops the learning process in organization as well as it is the pattern of objectives, purposes or goals and major policies and plans to achieve missions for any organization within a limited time prediction or expectation.

All business organizations are concerned with low which will survive and prosper in the future. A business strategy is often thought of as a plan or set of intentions that will set the long term direction of the actions. However, how organizational plans or how intent , an organization's strategy can only become a meaning reality to achieve include corporate, business and function three levels.

The top corporate level key issues concern that what businesses shall be in , acquire or divest, how allocate resources what the relationship businesses and center is . The middle business level key issues concern that how businesses compete, what the mission is, what the strategic objectives are. The low function level key issues concern that how the function contribute to the business strategy, what the strategic objectives are managed in the function, what technology is used in the function, what skills are required by workers in the function.

Organizations need to concern these questions. Is the strategy consistent between the organization's strategy and business strategy, between operation strategy and the other functional strategy, between the different decision areas of operation strategy? Does the strategy contribute to competitive advantage? Enabling operations to set priorities that enhance competitive advantage, high opportunities for operations to complement the business strategies, making operations strategy clear to the rest of the organization, providing the operating capabilities that will be required in the future.

Organizations need have operations performance objectives to measure which performance. It is a criterion against which to evaluate the performance of operations. There are considered to be five possible operations performance objectives, cost , quality, speed, dependability and flexibility. Such as, the ability to produce at low cost, the ability to produce with specification and without error, the ability to do things quality in response to customer demands and offer short lead times between a client orders and a product or service and when who receive it, the ability to deliver products and services with promises made to clients, e.g. in a quotation or other published information, the ability to change operations. Flexibility includes the ability to change the volume of production, to change the time taken to product, to change the mix of different products or services produced , to innovate and introduce new products and services. Thus, these are basic organization structure of strategic management.

How to apply strategic planning and management in public and private sector organizations and what are their differences?

Management issues can be divided in two groups: governmental or public, with its specific aims, methods and challenges, and private sector responsible for economical results, competitiveness and state revenues. How can strategic planning, management and leadership of public and private sectors identify opportunities to improve performance with differences? Concerning this research, some strategic management professional had attempted to do research to conclude that in public sector there is great emphasis on strategic planning part of management process, but implementing plan to clear activities delays or is even misled. In private sector enterprises tend to look short term. Otherwise, thus gaining results in small every day actions , but looking greater sight to future and therefore to get chance of greater growth . Government should implement more client-oriented approach using best example from entrepreneurial world. Private sector should learn how to generate concrete long term plans, delegate duties and not to mix responsibilities in enterprise for greater result. So , who concluded that strategic plan is considered that private sector prevails over the public sector in efficiency and result oriented actions. Although, this assumption reasoned with lots of practical examples and arguments and efficiency's prevalence of private sector over the public administration was proved.

Considering the public administration strategic plan, the strategic management professionals argument do not encourage public administration to work in its own self-interest, but who discovered more efficient environment where to find the best management practices, in stance in field of customer care, that can be adopted in a legal and rational way.

Public sector is advocated that intellectual work is more hierarchical , within the team work more knowledgeable team member for a special task will already to be an informal interim leader, regardless of the structure of hierarchy, to compare to private sector hierarchical structure. They showed that are subordinated hierarchically to the long term development planning documents. The short term development planning documents are subordinated hierarchically to the median term developed planning documents. According to the updated system all public administration situation should develop the action strategy from the period of three years that serves for the budget planning and allocation to compare to provide sector. Otherwise, strategic planning in private enterprises come within strategic management and contributes as part of it. Strategic management is focused defining of business mission, the company's development direction, objectives and the resources and long-term management decision -making for implementing the strategy .

Why is middle management important in strategic organizational chart structure? Middle level managers, their role no longer entails issuing orders to subordinates. In fact, middle level managers in flat organizations may have very few direct reports. The most successful middle managers must rely on strong influencing skills and the ability to a complex network of resources critical role in the ultimate ability of a company to achieve its strategic goals. For example, marketing managers and engineering directors, there are the middle level managers who are being asked to do more with fewer resources. They are being held responsible have no direct organizational authority. They are being asked to influence partners, drive into unfamiliar channels, and motivate complex networks of global resources to get results .

So, employers or top managers, leaders need to concern whether who have worked relative pressure from worked relative causes. And yet ongoing restructuring, the dissolution of the career ladder, and persistent job insecurity have eroded middle level managers' sense at loyalty, frequently leaving them feeling demoralized and disenfranchised. Because it has chance, these middle level managers who are at risk of leaving your organization, unless you provide the proper support and development to perform their new responsibilities. Higher turnover among this crucial middle manager group , risks undermining company performance and diminishing the vital connection between strategy and execution. With more pressure , greater responsibilities , less training and fewer resources at the command. IS it any wonder that many middle level managers are suffering from increasing levels of stress?

Companies recognize that such high turnover rates will significantly to implement to middle level management to hope them to achieve strategic objectives. So, it seems , instead of top and low levels management, middle level management ought to be the most important role in any organizations. Because these middle level managers are such as middle communication staffs , who need to listen top level management to let the top level managements to know how to do whose job duties in most efficient methods and effective final results to achieve organization's expectation. So, any strategic plan implement must need whose assistance to finish plan more easily.

● Management factors influence organizational strategic plans

Nowadays, many countries public institutions had implemented total quality management. For example, in the United States, strategic planning was introduced after the 1900 year with much of the early literature focusing on local government applications (Poister and Streib, 2005;45). The emphasis in strategic management approaches to be more in focused on a future time horizon. Ideally, strategic management attempts to achieve future goals by liking strategic initiatives to operational process. When total quality management is also forced looking and seeks long-range improvements, applications also emphasize attention to current quality and citizen satisfaction concerns.

So, strategy means the determination of the basic long-term goals and objectives of an enterprise, and the adoption of actions and the allocation of resources how to carrying and these goals. It is the pattern of decisions in a company that determines and reveals its objectives, purposes or goals, produces the principal policies and plant for achieving those goals, and defines the range of business, the company is to purpose, the kind of economic and human organization , it is or intends to be , and the nature of the economic and non-economic contribution , it intends to make to its shareholders, employees, customers and societies.

Is strategy implementation suitable to apply the public sector? It depends on whether perceived service is affective, efficient and equity to department departments. A logical incremental and mostly rational style of implementation are associated with better effectiveness, efficiency and equity, with the absence of an implementation style associated with worse performance.

Nowadays, strategy management tools and ideas been brought into play by governments across the world to enhance capacities and performance standards in the force of in face of increasingly challenging. In response, researchers have begun to investigate whether management can be applied to strategic public organizations. What are the relationship between different strategy implementation styles and the effectiveness and efficiency? Is a rational strategy implementation styles associated with good organizational performance? Does an incremental strategy implementation style have a stronger or weaker relationship with performance or weaker relationship with performance than a rational one? Does some combination of the two styles result in the best performance outcomes? What is relationship between strategy implementation styles and the perceived effectiveness, efficiency and equity to public sector?

To answer above questions. It is important to know that the actual content of those strategies and the way in which were initially formulated to public sector if any public organizational departments want staffs work efficient and effective and equity. The introduction of new public service delivery models, monitoring the effectiveness of how public departments operational evaluation system and culture requires to fit a distinction between more or less planned styles of implementation tends to be top-down and hierarchical, involving the use of prepared action plans, performance monitoring, and review processes to any government departments.

In theory, private and public organizations may adopt different implementation styles for different purpose, for example, using a highly formal process for introducing an efficiency, focused strategy, when adopting an incremental approach to the explanatory search for innovative solutions to service delivery problems to public needs for any public sector departments. An emphasis on a rational implementation style is thought to result in better public sector and department organizational performance because the goal clarity on which it facilities the on-going inter-department coordination of internal and external activities between public sector's different departments.

Overall, the evidence from the private sector suggests that a rational strategy implementation style is associated with better organizational performance. However, decisions from private and public organizations are found that strategic planning has a stronger positive influence on the success of implementation than a more ad-hoc approach in which decisions are made on an incremental basis as situations. For example, Hickson et al (2003) study exploring implementation style and performance in a sample of public and private organizations finds that a dual approach combination elements of both planned and adoptive implementation has a stronger positive association with organizational performance than an emphasis on either planning or adaptation. Thus, it beings this hypothesis, such as a logical incremental strategy implementation style will have a stronger positive relationship with organizational performance then either a rational or incremental implementation style.

Due to public organization is a hierarchical structure. I suggest that a logical incremental and a mostly rational implementation style are associated with higher levels of effectiveness, efficiency and equity than other implementation styles, with no clear approach associated with the lowest level of performance to any public departments. Strategic decision theory is an important school of thought in management studies. So, policy markers need to seek how to improve the effectiveness, efficiency, effectiveness and equity of local public services should therefore consider the extent to which it is possible to encourage incremental adaption of strategies.

● Organization strategic plan challenges

School strategic plan challenges

In researching this question how to achieve the greatest level of effectiveness to school organizations. This can be measured through a conceptualization process of the S.W.O.T. (strengths, weaknesses, opportunities, threats) environmental analysis, clearly defined mission statement, goals and objectives, specific strategy formulation outline, implementation of the strategies and control of the strategic plan. This conceptualization control process is the action that will link the independent variable of efficient strategic plans, through the original measurements of the steps of those plans.

Why do school organizations need an efficient strategic plan? School strategic plan is thinking and responding satisfy social education to adopt student and school cultural, and to adopt economic influence threat factors. Strategic planning is needed at the point when priorities begin to compete with another one school. It is necessary to have specific goals for any activities or decision to measure school effectiveness in addition to thinking strategically for long term education success.

There are many different dimensions to school planning classified according to :(i) the time involvement of the school plan, (ii) the school organizational level performing the plan, e.g. classroom control performing, teaching performance etc. (iii) the activities involved in the school plans, e.g. what is the standard (criteria) to decide school fee charge amount, each course of student maximum numbers per year, how to design each course content and (iv) the general characteristics of purpose of the school plans , e.g. mission, education development long term plan.

The criteria of school effectiveness include such as, significant relational student groups to foster a sense of close relationship between teachers and students, providing opportunities of each student group for learning sharing, each student personal psychological caring and belonging, strong teaching leadership resources that are characterized by the presence of a key teaching groups of strong experienced teaching leaders, that compliment the leading the lack experiences teachers, and who how a set of strategic educational objectives outlining what who are to accomplish each course teaching structure, participatory decision-making, characterized by ownership and openness to diverse beliefs and opinions between experienced teachers and lack experienced teachers, classroom space and teaching facilities that will provide flexibility as well as classroom to growth and expansion for the needs (demands) of student numbers increasing.

So, it seems an effective school strategic plan is broad in scope and identifies how a school organization will commit its resources over a pre-selected period. It is a long term plan analyzing and creating objectives to reach a specific set of education goals. When the school strategic plan is incorporated, it involves dividing and assigning the responsibilities of each education task with specified resources and completion target dates. The advantages of planning help schools adapt to changing education environments and specifies to whom the responsibilities belong. It gives a sense of direction for assessing the education market position and establishing education objectives, priorities and strategies to accomplish the education goals with motivation.

For educational strategic planning has these basic steps processes including: the external educational environment analysis internal and external analysis, a clearly defined education mission statement with educational goals and objectives, education formulation and implementation and control. The first stage of development, an education strategic plan is an analysis of the external educational environmental opportunities and threats of an educational organization, (strengths, weaknesses, opportunities, threats) analysis. This external overview includes analysis of the macro environmental forces, educational industry environment and trends. Macro environmental forces including: the political and legal , economic , technological and social forces. For example, school organizations can evaluate which countries economic situation to predict student family financial afford, if the country unemployment ratio is high, it is possible that students need more student loans in the year, if the country technological production industry 's need is much, then it is possible that engineering , computer subjects demand will increase, if the country's political and legal system is stable, it is possible that the low and policy subjects demand will increase. So, schools need to concern whether what external environment is occurring to predict what kinds of demands (needs) of including a schools' resources, mission statement and goals. It also entails the sustained competitive advantage, which is the structure of human (staffs), e.g. teachers, clerks, computer technicians etc. as well as school organizational and physical resources, e.g. classroom facilities, school library, classrooms and offices furniture and computer facilities etc. The mission statement is the reason for the existence of the organization. Such as school organization mission statement can be providing professional knowledge to prepare students career development, providing reasonable school fees to educate poor students. To be the top university at school world rank, providing high educational quality service to let students to study in an enjoyable environment. Following, schools need to know or plan what which short term plan educational goals and objectives are. For example, goals and objectives will be increased double student number in the end of this year or will be increased double school fee income more than 30% each course and it has no influence to reduce student current enrolling number in the end of year. For long term plan example, goals and objectives will be raised famous and loyal university rank within the 100 rank from world university rank between five and ten years. Finally, the most important reason why any school needs an effective strategic plan. Any school can revise what challenges which will encounter and which can find the reasons why which can not achieve to implement whose original educational goals and objectives and to attempt to find the methods to solve these challenges to achieve which objectives and goals more easily. Even, if the school ensures to achieve its goals and objectives. Strategic plan can let which to find what needs to be improved to adopt to satisfy which potential student needs. Thus, an effective strategic plan can let any school to achieve its objectives and goals more easier as well as to revise and either to find reasons why which can not achieve which objectives and goals or to measure what which needs to do to improve its strategic plan more effective when the school has achieve its objectives and goals ensure. Thus, it seems the school can achieve its objectives and goals more easier in a effective and logic attitude if the school can have an effective strategic plan to predict what challenges it will encounter during its strategic plan achievement process.

● Service organizationsveffectiveness
and efficiency challenges
The service concept plays role in service design and new service development in service or manufacturing industry. The service concept indicates the how and the what of service design and helps mediate between customer needs and an organization's strategic intent.
A service organization can only delivers a service after outsourcing investments in numerous assets, processes, people and materials. Much like manufacturing a product composed of components, services similarly consist of components. However, unlike a product, service components are often not physical entitles, but rather are a combination of processes, people skills and materials that must be appropriately planned or designed service. In designing a new service of redesigning can existing service, service managers must make decisions about each component of the service, from major decisions like facility location to seemingly minor decisions like supervising workers. For even a relatively simple service, numerous decisions are made in taking a new or redesigning service from the idea

stage.

In many cases, these processes are ongoing as service organization continue to invest in their physical assets , these processes are of their workforce as well as make changes and improvements. The strategic level to the operational and service encounter levels. A major challenge for service organization is ensuring that decisions each of these levels are made consistently, focused on delivering the reasonable or satisfactory service performance to targeted customers. Any services include physical and non-physical components both. Or do customers need a service as a singular outcome who are seeking when who obtain or purchase the service? e.g. restaurant waiter service, cinema ticket sale service and cinema seat seeking helper etc. Similarly how do service providers (i.e. service employee) provide excellent service attitude to satisfy customer expectation successful, such as one satisfy customer expectation successful, such as one package of restaurant or cinema watching movie of service. Customers have a preconceived notion of what a service is, even who have not experienced it previously (Johnston and Clack, 2001). So, service providers need to provide excellent service performance or attitude to satisfy any customers' real preconceived psychological needs if who hope customers must choose to consume whose service again, e.g. restaurant or cinema service etc. any shopping service consumption choices.

Before, during and after service delivery, service organizations need to arrange excellent service to satisfy consumer's needs or expectations. These expectations relate to the nature of the nature of the service package, as well as to the nature of service, during the service encounters. So, to ensure the service package and service encounter to satisfy the customer's needs and service organization, itself must focus on the design and delivery of whose service concept.

Some psychologists indicate service concept has three levels. First, the service concept is how it drives design decisions for new and redesigned services. An organization's definition of its service concept is necessary at the strategic level of planning. Second, who describe how the service concept is useful at the operational level during service concept is useful at the operational level during service design planning, particularly in service strategy into the service delivery system and in determining appropriate performance measures for evaluating service design. Third, who indicate service recovery, one component of service design it used to show the usefulness of applying the service concept in designing and enhancing service encounter interactions. They propose that it is critical to clearly define the service concept before and during the design and development of services. The service concept then serves as a driver of the many decisions made during the design of service delivery systems and service encounters. Johnston and Clark (2001) further defined the service concept as: service operation is the way in which the service is delivered; service experience is the customer's direct experience of the service; service outcome is the benefits and results of the service for the customer ; and the value of the service is the benefits to the customer perceives as inherent in the service weighed against the cost of the service. So, service concept includes operation, experience, outcome and value four aspects. The service concept is not only defined the how and the what of service design, but also ensures integration between the low and the what. Furthermore, the service concept can also help mediate between customer needs and the organization's strategic intent. One reason for poorly perceived service is the mismatch between what the organization intends to provide (its strategic intent) and what its customers may require to expect (customer needs).

Without a clear and shared understanding of the nature of service to be provided, i.e. the service concept, how can an service manager expect to design a successful service? For example, a car salesperson needs to explain the characteristics and quality and speed and safety issues to let the customer to understand what the functions are for the car. The car salesperson needs to know how to give the excellent customer feedback service to persuade the customer to choose to buy the car easily. So, the role of car salesperson (service provider) who needs to know what the car manufacturing technology, car engines physical facilities and equipment to prepare to give enough information of the car to let the customer to know. Then, the chance of successful sale will be increased.

In conclude, service concept includes these steps: The first step is service strategy, which includes inputs elements, such as staffs, technology, processes, physical facilities and equipment. Next step is service delivery system, which indicates how staffs perform whose service. The, the step is outputs, which include service outcomes and service experience. Finally, the step is performance, whether the performance is efficient and effective as well as how the service provider will measure and will give feedback to its performance. So, service concept is one system process and it is a cycle process.

● Electronic health record system
to health care organization challanges

Why strategic management concept (planning) is needed to apply to any hospital organizations , when which needs to apply electronic health record system to serve client records for administration. Nowadays, these factors have been facilities to new model of health care delivery to hospitals, such as electronic health record (EHR) system. Electronic health records care professionals, health care systems and governments. The use of EHR is growing rapidly in various countries including the UK, the USA, and Australia. Each country has developed its own methods of design, adoption and implementation. However, they face many challenges, particularly relating to interoperability, privacy and security. Thus, health care organizations need have good strategic plan to meet the electronic health record system chance needs to satisfy customer needs for excellent health care service. The strategic plan includes how to describe the definition and features of primary health care service, such as what is the health care service, such as what is the health care organization's core value(s), principle(s), objective(s), and elements of a primary health care system, how to arrange the primary health care team and how to give the benefits and how to solve the challenges of primary health care teams in the health care service organization.

Healthcare is influenced by a range of factors, like new technology, advances in medicine and society expectations. A healthcare delivery system is a way of organizing health services. It is finite resources. So, as patient's expectations grow, it has to be managed effectively and efficiently by government throughout the world. Primarily, healthcare is delivered through primary care centers, which deal with patients whose healthcare can be managed outside of the hospital. Secondary, healthcare is managed in hospital. Tertiary care providers more sophisticated care in specialist medical centers. So, health care strategic plan is needed to designed to follow who will manage it, such as government or hospital or medical centers. For example, to develop the electronic health record system, each health care service organization needs to concern how to apply the electronic health record system to provide the most fast speedy, the most safe and the most excellent quality care to serve patients satisfactory. Health was once defined and thought to be influenced by people's habit relating to lifestyle, exercise, the environment and food (Stanhope & Lancaster, 2000). Later, health was seen only as the freedom from disease (

physical or mental). So, patient service is related to physical or mental needs in any health care service organizations usually.

In the future, because electronic health record (EHR) system will be popular to be used to serve patients for any health care service organization, such as clinics, hospitals, medical centers, psychological illness health care clinics etc. It is therefore suggested that political leaders at the Ministry of health need to establish a broad vision for how EHR will be developed in the future. This vision must be influenced by all the main stakeholders. By consulting with these stakeholders and thus involving them in defining the EHRs, it development and maintenance of the EHRs. To ensure that the adoption process runs smooths and never loses direction. It is proposed that government staff should prepare a strategic roadmap, which will enable resources and actions to be prioritized to ensure effectiveness and efficiency. The strategic plan " tool" has become increasingly important in dealing with the continually changing environment of the health care setting. So, it is well placed to monitor the health system for any potential threats or challenges from encountering patients' needs immediately in any hospitals, clinics or medical centers. So, the strategic plan can also be used to coordinate stakeholder involvement, monitor and utilize policy changes, coordinate the involvement of potential users in the design and implementation of potential users in the design and implementation of the electronic health record system, assess and priorities finances and coordinate human resources. So, this health electronic record system will be a popular tool to sustain direction and action for any health care service organization in the future. Hence, any health care service organization need to use electronic health care system to adopt to the new change needs for patient service. As the same time, any health care service organizations' strategic plan ought to follow how to design its health care system to implement its strategic plan, then those health care service organizations will be more easy to achieve whose objectives or goals or missions. So, it means that how to design the health care service organization's electronic health record system. Then, it will know how to implement its strategic plan more easy.

● Benefits of rationalization from strategic plans

Reducing costs and improving service for strategic plan to service organizations

In general, organizations throughout the public and

private sectors face to improve support for operations, reduce costs, and improve efficiency. In most, organizations, the costs for operating and managing applications makes up from 75 % to 80% percent of the budget. The emphasis on ongoing portfolio governance, system that cost reduction strategic plan for operational plans to any departments.

Application rationalization means : selecting organizational application based on business and prioritizing related actions (choosing what the business will to and what which won't do), effectively managing the value of both existing and proposed applications, monitoring changing priorities and application value in real time, continually reviewing and adjusting as necessary, application inventory is the process of rationalizing the business applications begins with capturing in inventory of all applications currently in use.

One element that characterizes these efforts is that which one usually one-time events marked by a statistic method to collect application data, which results in a new statistic information that is probably different from and unrelated to the one collected 18 months earlier. Some painful meaning analysis is done on the collected data, and a few actions might be taken. The rationalization questions may include: How does the application fit with technical standards? Does staff have the necessary skills set to use it to best advantage? Are users satisfied with its performance and benefits? Are there better alternatives? What are the maintenance costs? Mergers and acquisitions, application rationalization can be performed before and after mergers and acquisitions to assess the best strategic fit. The value and impact to apply rationalization strategic plan method to reduce cost and improve service benefits for operational plans to any departments.

Business process management, application rationalization can provide insights into gaps or redundancies in the current application portfolio, enhancing an application's ability to finish any business process more efficiently. In doing so, the business can introduce innovation products, provide customer service, and manager risk more efficiently and effectively compliance management. Organizations need to know of their application rationalization at its every department from an aggregate compliance score perspective, how to manager the application investment from a lifecycle management perspective.

By consolidation technical strategic plan, organizations are able to reduce the costs of different departments. They provides cost reduction to overall business expenditures which enables new products and technologies that drive the bottom line. For example, vendor price reduction management rationalization can apply efficient management for vendor negotiations by giving them the advantage of a detailed application, e.g. inventory numbers. The risks associated with it, and its business value. Once on an even playing field, the organization can negotiate wisely and put terms into on agreement that place demands back on the vendor to reduce risk or add business value, going way part pursuing price reductions. For another example, prior to outsourcing strategy , experts say organizations should have a good sense of the value of investments, which have already made, the value and risks of outsourcing and specifically what whose money is accomplishing through their outsourcing negotiation. Knowing what assets are in their application portfolio and what services which need to acquire will ensure that business set up the right outsourcing agreement. Next example, audit prioritization and remediation is critical to know which aspects of operations run the highest business and technical risk, so which can be articulated and addressed. An efficient audit solution allows executive to share insight into such risk by enabling them to create a single system of audit and record that gives consistent live view of the business benefits of their application , e.g. inventory numbers. Quantifying these benefits will be specific to the particular organization. For example, if one large insurance company could discover that 15% of its insurance applications could be decommissioned immediately with no impact to its insurance business, resulting in substantial savings. Then, insurance company will choose to spend 37% of its time on maintenance of insurance applications and 63% of its time on new project development, a complete reversal from how the organization divided its time three years ago. Thus, prediction what will occur to cause any business loss or cost increasing that can influence the business have more benefits to decide to spend more time to choose to do the more beneficial projects in order to reduce long term cost spending and raise long term benefits. So, behavioral rationalization can influence the business's correct time spending to which aspects of investment projects to earn more returns.

● Brand strategy

Managers need to consider the customer and other stakeholder with their branding efforts to make appropriate making decisions because brands is such at the strategic organizational assets. Management at this valuable asset needs to strategic thinking and position. The fast innovation, increased service levels and diminishing brand loyalty characterizing today's marketplaces have led to corporate branding becoming a strategic marketing tool (Xie and Boggs, 2006).

A successful brand can be defined an identifiable product, service, person or place augmented in such a way that the buyer or user perceives relevant, unique added values which match their needs most closely. What kinds of product brand can influence consumer choice? For example, product like milk, tin, iron ore and potatoes , vegetables come to mind where purchase decisions tend to be taken on the basis of price or availability and not on the expensive products brand can influence consumer choice, e.g. cars , wash machines, televisions , air conditioners etc. manufacturing products.

Conceptually, branding appears to be a necessary means of building sales by identifying products and services. Branding is the initial means to build consumer awareness by naming the offer, but also by distinguishing the offer from other similar products or services within an established category. Branding is about being different (Kay, 2006).

When a company can create strong brand , it can attract customer preference and company is more protected against a company initiatives, and company can plan a growth through the penetration of new markets. So, if a business can have a strong brand, it can ensure a company's long-term success in possible. It can create goodwill value in consumption market to influence each consumer choice when who needs to buy the kind of manufacturing product. A brand combines physical and psychological element both. The physical aspect creates the linkage between differentiating them from other enterprises or products. The psychological aspect of a brand constitutes the maintenance of uniformity in terms of communications, guarantees ad behaviors as well as consistency and conformity to particular requirements (Chovancova, 2012).

Brand strategy refers to the ways that firms mix and match their brand's name on their products and a firms through its products, presents itself to the world. Corporate brand strategy must be developed to deliver the highest gains to all stakeholders and corporate public (Shahri, 2011). The brands as strategic assets and resources of competition advantages for organizations in changing and high competition world need to strategic attention and consideration from them. Strategic management organizational strengthens and weaknesses (internal factors) and environmental opportunities and threats (external factors) and environmental opportunities and threats (external factors). Also, strategic brand management can be viewed from these internal (identify) and external (image) perspective. So, establishment of balance is needed between the brand identity and image , e.g. LG brand mobile phones will be built different attractive mobile images, e.g. mobile phone products design of any model choices as well as correct identity attributes ,e.g. music sound choices attributes, internet attributes, phone call attributes by the LG brand mobile phone manufacturer. So, the suggested LG brand models can help multi-business companies operating and guideline to selection and choice of LG mobile phone branding strategy to enter the global competition mobile phone sale market, e.g. mobile phone mature market , e.g. Hong Kong, US, UK, mobile phone potential (developing market) , e.g. India, Africa.

It is evident that this LG brand different model mobile phone products can be chosen to enter to emerging or developing markets. It can be a proper guidance to individual (single) mobile phone business companies (from developed) economies entering to emerging or developing economies or companies operating in emerging markets. So, LG brand mobile phone can have the strength of relationship between influencing factors and choice of branding strategy is moderated by other situation-dependent influences if it chose to join to be another brand of mobile phone partner. Because of broader the stakeholders' interest, the LG non famous brand mobile phone firm can operate in emerging markets , e.g. US market more likely will phone corporate branding with any one famous brand mobile phone firm in US.

In emerging market, such as US mobile phone brand market, there are many different stakeholders that affect LG brand mobile phone organization enters to US mobile phone market. In this US mobile phone market , corporate image is emphasized by stakeholders more and more, therefore entrants from developed countries , such as US, is possible to choose corporate branding more likely. Developing economies experience political and legal instabilities daily, as a result, it can be suppose that corporate branding can manage these instabilities and decrease their effects. Because lack of valid and reliable information , media and other communication channels to Korea , LG brand mobile phone company, the marketing costs are very high in developing economies , such as Korea and companies prefer corporate branding strategy with US any one famous brand mobile phone company. So, such as one Korea, non famous LG brand mobile phone company which can choose to enter the developed country, such as US market to corporate with any one famous brand mobile phone company to build corporate brand strategy if which believed its LG brand mobile models have unique functions (attributes), when US any famous brand mobile phone companies' models of mobile phones have lack of these unique functions from LG brand mobile phone products.

● Human resource plans to space
exploration organization

The European space exploration decides on investment in space science. I shall indicate how it is carrying on implementing strategic human resource plan presence in space mission to achieve its space exploration aim. Application-oriented space programs, such as telecommunications, navigation and Earth observation are fully served by robotic (i.e. fully automated) satellites. Where a strategic human resource presence plan would be demanded environmental requirement of these state-of-the art instruments. Yet the exploration of the nearby solar system , for example, the Moon and Mar mission may be conducted in principle by either robotic vehicles and/or a human presence. Hence, an excellent strategic human resource plan is really needed if European space exploration expected its space exploration mission can be success. To justify future space exploration, especially in the area where robotic and human spaceflight capabilities overlap. To provide guidance, we must examine some strategy aspects of this potentially powerful robot-human partnerships long-term strategic human partnership plan.

Scientific enquiry(including life and engineering sciences), broader consideration of technology and economy as well as more philosophical and political aspects. European space exploration must need different international scientists cooperation from different scientific professionals to cooperate to research different scientific skills to achieve space exploration more easily. Because European space exploration mission is expected to earn economic and societal benefits of funding pure science and space science missions. Indeed, a strategic human resource plan for the cost share between robotic and manned missions in European space exploration, capitalizing on technological advance and international cooperation, but without negative impacting the future of pure scientific research, would be highly desirable. Hence international different scientists need to cooperate to achieve this space science exploration mission more easily. First European space exploration needs have clear strategic plan for human space flight missions. Such as: achieving scientific, political, and commercial activities dealing with the Earth, e.g. meteorology, climate , resources, communications, navigation, military and surveillance, achieving activities related to the exploration of the solar systems typically scientific , and which may be either robotic or manned. Thus, European policies and activities are needed reasonable well focused and organized of with the selections of missions in each of areas being determined by evolving scientific developments and commercial priorities, when European needs to cooperate with some space exploration countries, such as China, England, Japan, US, India etc. countries. For example, an objective and strategic consideration of some aspects of the future of solar system exploration might begin process with a significant impact on long-term European ambitions and policies.

European space exploration needs to consider how to develop a strategic view. The term space exploration represents to extension of human reach beyond the Earth's atmosphere using spacecraft to access unknown environments and to acquire knowledge about space planets, stars by human and robotic means.

From a purely scientific perspective, the exploration of the solar system mission is such as, understanding the formation of the solar system and of the Earth, and questions of plane more generally. It also addresses questions related to he beginning of life on Earth, and the search for evidence for (past) life and biological activity, elsewhere in the solar system and beyond.

From a human space flight perspective, space exploration mission represents the outward continuation of Earth based exploration, which has advanced over many centuries. These activities, ranging from the Apollo program, the current international space station activities, and future plans for manned missions to Mars have a strong impact on the public, at the same time, associated costs are very large.

From long term plan, from a economical benefit human space flight perspective, European space exploration organization objectives include: To raise students knowledge and learning to understand the solar system and of the universe as whole, to assist university to increase space science course (subjects school fee income and to encourage student numbers to choose to study this space exploration course (subjects as well as provides many different kinds of space exploration job chance for students space science employment market, for civilized and advanced society for universities education, employers capital investment and research to earn long term economic benefits to overall European economic development; space science research is as an extension of the pursuit of pure research , entirely unexpected and unpredictable economic development can eventually deliver substantial benefits to European society, and related economic dividend, more calculated approaches to exploiting potential arising from space research are being increasingly well coordinated.

Space technology transfer program (and its associated business incubations center), for example, has been set up to share the benefits of its research and development, making space sector technologies available to European industry, technology development has more immediately, space exploration provides new challenges, requiring the direct development of new technologies. These technological development can create new possibilities for innovation and economic growth , spanning business opportunities for industry as well as access to new resources. This provides the strong motivation both for politicians and tax payers to commit to their very high costs, space exploration encourages industrial development return is the strong industrial interest to develop large-scale facilities and capabilities for space exploration, space exploration has the capability of spectacularly demonstrating national and international capabilities, and has the potential of fostering international cooperation in ambitions projects of international human resource cooperation . At the same time, industrial countries and Europe as a whole, do not want to be left behind in the commercial aspects of space exploration, but rather want to be considered as viable collaborative partners by other space faring countries and organizations . For Europe, this means maintaining a level of space exploration know how such that other key players (USA, Japan, China, Russia, as well as emerging investors like India and Brazil) consider that it provides. Thus, European space exploration needs different countries scientists cooperation to achieve space business objectives, space research objectives, space education objections. It needs have human resources strategic plan to assist to any related space technological aspect research if European expected its space exploration mission can be achieves on one day. Thus, strategic human resource plan is very important to European space exploration organization.

For strategic human resource plan, I shall indicate these aspects as below:

In the area of human health, international space station (ISS) research is providing in the understanding of ageing, disease and the environment. Biological and human investigations have provided an improved understanding of basis physiological processes normally masked by gravity and the development of new medical technology driven by the need to support telemedicine, disease models, psychological stress response systems, nutrition, cell behavior and environmental health . So, human strategic plan needs this medical, biological, environmental health, psychological health, medicine, cell behavior, nutrition scientists employees in the world. In the area of micro-gravity science, the ISS has been central to the understanding of many phenomena in life sciences and technology.

In the area of human flight element of the European space program. It has become a reliable facility, with experiments that can be planned with experiments that can be planned with some confidence of execution. Fields now covered include micro-gravity research, medical and engineering sciences, chemistry, material developments, and fluid physics with the number of experiments carried out having increased substantially over recent years. The European program for life and physical sciences has produced many advanced in a variety of scientific disciplines since its inception in 2001 year, since the bulk of the substantial infrastructure costs for in the past, its use for science, which has been greatly improved in recent years, should continue to be optimized.

Thus, European space exploration human strategic plan can't only concentrate on flight (aviation) technology space professionals. It needs to seek other professionals, such as medical, psychology, science, biology, cell science, environment protection, life science , chemistry etc. professionals. Because this organization's mission is not only space science exploration, it includes other are related to space exploration research. If European space exploration only concentrate on researching space exploration, it will have risk , due to it spends existing funding be diverted from robotic missions to the intrinsically, even more expensive human space exploration program, single space exploration is much risk more than variety space exploration, e.g. space medicine, space medical, space tourism, space nature resource exploration, space cells exploration etc. different related space exploration businesses. Thus, strategic plan can't only concentrate on Moon or Mars space exploration . Because space has much potential business opportunities to let human to discover to gain any new business benefits to human.

In the future, human space exploration possible mission will include: defining the infrastructure priorities for servicing and cargo transportation whether by Ariane 5, by Soyuz launched from Centre Spatial Guyanais (CSG) , or by other commercial vehicles, strategically maintaining the options for human access to low Earth orbit more effective exploitation of the ISS for the physical , life science, engineering science and by the scientific community more generally (for example, involving announcements of opportunity for engineering sciences, articulating the role of the ISS in terms of human biology, especially in the context of future missions to the Moon or Mars, defining more what the ISS can contribute to the long term development of human space flight (such transportation systems, robot-human interfaces, and advanced life-support systems, expanding and enhancing its capabilities for education , which the astronauts on board have undertaken with great success, and further publishing its scientific work and potential.

Finally, how to reduce risk cost to space exploration, as soon as human space flight is considered the currently accepted wisdom is that risk to human life (in terms of launchers, survival systems, space tool and return to Earth) must be suppressed to extremely low levels of profitability. For example, the lowing possibility of a factor from 10% to 1% might increase the cost by a factor of 10 or more, but whether the formal probability estimates, significant advances in space exploration will always carry some risk to human life quantifying these risks will always be. However, difficult but a comparison with the historical levels of risk as commercial aviation development might provide a useful guide. Thus, why not single space exploration business (related space science businesses) can reduce risk as well as European and other countries space exploration cooperation can bring human benefits more than European (single) space exploration business investment. Thus, global strategic human resource plan must be need to European space exploration business.

Why does organizational development need strategic plan? Strategic plan is similar with a pyramid planning. At the low level of strategies/ tactics operations: How will the organization accomplish its goals? At the middle level of goals/objectives direction: what does the organization want to achieve? At the top level of principles beliefs: What does the organization mission and purpose? Why does the organization exist?

A well-developed strategic plan describes a vision for the future, strengths and weaknesses of the organization, the nature of the changes for sustainable growth and development, the sequence of these changes, those who are responsible for guiding change, the resources required, whether which currently exist within the organization or must be generated from external resources.

In a strategic plan, it consists mission , such as what we hope to accomplish , capabilities, resources, strengths and weaknesses, such as what you are capable of doing. Opportunities and threats , include needs of clients, and stakeholders, competitors and social , economic , political and technological forces. When all elements combine the strategic plan can be the fit. Long term strategic plan needs usually 5 to 10 years, focuses of future achievement, weighs a series of alternatives to make choices, resources mobilization with activities, operational plan needs short term (one year or less) , achievement to targets annual, alternatives are not considered, tend focus one unit or related such of activities, no formal action.

● The direction between business
and tactic models and tactics

Nowadays, business model has been used by strategy to refer to the logic of the firm, the way it operates and how it creates value for its stakeholders. What is the relationship between business model and strategy? Can business model reflect a clear separation between tactics and strategy. This distinction is possible because strategy and business model are different constructs.

Any strategy can help a firm to learn to analyze its competitive environments defined its position, develops competitive corporate advantages and understands threats to sustaining advantage in the face of challenging competitive threats. However, external environment changing (variable) factor can influence a firm's development. Such as globalization, deregulation to technological change. So, any firm can't neglect to change to compete differently and innovate in its business model. For examples, IBM computer firm's 2006 year and 2008 year " Global CEO study", showed that top management in a broad range of computer industries are actively seeking guidance on how to innovate to its computer business model to improve its ability to both create and capture value.

Advances in information and communication technologies have driven the recent interest on business model innovation. Many e-businesses constitute new business models. Of course, not all business model innovations are IT driven; other forces , such as globalization and deregulation, have also resulted in new business models and fed the interest on this area. In fact, socially motivated enterprises that aim to reach the bottom of the pyramid constitute an important source of business model innovations. In truth, there is not yet agreement on what are the distinctive features of super business models. We believe that the dispute has arisen, because of lack of clear distinction between the strategy and business model and tactics. Business model refers to the logic of the firm, the way, it operates and how it creates value of its stakeholders. Strategy refers to the choice of business model through which the firm will compete in the marketplace. Tactics refers to the residual choices open to a firm by the business model that it employs. What is the difference between the concepts of strategy , business models and tactics? In the first stage, firms need to choose a login of value creation and value capture (chose their business model). In the second stage, firms make tactical choices guided by their goals (in most cares, goals expect some form of stakeholder value maximization). So, the object of strategy is the choice of business model and the business model employed determines the tactics available to the firm to compete against, or cooperate with other firms in the marketplace. However, any business needs to know how the connection between strategy and business model and tactics can be clearly separated.

How to define a good business model? Two questions need to concern to answer : who is the customer and what does the customer value? what is the economic to customers at an appropriate cost? My idea is that business model refers to the logic by which that any business model should answer, one related to related to the value provided to the customer and the other to the organization's ability to capture value in the process of serving customers. For example, e-business can be an innovative technological business model to value chain analysis, the resource-based view of the firm, dynamic capabilities, transaction cost economies and strategic network. So, why business model is the first stage to design before strategy and tactics achievement.

Business model is similar to machine logic of operation system: any machine has a particular logic of operation (the way, the different components are assembled and related to one another), it runs in a particular way and in operating, it creates value for whomever uses it. For example, every automobile has a particular logic of operation, conventional automobiles operate quite differently than hybrids, and standard transmission automobiles. Different automobile models create different value for their stakeholders, the drivers. Some drivers may prefer standard transmission. Others may prefer a small car that allows them to easily navigate the streets of a congested city, others may prefer a powerful explosion engine to enjoy the countryside to the fullest. Different operation and create different value for their drivers. Likewise, to better understand business models, one needs to look at their component parts and understand how who relate to one another: The question arises: What are business models made of? I contend that business models are composed of two different elements. The concrete choices are made by management on how the organization must operate and the consequences of the choices both.

In fact, choices may include compensation, policy, contracts decision making, outsourcing decision, location of facilities, assets employed, extent of vertical integration, or sale and marketing methods. Every choice has consequence. For example, the provision of high-powered incentives (a choice) has implications regarding the willingness to exert effort or to cooperate with workers (consequences). Likewise, pricing policies (choices) regard sale volumes, affect the economies of scale and bargaining power is enjoyed by the firm both (two consequences).

In strategic plan view point, I indicate three types of choices: polices, assets and governance structure. Policies refer action that the firm adopts for all aspects of its operation, e.g. unions complain dealing, locating plants in rural or city areas choice, encouraging employees to fly tourist class, providing fee shares, bonus monetary incentives, or flying to secondary airports as a way to cut expenses to employee welfare. Asset refers to tangible resources, such as manufacturing facilities, a satellite system for communicating between offices or the use of a particular aircraft model by an airline. Governance of assets and policies refers to the structures of contractual arrangements that confer decision rights for policies or assets. For example, a given business model may contain as a choice to the certain assets, such as a fleet of tracks. The firm can own the fleet or lease it from a third part. The transaction cost economies can reduce the firm to pay asset purchase expenditure at same time because it only pay rent to lease to the fleet of trucks per month.

So, business model is as the logic of the firm, the way , it operates and how it creates value for its stakeholders. The make operational , we argue that business models are composed of choices (policies, assets, governance) and the consequences derived from the choices. For example, Ryanair airline business model includes: flying to secondary airports as lowest ticket prices, low commissions to travel agents, standardized fleet of Boeing 737s,treating all passengers equally, high powered incentives, none meals, nothing free. Consequences of these choices are: secondary airport changes low airport fees, lowest ticket prices can sell large volume, low commissions cost charges to travel agents, standardized fleet of Bosing 737 s has bargaining power with suppliers, all passengers treated equally to achieve economic of scale, high powered incentives to attract combative team, none meals provision to cause faster turnaround, nothing free causes addition revenue, headquarter is low fixed cost, and no unions will be flexibility.

Ryanair airline business model is similar to a machine is assembled and how it works. There are many ways in which a machine to performance a given task can be designed and assembled: Different levels of specific mechanisms, quality of components. Different machine have different direct consequences to affect the overall level of efficiency of the machine (speed, input, efficiency, noise, quality of output) etc. Other airlines are assembled differently than Ryanair airline , which have a different logic , a different way to operate and to create value for their stakeholders. These different ways to put together airlines correspond to different business models. In the case of Ryanair airline, the business model will have three cycles. The first cycle is : The lowest fares causes low quality service expected, to cause none meals, to cause low variable cost and to cause the consequence of lowest fares fare. The second cycles is: The lowest fare causes large volume, to cause high aircraft utilization, to cause low fixed cost/passenger, and to cause the consequence of lowest fares again. The third cycle is: The lowest fares causes large volume, to cause bargaining power with supplier, to cause low fixed fares again.

It is important to evaluate different cycles consequences. If the consequences are valuable , cycles develop valuable resources and capabilities. For example, as Ryanair airline's volume increases because of its low fares, bargaining power with its suppliers (airport authorities, Boeing, Airbus) grows resulting in improvement in Ryanair airline's advantage.

In fact, every organization has some business models. This is because organization makes some choices and these choices have the some consequences. Of course, this does not mean that every business model is satisfactory or even viable in long run. Some authors indicated business model has four elements: a customer value proposition, a profit formula, key resources ,and key processes. So, business model can articulate the value proposition. It can identify a market segment, if can define the structure of the value chain. It can estimate the cost structure and profit potential. How business model design involves assessment with respect to determine. It includes that the identify of market segment to be targeted, the benefits to rise to the enterprise will deliver to the clients, the technologies and features that are of the product and service, how the revenue and cost structure of a business design to meet client need, the way in which technologies are to be offered to the client. So, every organization will choose to decide how to determine the logic of the firm , the way in operates and how it creates value for its shareholders.

Tactics refers to the residual choices open to a firm of the business model that it employs. For example, for newspaper publishing's choice of tactics. A newspaper publishing firm can't change price of the newspaper because its business model is ad-sponsored and the newspaper must be sold at zero price. Put differently the newspaper publishing business model precludes from using "price of the newspaper" as a variable that can be changed depending on the intensity of competition and other external factors. Thus, price of the newspaper is not part of the newspaper publishing business's set of tactics. For another example, some business school for MBA student, every student gets a personalized MBA curriculum, depending on whose background and professional goals. Some business schools used in many of the school's executive education programs with several faculty members co-teaching the core courses and with assets, such as classrooms, with set up for case discussions for large groups educational method; another some business schools are impossible to provide similar education methods which business model do not have as an element in whose tactical set the offering of a tailored MBA course.

These business schools modify whose businesses models. So that those tactical choices would become available, but with the current businesses models, which are not possible for them to match the other business schools' similar business models for education method to MBA course. We conclude that different business models give rise to different tactics available for competition and /or cooperation. However, tactical play an important role in determining how and value is created and captured by firms. For newspaper publishing industry example, advertising rates and the precise number of ads. displayed in the free newspaper and up affecting the readership and advertising revenues. So, likewise, of some free charge newspaper publishing's advertising rate increases, fewer advertisers with want to advertise in these free charge newspaper publishing's revenue, profit and value capture. Therefore, not only the business model employed by the firm determines factor, but also tactics play a central role in how much value the firm will be able to create and capture of the end of the day. Tactical interaction refers to the way organizations affect each other by acting within the bounds set by their business models. Using this imagery of business model, representations, tactical interaction occur when one firm's business model is in contact will that of another firm. When this happens, there are consequences in both firms business models, where feedback to be determined not only by the focal firms choices, but by the choices of the other firm as well. For a discount retailer store example, it competes with another local retailer store, both engage in a tactical pricing competition to win customers. The interaction between the discounted and the non-discounted retailer stores can be captured to display both business models connected at market share. In this example of discount retailer stores and non-discount retailer stores, when both stores use prices in their tactical interaction. The discount retailer stores bring superior weapons to fight because of the business model that it employs to compete.

Specially, the range of prices, discount retailer stores can profitably set is much broader the profitability other non-discount retailer store competitors with a high cost operating model. So, the non-discount retailer stores can choose to sell the products or foods at higher or non-discounted price. When the discount retailer stores lack to sell whose same of similar products or foods. It means cooperation retail method of tactical interaction will be needed in this store retail market.

Strategy is often defined as a contingent plan of action designed to achieve a particular goal. Strategy is the creation of a unique and valuable position, involving a different set of activities. Creation implies choice of the particular way in which the firm competes. So, strategy is not the activity system itself, but the creation of the activity system itself, but the creation of the activity system. So, strategy refers in our development, for the contingent plan as to what business model to use. Strategy in a higher order choice that has profound implications on competitive outcomes. Choosing a particular business model means choosing a particular way to compete, a particular logic a particular way to compete, a particular logic of the firm, a particular way to operate and to create value for the firm's stakeholders. For example, model means choosing a particular way to compete, particular logic of the firm, a particular way to operate and to create value for the firm's stakeholders. For Ryanair airline example, it was encountering bankruptcy in the early 1990 year, its strategy was a plan of action to transform its airline business model from that of a standard full-service (through small) airline to a radically different one by adopting the Southwest's no-frills business model. In the mid 1990 year , after the transformation had taken place, Ryanair airline strategy. Ryanair 's top management considered four alternative plans of action to solve bankruptcy challenge. (1) becoming the Southwest of Europe, (2) Adding business class , (3) Becoming a feeder airline operating from Shannan 's airport, or (4) Existing the airline industry. Each of the entailed a different business model, a different logic of the airline firm, the way , it operates and how it creates value for its stakeholder. The high level election of becoming the Southwest of Europe (as opposed to adding business class or operating as a feeder airlines was strategy (a plan of action to create a unique and valuable position, involving a different set of activities).

Furthermore, the particular way in which Ryanair airline executed such plans was its realized strategy. The resulting new Ryanair airline with its new logic, new way to operate, and new way to create value for its stakeholders , was business model. What is the different between business model and strategy? A firm's business model is a reflection of its realized strategy. What do organization gain from having two separate concepts. There is the choice of business model because, there is a over time mapping from strategy onto business models. This means business model, an outside observer knows the firm's strategy. Some authors felt the substantive different between strategy and business models arises when the firm's plan of action calls for modifications to the business model (changes in policies and/or assets and/or governance) when particular contingencies take place. However, there are many possible sources of contingencies upon which strategies may be based. One such source is the realization of an event outside the control of the firm. For example, one contingency the many firm are currently considering is the possibility of a recovery from the recession. Firms have plans as to how their business models must be kept of a strong economic recovery (changes in polities, asset, and/or governance). Such as plans are part of firms' strategies.

How will business model be changes by firm's strategy? What is a strategy in this economic recession situation? so, business model is prior to achieve any strategic plans. It is a logic organization design or mind to prepare to achieve any strategic plans as well as tactical operation plans. Has it difference between strategy and strategic management? When reviewing strategic thinking , using realize how this phenomenon differs in any organizations. In military view point, strategy can be used in a military campaigns. It means a way of prevailing over the adversary, a fool of victory i war . In organization view point, strategy can be applied to human relations, political, economics, business. The concept of strategy has evolved into a field of knowledge in management. Otherwise, strategy management, with content, concepts and practical reasoning, role in the academic and business fields.

Whether do concept of strategy and strategic management are understood by business managers? What is strategy and strategic management to future managers? Are who understood and recognized? To answer these two questions? We need to seek these specific objectives. (i) To build a model explaining the definition of strategy (ii) To identify which concept of strategic management in the literature. To understand these difference of two concepts. We need to adopt organizational phenomenon in different situations. In this case, the development of organizational strategy depends on what strategy and strategic management depend on understanding the perceptions of their managers on what strategy and strategic management actually is. It concerns how to predict consumer behaviors. In the field of strategy, managers represent an innovation, and a new alternative for research.

Strategy and strategic management concepts can be explained what differ from historical perspective. In any enterprises, creating and managing strategic enable them to meet the challenges of the market, reaching their objectives in the short, medium and long term. Strategic concerns great development within the corporate environment. Phenomena , such as corporate restructuring , joint decisions and actions impacting on organization size, financing were driven by the technological advance in means of communication and transport and an interactive dynamic global level have become predominant. Nowadays, thinking strategically has acquired the status of a factor in leading and managing organizations, whether for profit or otherwise. After all, strategy addresses the link between the inner world of business and its external environment.

Considering strategy is as a business logic rational and sequential, to the most dynamic that understand this process is as associated with cultural and learning factors, political and power relations. Strategy is not only one way of dealing in competition environment or market, as treated not only summarize the ideas, proposal, guidelines, indicative of paths and solutions. It has the concept of operational efficiency. In summary, strategy is what matters for the effectiveness of the organization, the external point of view, which stresses the research of the objectives against the environment, in term of internal stresses, the balance communication between members of the organization and a willingness contribute towards actions and the achievement of the common objectives; it is a series of actions to a particular situation, it is analyzing the present situation and changing it whenever necessary. It is the determinant of the basis long term goals of a firm and the adoption of action how to allocate resource necessary for carrying out these goals; it is a rule for making decisions determined by product/market scope, growth competitive advantage and synergy, it is addition of the decisions taken by an organization in all aspects , as much commercial as structural with the learning process to management, it is the directional action decisions to achieve firm's objectives. Hence, strategy is long term or short term plan to aim to achieve any missions or objectives for any organizations.

Otherwise, strategic management defines key attributes: directed towards the overall organization objectives, includes multiple stakeholders in decision making, requires incorporating short and long term perspectives and involves the recognition of trade offs between effectiveness and efficiency. Strategy management is as an ongoing process involving the efforts of strategic managers to adjust the organization to the environment in which it operates when developing competitive advantages. These competitive advantages enable the company to seize opportunities and minimize environmental threats. It is a broad term that includes determining the mission and objective of the organization in the external and internal environment.

● Strategic communication plan

How can organizational communication influence effectiveness and efficiency? What are the most effective pathways for delivering organizational messages to priority audiences? Is it the suitable media? Face-to-face meeting? Direct mail? The internet ? How will organization deliver message efficiently?

Without a plan to guide organizational communication activities, the organization runs the risk of focusing on the wrong audiences, of using messages that simply do not work. In other words, without a well-thought-through plan, your organization runs the risk of becoming irrelevant with key audiences, even of failing to meet organizational mission.

How to strategic communication plan? Your organization needs to proactively focus the activities of your organization, where there is the greatest potential for success; ensures your limited resources (time and financial most effectively applied) imposes discipline and clear thinking about why it is the best interest for your communication method to your organization to pursue certain communication initiatives; to integrate all of your public relations efforts; media, government, donor to corporate etc. ; to ensure that every member in your organization staff board, volunteers are on the same level fairly, to achieve results that more your members towards realizing your organization's goals and to encourage creative thinking about new ways to address old challenges.

So, communication plan is simply a written statement that outlines communication goals, provides some situational analysis and proposes approaches and activities to achieve the identified goals given the identified current situation. An effective communication plan can be set out the timeframe for carrying and these activities, details the resources and supports that will be necessary to achieve your organizational goals, and identifies how results will be measured. It can be a summary document of only a few pages or a 40 pages on more. Part of length and depth of a plan depends on whether it is a five year organizational plan or a plan designed to support a particular campaign or strategic goal.

In the private and government sectors, communication plans are typically development on support of detailed organizational strategic plan. In the non-profit aim organization sector, it is most common to see strategic communication plans as a organizational and communication planning processes. An effective strategic communication plan focuses on many different ways of reaching all of the external and internal audiences, your organization will need to hear your messages.

How to create communication plan for your organization to improve: the ability to create a strong and positive reputation for your organization and public relations; building relationship and reputation with the media and with reputation with government at all levels; building relationship with employees and volunteer, e.g. internal communications; ability to attract an maintain strong donor support relations; building sponsorship and funding opportunities with business corporate relations; building organization's policies and direction board-staff relations; outreach about programs and services (constituency any client relations).

How to build morals within team by communication plan? Establishing goals to staff and volunteers, understanding every staff can meet is energized and ready to take on more ambitious goals. Communication plan aims to effective facilities meetings, a creative brainstorm and a focus group.

Organizing effective communication plan has these stages: Stage one includes that defining organization goals, defining communication objectives, situation analysis to organizational background and external environment. Stage two includes that determining who your organizational audiences are and what messages are delivered before you move to messages. Stage three determining what your organization strategies , what tactics are. Stage four, evaluation of ideas for strategies and tactics, implementation budget before investing time in developing the timing and timeline sections, identifying certain strategic and tactics resources, producing multiple communication opportunities having a communication plan will make it easier to determine whose to allocate limited resources.

How to develop strategic environment plan? It will largely be determined by the level of buy-in that key staff and board have for the plan. Buy-in is easiest to achieve when staff have had a role in developing the plan and feel some level of ownership of ideas contained within it. All of the pieces of a communication plan are represented in the following pages. They have been laid and in a logical order by moving from organizational goals to situation analysis to audiences and messages.

● Reasons need strategic plan

Why organizations need strategic plan

American Management Association defines and differentiates between strategy, policy and objective. It indicates that policies get procedures into roles. Strategies get into tactics, resulting in an-end-means. For example, it supposes a company decides upon a sales growth of between 35 and 45 per cent and desires to achieves this by acquiring other companies, instead of introducing new products, instead of introducing new products. So, it seems strategic plan can help organization has ability to predict how to achieve its strategy to achieve sale growth aim.

For example, acquisition can be considered as a strategy is chosen by the company. The company will then have to decide on the size of the firm to be required. If it decides on acquiring a small company. This becomes the objectives. In general, strategy means the determination of the basic long term goals and objectives of an enterprise and the adoption of the action and the allocation of resources necessary for carrying out these goals.

In micro organization view, strategy is the pattern of objectives and plans for achieving these goals, purposes and goals and the major policies and plans for achieving these goals stated in such a way, so it is defined what business, the company is in or is to be and the kind of company, it is or is to be. Also, some authors define a strategy is a set of decision-making rules for the guidance of organizational behaviors. Because firm's internal and external environment change over time, the strategy also changes consequently, the idea that strategy is dynamic.

Otherwise, in macro organization view, strategic management is a science of choosing the alternatives from the designed and available actions. The managers have to decide on a process that will be most suitable to their conditions and what could enable them to achieve a desired position of their organization in overall. Large organizations which use detailed strategic management models whereas smaller businesses concentrate on planning steps compared to larger companies in the same industry. In short, the most highly rated benefits of strategic management are: charity of strategic vision for the organization, focus on what is strategically important to the organization, better understanding of the rapidly changing business environment.

● What is strategic management?

How can strategic management assist organizational development? Some management psychologists indicate any large organizational participant members needed to be trained a widely varying traditions, some in economic departments, some in strategic management departments, some is organizational behavior, some in marketing etc. departments. Trained strategic management organizations can be more efficiently and effectively to compare to non-trained strategic management organizations.

Exactly what is it? Strategic management owning organizations can know how to raise internal strengths and reduce internal weaknesses as well as can know how to predict or avoid external threats occur and absorb or raise opportunities more easily.

Strategic management can be assumed that scientific knowledge is socially constructed and is the fundamental medium that makes that social construction possible. What are the differences between strategic management organization and non strategic organization? We were interested in identifying the fundamental definition , not the monetary fashions or cycles of the field, such as micro-organizational behavior or human resource to explain what differences are between of them.

In an effort to distinguish strategic management organizations from other subfields of management organizations, consideration of how strategic management differs from or relates to other academic fields, such as economy, marketing or sociology. We would have liked to include strategy-oriented organizations from these other related field, but which are too rare to allow the type of analysis we conducted.

Has it relationship between strategic management and top management team, capital intensity and market structure. We need to examine these existing definitions and comparing them to conceptual categories. Some management professionals defined strategic management is as imputed from the distinction of the field: The field of strategic management deals with the major intended and emergent initiatives, involving utilization of resources, enhancing the performance to their external environments. They also indicated six elements make up the definition of the fields of strategic management. The first definitional element is the major intended and emergent initiatives, such as strategy, acquisition and diversification, which refer to relatively deliberate, planned initiatives, but it also includes such as learning, and innovation, which represent the move emergent activities that occur in a firm. The second definitional element is taken by general managers on behalf of owners to concern the key actors who are the focus of attention strategy research. Terms such CEO, directors, board represents the upper level. The third definitional element is involving utilization of resources that managers use in their strategic initiatives, e.g. capability and knowledge represent the resources that are internal to the firm, whereas, terms , such primarily as ties resources that link the firm to its environment and the performance. The fourth element is enhanced the performance, conceptualizes the key objectives or outcomes that are of interest to strategic management scholars, e.g. growth performance to achieve advantages. The fifth definition element indicates firms which reflects the focal unit of analysis of strategic management. Finally, the sixth element is in their external environments and is represented by market competitor and industry, which refer to the immediate environment of a firm as well as by uncertainty environment contingency, which indicate a potentially broader external context.

Porter Michael (1986) , long time Harvard professor and editor of the Harvard Business Review, published the first edition of the competitive strategy, who explained "strategy means the pattern of decision in a company that determines and reveals its objective purposes or goals, produces the principal policies and plans for achieving these goals, and defines the range of business the company is to pursue, the kind of economic and human organization, it is or intends to be, and the nature of the economic and non-economic contribution it intends to make to its shareholders, employees, customers, and communities".

In the military, the strategy for a battle refers to a general plan of attack or defense. In civil terms, strategy is concerned with the deployment of resources, this is amounts to the allocation of resources. Tactics, then is concerned with the employment of resources already deployed. In the civilian sector, this equates to operations in the board sense of the terms. Generally speaking, tactical re-expected to occur in the context of strategy, so as to ensure the attainment of strategic intent. However, strategy can fail end, when it does tactics dominate the action. Execution becomes strategy. Thus, it is always one part intended (the plan as conceived beforehand) and one part emergent (on adaption to the conditions encountered). As a consequence, there are always two versions of a given strategy: (1) strategy is as intended and (2) strategy (c) realized.

In fact, a strategy or general plan of action might be formulated for broad, long-term corporate goals and objectives, for more specific business goals and objectives, or for a functional unit, even one as small as a cost center. Such goals might or might not cause the nature of the organization, its culture. The kind of company its leadership wants it to be the markets, it will or won't enter. The basic on which it will compete or any other attribute quality or characteristic of the organization. Because strategies can do exist at various levels of the organization, it is conceivable and appropriate for the corporation to have a strategic plan , for a business unit to have one too, and for a functional unit to have one. Strategic plan can import to all organizational levels. So, it is intended to address matters of great importance. For those concerned with the enterprise, strategic issues, initiatives and plans are those that affect the entire enterprise is important ways. So the top, middle and low levels ought need to have short term and long term strategic plans to implement.

What is the direction and destination of the firm? Where is it headed and what is it to become? Not all strategic issues are long term, although may be. A short term crisis can be of strategic significance and should be dealt with accordingly.

Plans of action, whether for business always have two fundamental aspects: ends and means . What is to be achieved and how it is to be achieved? What are the firm's future results, e.g. goals, aims , targets or objectives consequences . Firms can choose either program or action or step or initiative to achieve enterprise level or business unit level or functional level future result. Those combination of ends and means firm can find any plans in all these levels of organizations. Strategies are too exist at all three levels. Consequently, one can and should find strategic thinking, planning and management at all three levels.

However, planning has been defined in various ways, ranging from thinking about the future to specifying in advance who is to do what and when. For firm plan, it can define the activity of preparing a plan, a set of intended outcomes (ends). Planning can be formal or informal , an involve lots of documentation or very little. The information base can be large and captured in a wide range of reports, studies, databases and analyses, or it can rest entirely on the personal knowledge of a few people or even just one. Plans and thus the planning activities that produce them, frequently with address timeframe, either generally or in the form of perhaps detailed schedules, resources too, might be addressed, whether in terms of money, space, equipment or people. There are no predetermined guideline to follow, it is a matter of doing what is appropriate for the task at hand.

In conclusion, strategic planning characteristics includes: establishing and periodically confirming the organization's mission and its corporate strategy what has been termed the contest for managing ; setting strategic or enterprise level financial and non-financial goals and objective; developing broad plans of action necessary to attain these goals and objectives; allocating resources on a basis consistent with strategic directions and goals and objectives and managing the various lines of business as an investment portfolio; deploying the mission and strategy. That is articulating and communicating it, as well as developing action plans at lower levels that are supportive of those at the enterprise level , one very specific method of policy or strategy deployment; monitoring results, measuring progress, and making such adjustments as are required to achieve the strategic intent specified in the strategic goals and objectives; reassessing mission, strategy, strategic goals and objectives and plans at all levels and if requires , revising any or all of them.

● Why needs strategic versus non-strategic cooperation

On reason why organization needs strategic plan because it can not revist to compare whether what it can improve or change to be better between the strategic cooperation stage and non-strategic cooperation stage if it choose to achieve strategic plan. What are the difference between strategic cooperation and non-strategic cooperation within any organizations? What are the benefits to strategic cooperation organizations?

The strategic motivations are in play in finitely repeated in any organizations. Clearly, cooperation can drop because strategically-motivated individuals, who reciprocate others' cooperation solely when there is future interaction. However, it can also drop because non-strategically-motivated individuals, who reciprocate others' cooperation even in the absence of future interaction, believe others will stop cooperating in the last period. In other word, since both strategically - and non-strategically motivated individuals can cause the decline in cooperation , it is difficult to know what the contribution of each type of motivation is. So, it seems that if any organization can review to measure any staff individual motivated effect with team cooperation, it will improve strategic plan to be more successfully or more better to compare prior year and current year strategic plans.

Some psychologists have done this experiment, for example, one team member could take the increase in cooperation between repeated games and (repetitions of) one short game as being caused by strategically -motivated individuals who now have a reason to cooperate. However, this increase can also be driven by non-strategically-motivated individuals who cooperate more because who expect that within repeated interaction others will be more cooperative. Similarly, the observation that cooperation is more frequent when it is more profitable can be attributed to strategic behavior and the existence of additional cooperative equilibria. However, the increase in cooperation can able be , due to an increase in non-strategically-motivated cooperation that results from intrinsically-motivated individuals who now find cooperation relatively more attractive or from rational individual who make relatively more mistakes.

How to distinguish strategic from non-strategic motivations for cooperation in organizations? Psychologists conclude that strategic behavior has a more pronounced effect than learning in explaining the usually-observed decline in contributions in public good games. On the basis of experiment treatments, who observed cooperation is strategically motivated. However, the relative importance of non-strategic motivations increases with the profitability of cooperation. So, psychologists indicate different organization departments cooperation can encourage individual staff motivations after strategic cooperation. Otherwise, non-strategic cooperation different departments will be more unsuccessful. It seems that how to encourage department cooperation factor which can influence the organization can raise productivity or improve service performance more easily.

● Strategic plan tangible and intangible benefits

Why will inefficient and effective strategic plan bring disadvantages or lack benefits to any organizations? Motivating staff and volunteers, thinking about the future is a stimulating and energizing process. It can create a shared vision, with ideas about how to achieve that vision. Building a planning team with a common vision. The strategy plan that emerges from the process is generally more realistic and achievable and working or interdependent relationships within the organization are strengthened. Confronting key issues and solving problems. Strategic planning sets in motion a dynamic process that allows the organization to continually reassess, confront change, and grow within an agreed-upon framework. Defining roles and responsibilities , measurable performance objectives are set and the person(s) who is responsible for specific activities is identified. Challenging the status, the process creates an open atmosphere. How can organization do things better in a more systematic and thorough way. Allowing busy managers and policy makers to concentrate on the organization's future for a short period of time, meaning that who will be able to focus their expertise and insights on self-assessment and planning future directions. Explaining organization to others , a thoughtful and clear strategic plan is often a good marketing tool and can encourage shares issues support for the organizational mission that individual perspectives, roles and problems are subsumed by an overall plan that coordinates all staff members and volunteers , so that agreed upon goals and objectives are achieved in a timely manner.

The steps of strategic plan suggesting: First step, analyzing the shared valued and experiences of staff and board. Planning a meeting or workshop to facilitate strategic planning. Second step, review and update or prepare a mission statement for the organization. Third step, analyzing the organization's external environment, political , economic, social and technological factors and internal environment: resources or input, processes, and performance or outputs. Fourth step, conducting a SWOT analysis (assessing the organization's internal strengths and weaknesses and its external opportunities and threats). Fifth step, creating smaller groups for in-depth planning activities in key areas. Sixth step, reviewing the organization's existing strategic plan if there is one to identify aspects of the plan that are still strategic, those are as longer strategic plan, due to changing environments, and gaps or new issues that should be addressed in a revised plan. Seventh step, outlining a vision of where the organization should be outlining three to five years from today (the vision of success). Eighth step, identifying the strategic issues facing the organization. Ninth step, formulating goals and strategic objectives to address major issues facing the organization and ensuring its longer term growth and sustainability. Tenth step, developing work plans showing specific activities, persons responsibility resources needed and indicators why which performance will be measured. Eleventh step, identifying next step for resource mobilization and creating a approaches for generating sufficient revenue funding. Twelve step, preparing the written detailed 5 years strategic plan mission statements. Final step, identifying next steps for resources mobilization and creating a financial plan that cost, and outlines approaches for sufficient revenue or funding .

Reference

Chovancova, M. (2012), " Building a strong brand to support company competitiveness"., from www.sba.org.pl.content/50647.

Davis, Gerald, 1991, " Agents without principles: The Spread Of The Poison Pill Through The Intercorporate Network." Administrative Science Quarterly, 36: 583-613.

Obembe, D. understanding individual action: when employees contravence management directives to faster knowledge sharing. Management research review. 2010, vol. 33, issue. 6 , pp. 656-666. ISSN 2040-8269.

Poister, Theodore H. Streib, gregory (2005), "Elements of strategic planning and management in municipal government, Status after two decades", Public Administration Review, 65(1), pp.45.

Hickson, D. J. Miller, S.C. , Wilson , D.C. Planned on prioritized, implementation of strategic decisions. J. Manage, Stud , 2003, 40, 1803-1836.

Johnston, R., Clack, G., 2001. Service operations management, Prentice-Hall, Harlow, UK.

Kay, J.M. (2006). "Strong brands and corporate brands", European Journal Of Marketing, vol. 40, no.7/8, pp. 742-760.

Porter, Michael (1986). Competitive Strategies. Harvard Business School Press.

Shahri, M.H. (2011), " The effectiveness of corporate branding strategy in multi- business companies", Australia Journal of Business And Management Research, vol. 1 no 6, pp. 51-59.

Stanhope, M. & Lancaster, J. (2000). Community & Public Health, St. Louis, Mo, Mobsy.

Xie, Y.H. and Boggs, J.D. (2006), " corporate branding vs. product branding in emerging markets, a conceptual framework", Marketing intelligence & planning, vol. 24 no. 24, pp. 347-364.

www.ingramcontent.com/pod-product-compliance
Lightning Source LLC
Chambersburg PA
CBHW021350150726
47989CB00005B/2185